D1026717

ECM Methods
What you need to know

Tom Jenkins
Walter Köhler
John Shackleton

This book is dedicated to the staff, partners and customers of
Open Text Corporation and its subsidiaries. This book is possible
due to their combined efforts, experimentation, and collective vision.

We would like to thank the staff, users and partners
of Open Text for their contributions to this book.

Special thanks go out to the contributors:

Evelyn Astor-Hack, Randy Baird, Virginia Bartosek, Adrian Butcher, Charles Charter,
Jonny Coombes, Lisa Dekker, Joe Dwyer, Nick Gilbert, Adam Howatson,
David Howatson, Anton Huenermann, Toby Jenkins, Dave Kinchlea, Stephen Knox,
Agnes Kolkiewicz, Mandy Lam, Jennifer McCredie, Darren Meister, Tony Niederer,
Kevin Northover, Donna Pearson, Elizabeth Rogers, Jacky Saayman,
Benjamin Shapiro, Renee Tremblay, Annemarie Vander Veen,
Doug Varley, Rolf Wiedemann, Patrick A. Windsor II.
Graphic Artists: Janet Catipi, Sabrina Prudham, and David Rees.

Specific resources are accredited in the Bibliography
and the User Case Study Bibliography.

Jenkins, Tom
Köhler, Walter
Shackleton, John

ECM Methods

Second Printing, July, 2006
Printed in Canada

ISBN
0-9730662-7-X

$29.00 U.S.

Published by
Open Text Corporation
275 Frank Tompa Drive
Waterloo, Ontario, Canada
N2L 0A1

(519) 888-7111
info@opentext.com
www.opentext.com

All rights reserved. Copyright © 2006 Open Text Corporation. No part of this book may be reproduced
or transmitted in any form or by any means, electronic or mechanical, including photocopying, recording,
scanning, or by any information or retrieval system, without the express written consent of Open Text Corporation.
Open Text Corporation will seriously consider any request to reproduce or use portions of this book, and would
encourage any party interested in doing so to contact: ecmbook@opentext.com. In the event such
consent is provided, Open Text Corporation will reserve the right to review and approve the final form and
manner in which the portion of this book reproduced and used.

WHAT YOU NEED TO KNOW

The largest corporations in the world have been actively taking advantage of the Internet in very quiet yet transforming ways. They have embraced an area known as Enterprise Content Management, or ECM, as the next most vital area of their IT activities to enable their organizations to gain competitive advantage. We believe that this process will transform the organization in a similar way to ERP and that the impact will be even more significant.

In a business climate that demands structure and control, ECM creates a safe and transparent environment for organizations to foster innovation and growth. ECM leverages the power of the Internet to transform the way people interact. It creates secure and regulated environments, ensuring that protected content remains behind closed doors. At the same time, ECM unlocks the true potential of the enterprise by enabling people to transform content into knowledge, creating new possibilities and business opportunities.

This book is the third in a trilogy called "Turning Content into Competitive Advantage." The first book of the series, **ECM Solutions**, examines how ECM applications change the business processes of corporate enterprises to gain competitive advantage. The second book, **ECM Technology**, provides the reader with a solid foundation in the principal technology elements that make up ECM. This last book, **ECM Methods**, is the story of **how** leading organizations have achieved effective change using ECM.

It begins with an overview of the critical business needs found in every company and the basics of the ECM technology that can be used to satisfy these needs. It then takes a close look at the most critical success factor of any ECM deployment in an organization: the change of people's behaviors in working with non-structured information. Bringing the virtues of real collaboration, which form the foundation of many successful public

Internet projects (such as LINUX, for example) into the structured, hierarchical universe of a profit-driven company has more cultural than IT challenges.

Based on that knowledge, we examine why some ECM deployments are more successful than others when the same technology is applied to the same set of problems. The majority of the book concentrates on two fundamental deployment strategies:

• Application centric

• Enterprise centric

While both strategies are similar in their need for a methodical approach, they differ in the methods required to be successful. One of the biggest differences is the scale and scope of the problem to be solved. We review both in detail and identify seven distinct stages that involve different mechanisms to satisfy the requirements of that particular type of deployment. At each stage, we compare and contrast both approaches and make observations as to the characteristics of the most successful evolutions, from application-centric deployments to enterprise-centric deployments.

Throughout the book, there are illustrations of user experiences expressed in short case studies based on actual experiences. Most applications begin due to a compliance requirement and quickly evolve into ROI models as organizations seek to gain an advantage from archives that they have been required to create and maintain.

Finally, the book reviews the future of ECM in terms of expansion into online communities and extranets that bring together corporate entities into a marketplace.

ECM represents a critical new stage in the advance of the information age. It describes both a philosophical approach and the underlying technologies used to help businesses transform their content into competitive advantage.

In today's business world, ECM is about more than managing content. Society is now demanding higher standards for the accuracy and availability of content:

> *In the two years following 2001, more than 20 new laws were enacted throughout the world that impacted how organizations gather and disseminate information. Government reaction to events such as 9/11 and Enron have been to demand greater transparency in collaboration and content. Regulators are relying on recent advances in electronic content management technology to provide this greater transparency in an efficient manner.*

In the past few years, more regulations were passed in some industries than have been written in almost a century. From the Patriot Act, to Sarbanes Oxley and FDA (Food & Drug Administration) regulations, government regulations are creating more secure living conditions for consumers. Across many industries, individuals and companies have already been penalized for not complying with these regulations and mismanaging critical business content.

Deploying ECM will help to transform your organization into a more knowledgeable and agile enterprise that is a global competitor in any jurisdiction in the world. This book describes the creation of a new approach to data by some of the greatest minds in the world of information technology—a collective vision determined to solve the challenge of managing structured and unstructured information. Each chapter in the book focuses on a specific step in the process of realizing an effective ECM deployment and provides insight into the many aspects and complexities of change management surrounding ECM methods.

We hope you enjoy this story about the deployment of new and exciting technologies, and will be encouraged to make your own journey to bring ECM technology to your business.

Tom Jenkins

Walter Köhler

John Shackleton

Open Text Corporation

CONTENTS

Part 1: The Content Needs of the Organization

Part 2: ECM Deployments

Part 3: ECM Application Deployments

Part 4: ECM Enterprise Deployments

Part 5: ECM Extranet Deployment

Part 6: The Future of ECM

Compliance Grid

Compliance Solutions Map	Gov	Pharma	Energy	Finance	Mfg	Services
Research	U.S. Army S 111	AG S 221	Energen S 231	UBS S 76	Holcim S 271	LMU S 205
Admin	Fluor Hanford S 59	Aventis S 219	Vintage M 58	LVA M 142	Sony M 21	Translink T 119
Mfg	Northrop Grumman T 65	Genzyme T 238	Sasol M 98	Winterthur S 247	Arup S 269	Johnson S 74
Services	Calgary S 199	FSMB S 195	PG&E S 237	Shenandoah Life T 233	CAS S 279	Giant Eagle M 186
Enterprise	GD S 291	Roche S 215	South East Water M 158	EIB T 265	Distell S 6	ISO S 297
Extranet	FMI S 187	Aventis S 219	Kerr-McGee M 216	OSFI T 54	DMJM S 267	LMU S 205

For information regarding additional solutions please go to:
www.opentext.com/ecmtrilogy/innovator/index.html

M = Methods Book
S = Solutions Book
T = Technology Book

Company Name	Page Number

Innovator Stories

ROI Grid

ROI Solutions Map	Media	Gov	Edu	Pharma	Energy	Finance	Telco	AEC	Auto	Mfg	Services
R&D	HBO T 29	U.S. Army S 111	FOIC S 109	AG S 221	Murphy Oil S 235	NERA T 58	HP S 47	Miller T 167	Volvo Aero S 121	Distell S 6	TRL M 164
Admin	CBC S 23	ILR S 185	Broward T 225	Novo Nordisk M 134	PG&E S 237	LawPRO S 13	Sony S 21	M+W Zander T 177	BMW S 119	Reebok S 43	Translink T 119
Mfg	TWBG S 169	Northrop Grumman M 200	Turner T 75	Roche S 215	Energen S 231	Alte Leipziger T 185	BT S 259	Holcim S 271	Fiat S 281	Miele S 123	Dow Corning S 143
Services	TSR S 173	DRC M 228	Emory U. S 209	Aventis S 219	South East Water M 158	Barclays T 148	T-Systems M 92	DMJM S 267	Daimler T 7	Owens Corning T 145	Mercer S 151
Sales	EA T 201	Lockheed T 164	LMU S 205	Novartis S 155	Sasol M 98	AGVA S 245	Siemens S 85	Johnson S 74	Audi T 85	Siemens S 85	Swiss Air M 71
Executive	TSR S 173	Fluor Hanford S 59	Clark S 207	Roche S 215	Shell S 229	UBS S 76	C&W S 81	Holcim S 271	CAS S 279	Motorola S 83	SKM S 40
Enterprise	Standard S 173	USPTO T 68	Open U. T 220	Genzyme T 238	Kerr-McGee M 216	Shenandoah T 233	Motorola M 232	Arup S 269	CAS S 279	Motorola S 83	CARE M 112
Extranet	20th C. Fox S 171	USAF T 240	Broward T 225	Novartis S 155	Shell S 229	Federated Investors M 178	Cisco S 257	M+W Zander M 206	BMW T 124	Unilever M 170	ISO S 297

For information regarding additional solutions please go to:
www.opentext.com/ecmtrilogy/innovator/index.html

Company Name | Page Number

M = Methods Book
S = Solutions Book
T = Technology Book

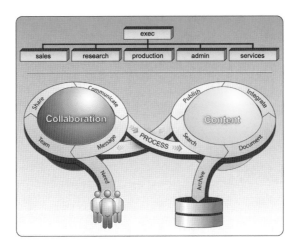

Figure 1.1: ECM Applications

A sign of organizational maturity occurs when multiple departments carry out their work with a single application platform. It is obvious that everyone in the company wishing to spend money should use the same Purchase Order System. If each department had its own system for authorizing purchases, it would be chaotic. Yet most organizations are doing just that when it comes to Enterprise Content Management (ECM) applications. The deployments tend to be isolated in pockets within departments of the company. But increased pressure to comply with new regulations is forcing organizations to consider ECM more strategically.

Take the Sarbanes-Oxley Act (SOX) as an example. This regulation is designed to restore (or maintain, depending on your views) the confidence of investors in public markets. Compliance to Sarbanes-Oxley is cross-departmental by its very nature. This type of cross-departmental application highlights the need for companies to invest in applications delivered by a common set of technologies. This chapter focuses on how ECM enables organizations to lower their total cost of ownership by delivering an enterprise data model and core applications that provide an infrastructure for additional business applications.

CHAPTER 1

THE BUSINESS NEEDS

The primary objective of any business is to generate wealth. Businesses are continuously examining ways to become more efficient than their competitors. This is the premise upon which the free market economy is based.

To succeed, companies need to manage their organizational assets. Systems to manage human, capital and financial assets have been part of the IT landscape for the last 40 years. Systems may have existed to manage the information assets of an organization, but many have been rendered woefully inadequate by the exponential rate of information creation. How can a company use the information and content that exists within and around it? What information should they know? How do they establish an infrastructure that enables them to understand their content?

Enterprise Content Management is technology that provides a means to create, store, manage, secure, distribute and publish any digital content for enterprise use. ECM is not about numbers; it is about words. Much of the IT industry in the past 50 years has focused on back-office databases and their management in Enterprise Resource Planning (ERP) systems.

ECM is unique in that it was developed to manage the proliferation of non-numeric content such as documents, Web pages, spreadsheets, diagrams and images, all largely driven by the pervasiveness of the Internet.

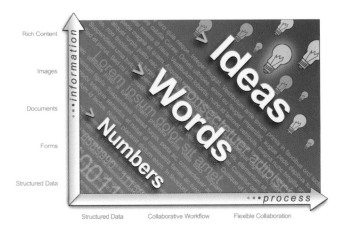

Figure 1.2: Working With Information

For ECM systems to be widely adopted, they need to emulate the way people work without disrupting their daily routines. This involves creating a digital place for people to work in much the same way they work together in departments or at office locations. For ECM to be effective, it needs to automatically capture the content produced as a byproduct of this work. The very best ECM solutions deliver applications that integrate content management invisibly within the very act of collaboration. The transparent combination of content and collaboration benefits organizations tremendously by providing a place where simple ideas take root, are nurtured, and mature into market-leading innovations. This critical point is one we will explore in detail in this book.

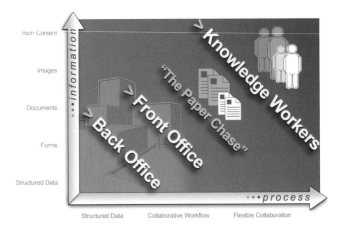

Figure 1.3: The Evolving Challenge

People work together within a particular line of business or work group. Companies are normally organized by departments around these lines of business, such as sales or manufacturing or administration. Typical ECM applications are built to meet the content management needs of a particular department and are driven by the specific needs of a line of business manager facing a particular productivity problem. These departmental solutions provide the foundation for subsequent larger enterprise installations.

ECM as a set of departmental applications is most effective when supported by a common data structure and a combined set of technologies. In other words, each departmental application typically requires the same basic technologies and infrastructure, but has a specific set of needs that are unique to that line of business. ECM systems that can be easily adapted to meet each department's unique needs, while maintaining a common data model, are inherently more flexible and future proof. Implementing ECM applications on a common data model results in lower total cost of ownership and faster implementation, leading to greater productivity and higher returns on technology investments.

Content-Based Applications

Consider group-level applications that are closely aligned to the way people work. The following represents a typical organizational chart for a company:

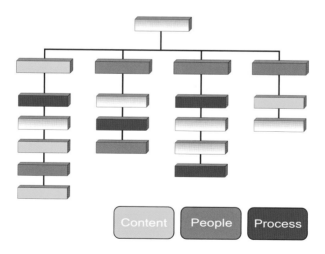

Figure 1.4: Typical Organization Chart

> ## Murphy Oil

Murphy Oil, an oil and gas organization, found that non-integration of its front-end processes with the back-end ERP system caused time delays and cost accruals for the Accounts Payable department. Too much time was spent on invoice processing, which complicated invoice status determination and resulted in dismal customer service.

An ECM solution now provides Murphy Oil with a central repository, offering online access to documents and reports. The integration of the system with ERP software has automated workflow processes and instilled a greater process and resource visibility, reducing invoice cycle time, lowering average vendor inquiry resolution time, improving vendor relations, and reducing administrative costs.

"Prior to the integration with the [ERP] software, vendor inquiries about invoices typically took about 15 minutes to complete; now it rarely takes more than a two-minute phone call. Our AP staff has more time to spend on activities that create value for our organization. The savings have added up," says the Systems Project Coordinator from the Controllers Department at Murphy Oil.

Figure 1.5: Three-way Invoice Matching at Murphy Oil

Companies consist of many separate departments—Accounting and Finance, Legal, Administration, Marketing, Sales, IT, Research and Development, and so on. Each department has specific requirements for content management. ECM business solutions have been designed to meet many of these requirements and solve problems specific to a particular department. Typically, these solutions are driven by the need to improve efficiency or save money. Examples include purchase order processing, invoicing, project management, claims processing, Food and Drug Administration (FDA) compliance, product lifecycle management (PLM), and sales readiness.

ECM solutions often support core business functions. That is, if the solution was used inappropriately or did not exist, the business would not function. In the Pharmaceutical industry, for example, the development of new drugs must follow a regulated content management and approval process known as 21 CFR Part 11. The entire corporation is at risk if this process is not precisely followed. ECM business solutions for Pharmaceutical companies must therefore support 21 CFR Part 11. Other industries such as Financial Services and Healthcare have similar needs controlled by their own industry regulations.

Figure 1.6: ECM Architecture Simplified

Once an application has been deployed at the departmental or group level, the IT Department involved in implementing the first application can use the lessons learned to solve content issues in other departments. While the first deployment may take place in the Sales Department, the next deployment may occur in the Manufacturing Department, and so on. Some of the most advanced ECM-enabled organizations in the world today have more than 20 distinct department-level applications supported by a common underlying suite of technologies and a common data model.

Figure 1.7: ECM Applications

Some of the solutions that have been developed for ECM include:

- Accounts payable administration
- Bid management
- Content management
- Court case management
- Customer care centers
- Customer due diligence
- Derivatives management
- Digital asset management
- Engineering change management
- Government publications management
- Vendor communications

- Human resources
- ISO 9000 quality assurance
- Managing marketing extranets
- Manufacturing processes
- New hire induction/education
- New product development
- Policies and procedures
- Project collaboration
- Records management
- Vacation time management

As organizations move to leverage the same infrastructure for process improvements company wide, finding the best solution often leads to a long-term, strategic Enterprise Content Management solution. This involves deploying a complete series of applications across an entire organization. To make them simple to deploy and cost effective to replicate, a common set of technologies with the same content model is required as an underlying infrastructure. This means that the suite of technologies must be sufficient to deliver all applications across the enterprise.

Hundreds of ECM solutions are implemented in the leading organizations of major industries throughout the world. This book profiles many of those ECM success stories.

As ECM deployments reach a critical mass within major corporations, ECM applications are finding their way into every department. At the time of writing this book, there were more than 100 different applications using ECM technologies known to the authors.

On average, a single, enterprise-wide deployment of ECM involves more than 20 unique solutions, ranging from Engineering departments using ECM applications for new product development to Accounting departments using it to track changes to contract bid documents.

Inter-Departmental Requirements

With many applications that are critical to the operation and success of an organization, collaboration requires cross-departmental cooperation. In many companies, achieving this cooperation is the very basis for long-term competitive advantage. For example, when planning and implementing New Product Development (NPD) within a research group, the interaction between this group, manufacturing, and marketing is vital to the project's success. This implies strong cross-functional cooperation and collaboration, plus the sharing of critical documents among all three departments.

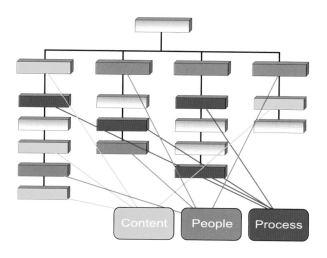

Figure 1.8: ECM Crosses Departments

> E-Plus MobilFunk

A subsidiary of the Dutch company KPN, E-Plus is the third-largest cellular phone network in Germany. This innovative organization is continually offering its customers new services and expanding its network; as a result, speedy business processes are essential at E-Plus. A powerful inventory system was needed to track the vast inventory in the 150 E-Plus shops.

E-Plus deployed an ECM system that links the shops with the central ERP application so that Sales personnel can use the intranet to directly and in real time access the ERP application when submitting an order or handling inventory. Prior to this, E-Plus employees had to synchronize this data daily with the ERP system. The new solution has enabled them to significantly reduce the cost of inventory control, says the Project Manager at E-Plus.

Customized system features have considerably accelerated business processes at E-Plus, enabling the staff to respond immediately to customers' needs, significantly reducing costs and producing a quick ROI. However, the E-Plus customers are the real winners, as their orders are now processed much faster—processing time has decreased from five days to 30 minutes.

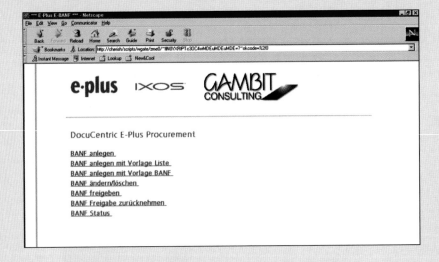

Figure 1.9: Procurement Management at E-Plus

The issue of cross-departmental functionality raises two important concerns for the ECM architecture. First, for diverse departments to collaborate efficiently, both business and IT people outside of a particular department require infrastructure support. Second, an underlying common data model is required to let people in different departments share information contained in separate applications at a cost-effective rate. While some applications can be delivered within a department, most ECM applications must be enterprise wide in nature so that they can be accessed easily across departments. Otherwise, organizations are fragmented into isolated islands of information and critical content remains buried. Departmental implementations are limited in scope and are eventually replaced by similar applications based on a broad underlying set of technologies that scale the entire organization.

Industry Requirements

ECM customers are looking for a solution that provides a common technology for many different applications. Departmental applications have evolved by adding elements that address specific vertical market needs. Many ECM vendors today are delivering solutions in specific industries based on their initial success in developing solutions in one or more markets. An organization's pain points are often specific to a industry, so customers prefer a vendor that has expertise in their particular industry. An ECM solution gains traction in an industry when one organization begins to use a solution and other organizations look to this solution to resolve their issues as well.

Within many industries, managing content is absolutely critical. Pharmaceutical companies have been early adopters of ECM because managing documents is a regulatory requirement for doing business. The New Drug Application (NDA) challenges organizations to provide detailed information about what happened during clinical tests, what the ingredients of a drug are, the results of animal studies, potential adverse effects, and how a drug is manufactured, processed and packaged. The integrated document and records management, collaboration and workflow functionality of a comprehensive ECM solution enables pharmaceutical companies to detail the product from start to finish. Using a comprehensive ECM suite, pharmaceutical companies can seamlessly review new drug targets, deploy personnel and resources, manage drug discovery projects, and accelerate time to market.

Productivity Gains

ECM has its roots in document management. In the early 1980s, the benefits of investing in a document management system were lower print or paper costs, reduced storage needs, and increased productivity. Today, ECM is evolving into a blend of proven technologies designed to solve a variety of content and process-centric problems. It follows that customer investment is moving from departmental solutions to entire enterprise infrastructures that promise return on investment on many levels.

The key to success of the earlier implementations has been to recognize collaboration and its role in creating context for content. It is simply not enough to know that content exists, without being aware of how, when and why it was created. Collaboration provides this context since it records what was happening at the time of content creation. This provides far greater insight into the relevancy of information.

The current trend in collaboration and content management is toward departmental or group-level solutions. Currently, the Internet is still new and very technically driven. In the future, companies will hide the technology beneath purpose-built solutions. Functionality will be there but virtually transparent. Internet software will evolve in the same way, and ECM will lead the evolution in collaboration by making solutions easier to use, without users needing to know anything more about the Web than how to click on a hyperlink.

While many organizations still regard content management solutions as self-contained solutions, they will increasingly deploy technology with an enterprise-wide ECM strategy in mind. Leading ECM solutions will evolve into comprehensive infrastructures offering fully integrated collaboration and content management functionality deployed at the departmental level and then rolled out to the entire enterprise. More and more customers will embrace an ECM approach that is aligned with business needs on many levels. Companies will be encouraged to grow their ECM solution—whether by improving corporate governance, streamlining processes or effectively managing content—as their business requirements evolve.

> LawPRO

Professional Indemnity Company (LAWPRO) is an insurance firm that is licensed to provide professional liability and title insurance. The organization, which relied heavily on paper, sought an alternative to this inefficient, innovation-stifling medium for storage and communication.

Workflow improvement reduced paper usage at LAWPRO, offering tracking functionality and the ability to work with diverse systems that span, organize, and connect them. LAWPRO automated paper-based processes using a centralized data entry and repository for documents, pulling business processes from a variety of systems into one cohesive unit.

The solution has caused a profound shift in the original project motivation—the paperless office almost became a by-product, not a goal. Workflow implementation has simplified existing processes and increased efficiency. As a result of the implementation, LAWPRO has realized benefits far beyond initial project expectations.

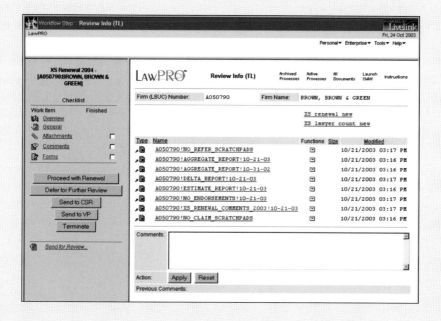

Figure 1.10: LawPRO's Client Review Workflow

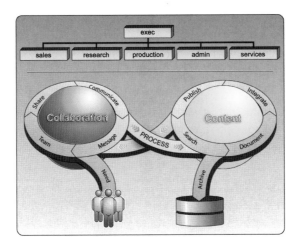

Figure 1.11: ECM Applications

From a more academic standpoint, a new market is emerging which addresses the higher-level needs of the knowledge-intensive organization, namely, how to increase overall organizational effectiveness in a volatile business environment. In order to realize return on investment in technology—and to adhere to new regulations and legislation—smart organizations will move toward implementing an underlying infrastructure that supports many repositories and combines key applications.

Vendors will offer customized views and applications for specific departments and processes that are cross-industry applicable. The infrastructure will have to scale and support new technologies. Customers of ECM solutions will become interested in newer technologies and expanding these systems to support more content types such as email and rich media files.

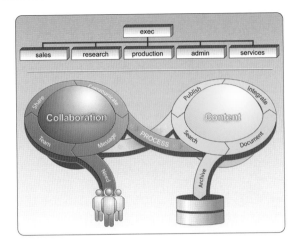

Figure 2.1: ECM Technologies

ECM technologies are all about connecting the right people to the right information in the right context. Historically, most ECM adopters have done so on a piecemeal basis—focusing on a specific business pain point and single technology solution. But this approach is expensive when you consider that achieving compliance with today's new regulations requires visibility on processes that span multiple departments and functions. These processes cross multiple systems, and each cross-over point represents a potential point of failure, additional manual labor, expensive and customized integrations, and additional internal controls for safeguarding. Progressive organizations are adopting ECM as a strategic platform to avoid these unnecessary costs. Understanding each of the component technologies is important to develop a more comprehensive ECM strategy.

CHAPTER 2

ECM TECHNOLOGIES

During the 21st century, companies in the Enterprise Content Management market will dominate the Information Technology agenda as corporations seek advances in technology to better manage content, people and processes.

We can trace ECM's evolution by examining major developments in the industry as early as the 1960s. At this time, companies such as Honeywell and IBM were major vendors. Their mainframe computer systems automated basic computations previously made by floors of workers.

In the 1980s, the introduction of the personal computer (PC) started the client-server revolution and personal productivity drove the creation of digital content. This content, created mostly by knowledge workers, complemented the automated generation of content that belonged in the mini-computer era. Intel and Microsoft became major vendors in this era.

	1970s	1980s	1990s	2000s
Who	IBM	Microsoft	SAP	Open Text
Why	Clerical Productivity	Personal Productivity	Departmental Productivity	Org. Compliance & Productivity
How	Data Processing	Email; Desktop Publishing	ERP	ECM
Computing Environment	Mainframe	Personal Computer	LAN	Ubiquitous Computing

Figure 2.2: Eras of Computing

In the 1990s, Enterprise Resource Planning (ERP) programs further automated transactional business processes within organizations, allowing more efficient management of numbers through a database. Companies such as SAP and Oracle were leading innovators in this era.

ECM suites are made up of a number of technology pieces working harmoniously to manage the complete lifecycle of electronic documents, from creation to archive and eventual deletion. You can compare ECM suites with other suite-based software products, such as Microsoft® Office. Microsoft Office includes different tools that work together to provide personal productivity for office workers. Likewise, ECM suites offer a set of tightly integrated facilities for searching, managing, distributing, publishing and archiving electronic documents to achieve organizational productivity.

Unlike Microsoft Office, ECM suites require little to no software to be installed on a personal computer. ECM software leverages Internet technology to deliver services to people, meaning that accessing the software requires only a Web browser, a username, and a password.

ECM suites provide secure access, storage, publication and archiving of large volumes of business content. ECM allows organizations to manage the processes for working with different types of content, while tracking and controlling content changes. Content management is not confined to organizing computer directories; it involves exploiting your business know-how to avoid critical failures, to operate more efficiently, and to become more productive and profitable.

Structured vs. Unstructured Information

To introduce the technologies that underpin ECM, you must to understand the difference between structured and unstructured content and why managing unstructured content is such a challenge.

Structured data is based on numbers organized into tables. These database tables can be quickly manipulated to find data that refers to the numbers in the table. Unstructured data is not as easy to organize and retrieve. Words, an example of unstructured data, are organized into tables similar to an index found at the back of a book. Because the data model for words (unstructured data) is fundamentally different from the data model for numbers (structured data), the technologies that support each must differ.

Computers have fundamentally changed the way we work; most office workers today require a computer to do their jobs. Managing payroll, processing orders and invoices, inventory control and financial accounting all rely heavily on the numeric processing capabilities of computers. Computers are exceptional at crunching numbers, but the challenge for ECM applications is to use information technology to manage documents and pictures, or what is termed "unstructured data."

Individual productivity tools such as word-processing systems, spreadsheets, presentation tools, Web editors and email have created an explosion of unstructured data that must be managed. Organizations need to store this information, make it accessible, and ensure that it is up to date and secure, as well as appropriately distributed, published and consumed.

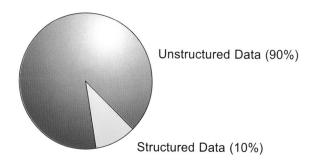

Figure 2.3: The Ratio of Structured Versus Unstructured
Information in an Organization

Unstructured data matters because of its sheer size and recent growth rate. While this is important, what makes unstructured data the focus of IT for the future is the astounding growth rates of digital content that are being reported with main stream adoption of the Internet. Various industry observers estimate that large corporations are doubling their unstructured data every two months! Even if this rate slowed to every 3 or 6 months, it represents an enormous change in the type of information available for use within an organization. This exponential growth is shown in Figure 2.4.

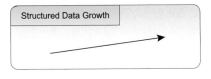

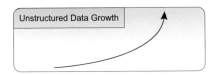

*Current Structured
Data Growth is Linear*

*Current Unstructured
Data Growth is Exponential*

Figure 2.4: Structured Versus Unstructured Data Growth

Think about this rate for a minute. Consider all of the digital information created by corporations since the start of computing and then consider that all that information will be created all over again in the next few months!

Our every-day experience confirms this when we consider the incredible growth in the size of our email inboxes and the scope and scale of the public Internet.

As a comparison, consider that unstructured information probably tracks transactions and that tracks the economy. A very strong global economy grows by an average of 4 percent per year. ERP growth is commensurate with that, and probably in the 10 percent range, or linear as shown in Figure 2.5.

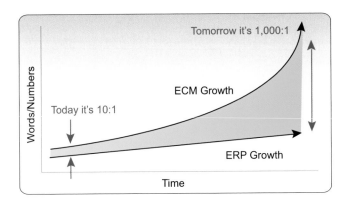

*Figure 2.5: Estimate of the Relative Growth Rates
of Unstructured Data and Structured Data*

It is well documented that legacy systems are extremely expensive to maintain, costing enterprises thousands of dollars a year in support, maintenance, and location and staffing costs. Faced with the need to decrease costs and comply with data retention regulations, Sony Global Treasury Services (GTS), an internal banking system for the Sony Group, opted to archive data from its legacy IT systems.

A legacy decommissioning solution that is fully integrated with Sony's SAP system has enabled the migration of over 2 million invoices in less than two weeks using a batch import interface. Remote access to structured and unstructured information ensures that billing documents can be accessed from any location, eliminating the previously cumbersome data retrieval methods.

The challenge of dealing with an array of legacy systems has been fully overcome. All data and documents are now available from a single point of access, delivering significant customer service benefits. As a result of the implementation, Sony has observed a faster and more visible return on its SAP investment.

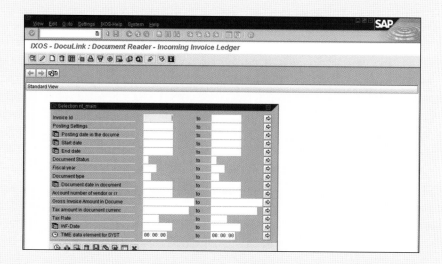

Figure 2.6: An Example of a Legacy Decommissioning Solution

Now consider the two growth rates together. Today there is probably 10 times more unstructured data. Consider the impact of a few years of hyper growth by ECM (unstructured) and steady growth by ERP (structured). The gap will be 1,000 times the size of what it is today. With this rate of growth, whatever problems IT currently faces with unstructured data will only become worse over time. It is better to start solving issues with Web sites and email management early since they will only be larger problems if they are left for another year to grow bigger. Clearly, the ECM repository of web sites and email will dominate the IT agenda for the foreseeable future.

Basic Components of ECM

The quest for solutions to these problems created the ECM market. The following provides an overview of the fundamental technology components of ECM.

Search

It is not easy to search unstructured data. While numbers obey very rigid rules that can be interpreted easily by computer programs (one plus one always equals two), words and pictures have few formal rules and are open to different interpretations based on context. Take the task of cataloging a book called "Lemons." Should the book be cataloged in the section on cooking, fine arts or cars? Opening the book would immediately reveal to the reader the subject matter and therefore, the correct placement. Computers cannot read yet, so the challenge is to design a system that makes the same interpretations that humans do. If this all sounds too theoretical, try searching the Web for "ECM." Search results will identify more than 800,000 hits, including everything from software products to publishing companies, electronic countermeasures to espresso coffee machines and even the European Crystallographic Meeting in Durban, South Africa.

ECM systems manage huge amounts of unstructured data. Motorola, for example, manages 4.8 terabytes of documents in their ECM repository. The electronic version of this book uses about 0.5 megabytes of disk space, so Motorola's repository would hold 88 million books like this one! ECM systems must not only manage huge amounts of data; they must also allow users to quickly find the documents they need. Modern search tools can learn concepts that allow them to automatically catalog documents, making them easier to find. Search technology also makes it possible to identify subject matter experts and readers with similar interests by tracking user behavior. Searching unstructured data is the first and one of the most fundamental disciplines of ECM.

> CBC Radio Canada

Canada's national public broadcaster, CBC Radio Canada, provides services to Canadians in English, French and eight aboriginal languages. Dedication to the ideals of public broadcasting has made the organization one of the country's largest cultural institutions. The same dedication has also prompted CBC to implement an ECM solution to enforce consistent business standards and practices across the enterprise.

Custom enhancements to its ECM system provide a number of Web-based solutions including an all-in-one, online contract management system that collects data and generates more than 25,000 contracts a year; an audience relations repository for communications documenting audience reactions; and a collaboration tool that allows various departments to plan programs and add their own information describing CBC's program offerings.

A single system enables the creation of all contract and rights licenses, and one repository holds contracts for all networks. CBC has been able to automate labor-intensive business processes such as negotiation, contract creation, amendments, and renewals and obtain support for research of audience reaction. Workflow technology now enforces the use of well-defined business processes across the enterprise.

Figure 2.7: Capturing Audience Reaction at CBC

Document Management (DM)

We have all experienced the effect on a sentence as it is passed by word-of-mouth around a room full of people. The sentence inevitably changes significantly from person to person and soon loses its original meaning. The same can happen with business-critical documents that are mismanaged, with disastrous consequences. Take for example NASA's embarrassment over a space telescope. Its giant lens had been improperly ground because of a mix-up involving one team member working in centimeters, meters, and kilograms while another used inches, feet and pounds. As a result, the telescope was out of focus and inoperable. Another case involved confusion between different versions of an aircraft maintenance manual, causing the cockpit window of a passenger aircraft to fall out of the plane at 16,000 feet—the accident apparently caused by engineers using the wrong size screws.

When a document is reviewed by a number of authors, it is easy to lose track of who has the most up-to-date version. Documents can get lost, deleted or fall into the wrong hands.

Document management systems allow businesses to control the production, storage, revision management, and distribution of electronic documents, yielding greater efficiencies in information re-use and document flow control. Managing electronic documents is a key technology of Enterprise Content Management.

Archiving and Document Lifecycle Management (DLM)

The accounting scandals at Enron Corporation made the world aware of the need for records management. When an employee of Andersen, Enron's outside auditor, admitted to destroying a significant number of documents related to the Enron investigation, it made people wonder, "How could that possibly happen?" It happened because prior to the court investigation, the documents were being destroyed properly and according to an established procedure within the company. However, a court order necessitated a change to that established procedure which, evidently, wasn't properly communicated or enforced. Systems today must be immediately adaptable to change and enforce new behaviors, either sternly or delicately, depending on the situation.

Everyone has experienced the sense of panic that hits when a spreadsheet or document somehow gets deleted. No amount of screaming at the screen, banging on the keyboard or shaking the motherboard will bring it back. Now imagine that the document you lost contained proof of an accounting infraction or was the only copy of a sales agreement for a million-dollar order.

> General Dynamics

General Dynamics C4 Systems, a leading integrator of secure communication and information systems and technology, had many methods for distributing news and information across the company. Email was becoming more prevalent, but users were being overwhelmed by volume and spam mail, and distribution lists were getting harder to manage. Also, the Web site had static content. The process was highly manual, decentralized, labor-intensive, and inconsistent.

To solve the problem, the organization began taking advantage of the key features of its ECM solution—using news channels and tickers to "push" information to users and establishing notifications to "pull" items of interest. Next, GDC4 worked with various departments to help them maintain their own content. Finally, the static Web site content was migrated to a completely automated presentation of general news and information—the GDC4S News Stand.

Visits to the News Stand have increased steadily, while the labor required to post items and keep content up to date has decreased significantly. Archived stories are available for searching, providing an easy resource for people looking for an item of interest they remember seeing.

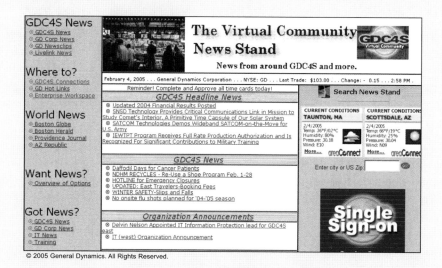

© 2005 General Dynamics. All Rights Reserved.

*Figure 2.8: Virtual Community News Stand
at General Dynamics C4 Systems*

Records Management (RM)

Records management is the discipline of managing records to meet operational needs, accountability requirements, and community expectations. Records management software works by allowing you to attach rules to electronic documents. These rules tell the system when it is okay to delete documents or move them to a data archive, either physically in boxes or electronically on storage devices such as CD-ROMs.

Government offices are superb at record keeping. When we are born, when we are married, when we have children, when we get divorced and when we die, a record is created at a government office. The rules that determine when those records can be archived and deleted are stipulated in government regulations and policies. Records management systems enforce these policies for government organizations, and for the equivalent form of vital records in an organization.

With daily pressure to comply with regulations and with changes to legislation, managing records and the lifecycle of documents have become crucial components of ECM.

Web Content Management (WCM)

How many Web sites does your company have? One? Twenty? These days, there are Web sites for every subject or product and many organizations host at least a dozen.

The first Web sites were created by computer geeks and academics. Because they were used mainly to share technical information, they were text-based and not visually stimulating. The World Wide Web and its support for graphic images and animation moved the Internet into the realm of art, and graphic designers became the new Web Masters. Corporations soon discovered that Web sites could be more than just a place for casual visitors to browse; they could be used to sell products, attract investors, inter-act with customers and engage with suppliers.

In today's organization, every department wants representation on the corporate Web site: Human Resources wants to advertise job vacancies; Marketing wants to promote events; Sales wants to sell product; and Investor Relations wants to inform shareholders. Furthermore, the CEO wants to have the site available in seven languages. Requests for site updates can overwhelm a single Web Master and create bottlenecks that result in information not being posted in a timely manner. The solution is to enable Web content to be owned and managed by individual content and authorities.

Web Content Management (WCM) software was created to allow multiple content contributors to make changes to Web sites, removing typical Web Master bottlenecks. WCM systems conceal all internal workings of a Web page, allowing users with little or no technical experience to add and modify content. WCM enables data fragments to be easily reused, so that updating the company's logo involves changing only one or two

More than one in eight Americans rely on VSP (Vision Service Plan) for eye care health coverage and thousands of companies trust the organization to provide a variety of eye care benefit plans. VSP teams with an extensive network of doctors across the country to deliver high quality and value, which creates significant challenges in managing information and communications. Some of the affected areas include credentialing and re-credentialing, doctor/practice information, and frequent communication with doctors. A unified ECM-based system allows VSP to manage the collection and dissemination of information more effectively.

The ECM system consolidates the newsletter creation process at VSP from ideas for content to final distribution to doctors. Integration with back-end systems automates the process and provides support for creating, revising, managing, versioning, and archiving the newsletter content. The system provides the functionality to generate a newsletter for each office, customizing content based on user requests, geography, and/or plan participation. It includes a repository for doctor credentials and information that aids with the doctor certification process. The repository has also been integrated with VSP's Web site to enable doctors to change practice information online.

Doctor satisfaction has improved considerably, as they now receive a single newsletter and only relevant, preference-based news and information. Automating manual processes has generated costs savings for VSP; mailing costs alone have decreased tenfold.

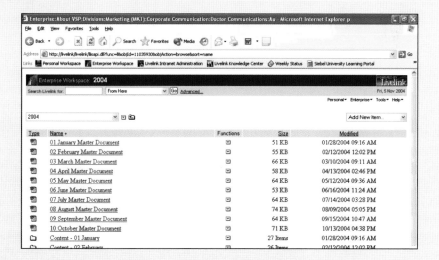

Figure 2.9: Vision Service Plan's Doctor
Communication Newsletter Overview

files, magically transforming the whole Web site. The technology behind Web content management is very similar to the technology required to manage documents. Most ECM suites include Web content management capabilities.

Teams and Collaboration

We have quickly grown accustomed to being able to phone each other anywhere at any time and in a matter of seconds. Cell phones and mobile telephony are so entrenched in our daily lives that it is hard to imagine life before they existed. The Internet has also revolutionized our ability to connect with others. We send documents over the Web and drum our finger impatiently awaiting their delivery. Being able to connect so easily with our colleagues over the Internet has made it possible to work effectively in virtual teams, with geography no longer a concern.

The Human Genome Project began in 1990 as a collaborative effort by research establishments around the globe to identify the 30,000 genes in human DNA. The project required the collaboration of scientists from many fields, including molecular biologists, engineers, physicists, chemists, and mathematicians at the U.S. Department of Energy. Technology had a huge role in the project; the Genome Data Base (GDB) is the worldwide repository for genome mapping data. Researchers around the world used the Internet to share research and answer questions. The project successfully concluded in April, 2003 and would not have been possible before the creation of the World Wide Web.

Global organizations can now capitalize on Web-based collaboration facilities to empower their workforces, working as virtual project teams to bring expertise from different areas and office locations to tackle business-critical problems. ECM systems include collaboration tools that enable the best minds within organizations to work together more efficiently—sharing information, capturing and preserving knowledge, managing collaborative processes and projects, and resolving issues.

Portals

The word portal immediately brings to mind science fiction movies or books in which a portal is depicted as a dimensional doorway in space that connects two or more worlds. Software portals are designed to perform a similar role by providing a place that connects multiple Web-based software applications. Portals are often the glue that pulls all of the bits of an ECM suite together, providing a contextual shop window to underlying applications.

Portal technology was designed to make the user's life easier by providing all the tools needed in a single, unified Web page. Most of us use portal tools to make sense of the Internet; Yahoo!®, MSN® and AOL® are all portals. They link us to places of interest very quickly, whether to book a vacation, check out the latest movie release or view the stats of our favorite football team. Most portals also let you personalize your experience; My Yahoo!®, for instance, allows you to build your own home page by picking from your favorite places and pages on the Web.

Rich Media and Digital Asset Management (DAM)

High-speed Internet connections now allow rich media types such as voice and video to be used over Internet connections. Software applications are rapidly emerging to take advantage of this technology for business use. Imagine sitting in traffic on your way to a business meeting and hearing your email messages read to you over your cell phone. Or picture yourself in an online meeting watching a presentation by a colleague overseas from the comfort of your home office. These are not pipe dreams; these technologies are part of the way we do business today.

CARE Canada, a humanitarian organization fighting global poverty, uses collaborative technology to save lives. When CARE relief workers operating in Kosovo came across an uncharted minefield, they transmitted live video over the Internet back to CARE headquarters to update their pilots on safe locations to drop food and medical supplies.

As telephony networks develop to support unlimited bandwidth, rich media applications will become more popular and integral to conducting business. Consequently, the need to manage rich media within ECM applications is steadily increasing.

Workflow and Business Process Management (BPM)

Business Process Management is a technology and an approach that connects people and content. BPM helps organizations combine content and collaboration to support structured and unstructured ways of working together.

Every organization conducts numerous business processes daily—from filling out a purchase request, to assigning documents for review and approval. The effectiveness of each process and the overall efficiency of an organization depend on business process automation tools. BPM provides powerful tools for defining and reusing business logic, simplifying business processes, and helping employees coordinate effectively with the organization and one another.

ECM solutions integrate with BPM systems to optimize business processes and improve performance. By linking processes with content creation, ECM enables organizations to exchange transactional information and respond more quickly to new or changing business requirements. BPM is a fundamental component of Enterprise Content Management.

Enterprise Application Extensions (EAE)

Enterprise applications such as Enterprise Resource Planning (ERP) and Customer Relationship Management (CRM) effectively perform transaction-based processing. However, data residing in these applications is the result of work that has been completed and, in many cases, cannot effectively support other business processes. Many processes, like contract creation, still require collaborative efforts of employees in multiple departments. To maximize content's effectiveness, organizations must connect content to the appropriate business processes and make it accessible to people participating in the process. Enterprise Application Extensions provide the underlying business structure that supports these business processes. Allocating unstructured content to business processes puts the information that people need at their fingertips without searching across many systems for content.

ECM extends enterprise applications by providing links between key processes and transactional information. Making this information secure and accessible across a variety of processes helps companies lower the costs and risks associated with meeting data retention and disposal requirements.

Bringing all the Technologies Together

Enterprise Content Management (ECM) is an amalgamation of the different technologies previously discussed. The component technologies that underpin ECM are shown in the grid in Figure 2.10. The grid separates technologies that connect people with people, such as email systems, from technologies that connect people with information, such as search functions. The vertical axis is divided into applications that deal with structured business processes, such as document management, and those that deal with unstructured processes, such as Web conferencing.

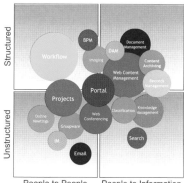

Figure 2.10: ECM Technologies

Making sense of all this technology is a challenge, so let's simplify the picture.

Everything on the left-hand side of the grid describes a technology that deals with working collaboratively. Collaboration technology links processes and individuals across the enterprise and creates a work environment in which teams can circulate ideas, experiences, and knowledge.

All the information, ideas, and data created as a by-product of collaborative work must be securely captured, managed and made available to others. The technologies on the right side of the grid deal with all content accumulated by business, such as memos, spread-sheets, reports, email messages, images, audio and video files, and transactional data.

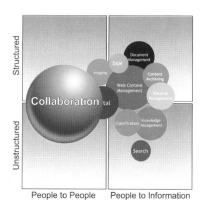

Figure 2.11: Collaboration Technologies

Connecting the content and collaboration bubbles is the genius behind ECM software suites. With ECM, knowledge is automatically captured as a by-product of collaborative work and is transformed into invaluable corporate knowledge. This knowledge is information that enables action, or further collaboration. ECM enables you to effortlessly capture ideas generated during an online meeting, or store plans and other documents created by virtual project teams. These knowledge assets are preserved in a secure knowledge repository, where they can be easily accessed, shared, or reused throughout an organization. People and content are interconnected by the productive work carried out by the business processes.

The "double bubble" motif is used throughout the book to illustrate ECM's value proposition of combined collaboration, content, and process.

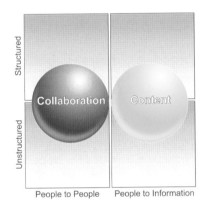

Figure 2.12: Content Technologies

The core technologies of an ECM suite must work together to address a vast range of business needs. While it may be possible to buy each of the technology pieces separately, bringing the pieces together in a suite provides a more efficient way to access and use information across multiple applications—making it easier to move content from one application to another (as shown in Figure 2.13).

Figure 2.13: ECM Value Proposition

ECM Solutions Framework

The diagram below shows the technologies that form the framework for ECM solutions. The framework provides a layer of ECM Lifecycle Management Services that link information workers to an Enterprise Library of information, which integrates content from multiple sources. The ECM Lifecycle Management services include: Collaboration, Content and Process. Collaboration services support person-to-person interaction and facilitate cross-application collaboration, including community and project workspaces, discussion forums, blogs, FAQs and polls. Content services provide a single point of access to all content, either in Web-based portals or the desktop applications with which information workers are most familiar. The ECM Solutions Framework provides access to content across the enterprise and supports storing the content on any mix of storage devices. Business process services deliver a common framework for automating the routing of information and documents, entering information via forms and notifying information workers of critical tasks and events via email. The ECM Solutions Framework facilitates the smooth evolution of existing solutions, speeds the development of new solutions and provides agility for the business to be responsive to change.

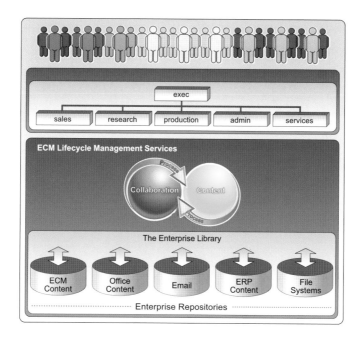

Figure 2.14: ECM Solutions Framework

Now that you are familiar with the fundamental technologies of Enterprise Content Management, we can begin the journey of discovery that led to the creation of a market. The following chapters focus on the stages of ECM adoption. In them, you'll be able to trace the adoption of ECM within the enterprise from start to finish with practical, real-life examples.

CHAPTER 3

RETURN ON INVESTMENT AND COMPLIANCE

This chapter will deal with the main reasons why ECM is deployed to solve problems—return on investment (ROI) and compliance. In order to succeed, companies need to know how to use the information and content that exists within their organizations to deliver better productivity and achieve competitive advantage. How can they understand the ROI of ECM in their organization?

Companies also must comply with an ever-growing list of regulatory requirements that govern how they run their business. These regulations require them to sort, collect, manage, and archive critical business information. How can they invest the resources to do this without it negatively affecting ROI?

Return on investment as a driver for deploying ECM is addressed in first part of this chapter, demonstrating methodologies, measures, and gains in productivity that lead to realizing ROI. Compliance is addressed in the latter half of the chapter.

Figure 3.1: Applications that Drive ROI in Departments

Figure 3.1 displays a grid of applications that drive ROI by department. All ECM technologies and applications can be mapped to an organizational chart. The figure shows a simplified representation of such an organizational chart to include Sales, Services, Research, Manufacturing and Administration.

With some ECM solutions, multiple departments work within a single application. This delivers a greater ROI than multiple departments working across multiple applications. The increase in ROI highlights the need for companies to invest in ECM solutions that deliver a variety of technologies to the organization through a standard platform. ROI, as opposed to perceived need, drives the spread of ECM solutions throughout the company. Senior management can deliver value to shareholders by making employees' daily tasks simpler and more effective.

Much of the IT industry in the past 50 years has focused on back-office databases and their management in Enterprise Resource Planning (ERP) systems. ERP has driven exceptional ROI by reducing inventory costs, increasing on-time performance, and improving decision making. In the same way, ECM delivers ROI by reducing the time it takes to make decisions because the decision makers are properly equipped.

In addition to the indirect savings from increased productivity, companies can realize ROI through more direct savings measurements. Immediate, real-time access to up-to-date and accurate electronic file folders containing critical business information reduces the need to physically store documents, which reduces document costs, storage space and the need for copiers. Of all missing and lost documents, 7.5 percent of paper documents are lost completely, 3 percent of the remainder is misfiled, and approximately $20.00 U.S. in labor is spent filing or retrieving a single document. Just think about the time it takes to find an email from last month!

Faster response times through more efficient operations will noticeably improve customer satisfaction. Whether it is an improved invoicing system or an organized knowledge base for customer self service, ECM ROI can also be measured in terms of overall customer satisfaction. This means happier customers and a well-protected brand image for the company.

The financial worksheet on the following page illustrates the annual impact that implementing a software solution has on profitability, cash flows, ROI and payback period.

FINANCIAL WORKSHEET FOR:

Pharmaceutical Company A*

Annual Savings	Base	Year 1	Year 2	Year 3
Savings In Printing Costs	$0	$6,075	$6,075	$6,075
Additional Work Productivity	$0	$47,957	$47,957	$47,957
Total Savings Per Period	**$0**	**$54,032**	**$54,032**	**$54,032**

Depreciation Schedule**	Initial	Year 1	Year 2	Year 3
Software	$100,000	$20,000	$20,000	$20,000
Hardware	$0	$0	$0	$0
Total Per Period	**$100,000**	**$20,000**	**$20,000**	**$20,000**

Expensed Costs	Initial	Year 1	Year 2	Year 3
Software	$50,000	$0	$0	$0
Hardware	$0	$0	$0	$0
Batteries	$0	$208	$208	$208
Personnel	$0	$600	$600	$600
Consulting	$0	$0	$0	$0
Training	$0	$202	$0	$0
Total Per Period	**$50,000**	**$1,010**	**$808**	**$808**

Basic Financial Assumptions				
All Federal and State Taxes	50%			
Discount Rate	15%			
Depreciation - Straight Line (Years)	5			

Net Cash Flows	Initial	Year 1	Year 2	Year 3
Total Benefits		$54,032	$54,032	$54,032
Less: Total Costs		$1,010	$808	$808
Less: Depreciation		$20,000	$20,000	$20,000
Net Profit Before Tax		$33,022	$33,224	$33,224
Net Profit After Tax		$16,511	$16,612	$16,612
Add: Depreciation		$20,000	$20,000	$20,000
Net Cash Flow After Taxes	**($115,000)**	**$36,511**	**$36,612**	**$36,612**

Financial Analysis	Results	Year 1	Year 2	Year 3
Annual ROI		28%	52%	73%
3-Year ROI	**73%**			
Discounted cash flows	($115,000)	$31,749	$27,684	$24,073
Cumulative cash flow		($83,251)	($55,568)	($31,495)
Payback (Years)	**3+**	**NA**	**NA**	**NA**
3-Year IRR	-2%			
3-Year NPV	($31,495)			

Figure 3.2: The Annual Impact of Implementing a Software Solution

ROI by Department

Consider group-level applications that are closely aligned to the way people work to achieve ROI. Figure 3.3 represents a typical organizational chart for a company.

Companies consist of many separate departments—Accounting and Finance, Legal, Administration, Marketing, Sales, IT, Research and Development, and so on. Each department has its own productivity requirements, and solutions must be designed to meet them and solve problems specific to a particular department. Typically, these solutions are driven by the need to improve efficiency or save money. Examples include Purchase Order Processing, Invoicing, Project Management, Claims Processing, FDA Compliance, Product Lifecycle Management (PLM), and Sales Readiness, just to mention a few.

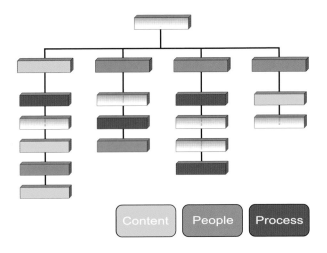

Figure 3.3: Typical Organization

Increasing Productivity

ECM has been increasing productivity within organizations since the early 1980s. Document management systems dramatically reduced paper and storage cost, but perhaps more importantly, increased productivity within the departments that embraced these systems. Now, ECM solutions are a blend of technologies that have come together to create an enterprise infrastructure able to extract ROI in many ways.

> Sinclair Knight Merz

Dispersed across geographic boundaries, time zones, and companies, Sinclair Knight Merz relies heavily on the effective performance of its virtual teams. Managing documents across all projects and offices was essential, but the high bandwidth cost of a decentralized, global document management system was a major constraint for SKM.

As the company continues to grow, a dedicated wide area network (WAN) represents an increasingly significant component of the IT expenditure. Using leading edge technology to provide best price performance is paramount. A document management system based on a distributed model with partial replication and a single server proved to be the solution. The system optimized bandwidth and maximized performance, while curbing associated costs.

SKM applied a cost-benefit analysis to the ECM implementation, and estimates a 167 percent internal rate of return on investment over a five-year period. The benefits were predominantly derived from re-use of work and the promotion of virtual teams. These factors allowed SKM's worldwide community to use best practices and enabled greater team collaboration.

Business Case Benefits and Savings

Internal rate of return 167%

	Year 1	Year 2	Year 3	Year 4	Year 5
Costs	$1.9M	$1.7M	$1.3M	$1.2M	$1.2M
Benefits	$1.5M	$3.1M	$4.6M	$5.2M	$5.5M
Profit/(Loss)	($0.4M)	$1.4M	$3.3M	$4.0M	$4.3M

Re-use of work · · · Best Practice

Virtual Teams · · · Document Tracking

Project Focus · · · Revision Control

Extranets

Figure 3.4: SKM's Business Benefits and ROI

One of ECM's underlying principles is the realization that collaboration has an important role in lending context to content. Capturing the how, when, and why content was generated provides an excellent picture as to how relevant the information is to future undertakings. Being able to easily access accurate information leads to better decisions. Better decisions save time and money. The graph in Figure 3.5 shows the value of making a better decision faster. The area represented by the savings of time shows the true return on investment for an ECM system.

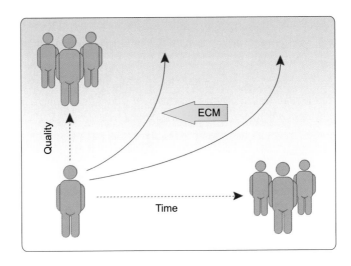

Figure 3.5: The ROI Impact of ECM

The diagram shows that a group normally makes a better decision than a single person, but that they also take a much longer time to do it. The trade-off between the time and the quality of a decision is the basis for managing individuals and groups in many industries. The impact of ECM on changing this equation is shown by the shifting of the tradeoff arrows over to the left. The area saved in time by the quality of decisions is the ROI achieved for any given ECM solution.

Today, content and collaboration management is still largely being adopted on a depart-mental or group level. As infrastructure such as the Internet develops and becomes more transparent and less technically driven, it will become easier to deploy across entire organizations and beyond. Collaborating through ECM solutions will become as simple as clicking on a hyperlink. Simple, effective technology will lead the way to increased ROI.

A new market is emerging to address the needs of knowledge-intensive organizations. Increasing overall organizational effectiveness in a turbulent business world has become a great challenge that ECM can play a role in solving. To achieve ROI while adhering to strict new regulations and legislation, ECM developers will offer applications specific to individual industries. These customized solutions will be of the greatest value if they can deploy across multiple departments, support new technologies, and scale to meet the growing needs within the enterprise. The unique ability of ECM to support additional content such as email and rich media files will also increase the solution's value.

Measuring Results

There are many ways to achieve ROI with ECM solutions. To justify the original investment and any further expansion into ECM, organizations must quantify their results. They must capture a baseline measurement of the processes that are to be improved as well as any others that might be affected before adopting an ECM solution. Specific goals must be set and results must be carefully measured. While most organizations will have some type of measurement before deploying a solution to justify the investment, many will not continue to measure after the deployment. This typically occurs when the savings have become so apparent to all involved that they do not feel it is necessary to measure the obvious. Sometimes, the value of the ECM solution is generated in ways not anticipated by the original justification and there is no easy reference point. This is unfortunate since most ECM solutions result in benefits that far exceed the initial estimate and in ways that were not originally intended. Measuring productivity gains from ECM will normally lead to greater adoption in the future.

Saving Time

Corporate reorganization and mergers often create opportunities for ECM solutions to generate ROI. Bringing together disparate accounting systems and managing the paper documents involved can be a difficult task. There is a constant need to refer to paper-based documents under these circumstances. ECM solutions can help with process.

An easy area to measure ROI is document retrieval. It can take anywhere from 10 to 15 minutes to retrieve a paper document, assuming that it is stored on site. To retrieve a document that has been scanned and archived within an ECM solution can take as little as 10 seconds. This resulted in working hours savings of 97 percent in the case of a global leader in the life sciences industry, generating ROI rapidly and creating payback within nine months.

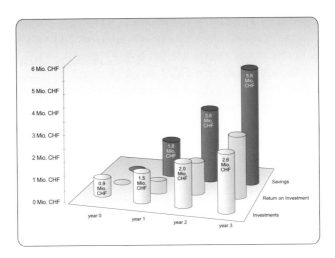

Figure 3.6: Cumulative Investments and Savings

Lowering Distribution Costs

Federations and cooperatives need to report to their members in great detail. The cost to print and courier these reports adds up quickly. Time is lost as paper documents are manufactured and distributed. Waiting an extra week to make an important decision can be costly. Finding information within these reports can be time consuming. Storing them for the legislated period of time requires expensive physical space.

One such cooperative in the Financial Services Industry was called upon to generate 15 monthly reports and distribute them to 243 members—over 8 million pages annually. Today, an ECM solution relieves their database by storing their reports in an electronic archive. The information is now closer at hand, and it requires only seconds to find a particular piece of information, whereas it would sometimes take several days in the past. The reports are distributed electronically in seconds, saving time and eliminating printing and courier costs.

Increasing Efficiency in Manufacturing

While the time to retrieve documents and the cost to produce and distribute them are tangible savings that are easily measured, they are just the tip of the iceberg. In both Manufacturing and Construction, the savings to be realized by improving change management can far exceed these initially obvious areas.

By using an electronic repository with versioning functionality for improved drawing management, engineers are no longer plagued by the circulation of outdated plans.

Workflow improves task management. Project status is visible through the solution's accountability and tracking functions. Perhaps harder to measure since these tools are used to avoid mistakes, as opposed to reducing tangible costs, they are certainly major generators of ROI.

A major European bank engaged in two construction projects but only used ECM to manage one of them. This created a unique opportunity to benchmark traditional versus ECM tools and workflows. Contractor management improved, since changes made during the ECM-based project were immediately communicated to all concerned parties. The changes were fully traceable, which reduced the risk of claims and overspending by an estimated 30 percent. Improved change management enabled more efficient planning, resulting in approximate savings of 50 percent. Over five years, a cumulative ROI of 437 percent was realized. The ECM system provided the project team with an efficient tool for information management and dissemination as well as collaboration.

Eliminating Duplication of Effort

In many enterprises, the Marketing Department develops, distributes and archives brand assets that are used for a variety of mediums, including print and the Web. Increasing productivity, controlling distribution, and improving market share are all key goals for the Marketing Department—a group that often works within tight budgets. Each day, hours can be wasted by manually searching for files on CDs, desktop systems and servers. Content is often in the wrong file format for its intended use. Marketing content is typically both structured and unstructured data, including desktop publishing files, vector images, bitmap images, and rich media files. ECM systems that manage digital assets can dramatically reduce the time it takes to find the right marketing images and collateral. They also eliminate the costly, often error-prone practice of re-creating content. ROI is easily calculated in this case if Marketing staff track their time.

Decreasing Labor Costs

In the Manufacturing sector, the salaries and benefits of employees manufacturing and/or assembling products are often the highest single cost. ECM solutions that support efficient methodologies (e.g., Lean Manufacturing, Product Compliance) generate excellent ROI when they can shorten the process and reduce the human expense. Faster product development and higher responsiveness to change are also outcomes typically derived by using ECM solutions effectively. Another source of ECM solution ROI is the reduction of waste, rework and warranty claims by assuring compliance to corporate, customer, and government standards at the design and manufacturing stages.

Retaining Staff Reduces Hiring Expenses

Leading edge technology organizations evolve quickly. This can mean long hours, extended travel and high stress situations for employees. Keeping staff happy is often difficult, but the knowledge and experience that they bring to the organization is key to its success. ECM solutions can help retain employees and the knowledge assets that they have either developed or brought with them.

Ensuring that employees are provided with all the tools necessary to do their jobs is important in keeping them happy. Creating an environment in which it is easy to find and share information was the major focus of technology spending after a leading North American telecommunications company conducted an employee satisfaction survey in 1997. A 1.2 million-page intranet was transitioned into a system that pulled all support services information together in one place.

In addition to the benefits of reduced network hardware and software costs, network management savings, HR and incoming personnel productivity savings, this organiza-tion recognized a number of qualitative benefits from deploying the ECM solution. Providing rapid access to information and resources helped the company improve the work experience and reduce frustration for staff, thereby improving employee satisfaction. Organized information resources and applications along with integrated search tools reduced the time required for employees to complete standard tasks, such as ordering a mobile phone or reserving facilities, which increased productivity and ROI.

ROI and Compliance

To comply with government regulations throughout the world, organizations must collect, manage, and archive critical business information. Records of all types must be easy to find and present ECM solutions can create ROI by managing this process efficiently. Solutions that play a proactive role by securely storing records for a designated period of time as well as cross referencing records to related information and facilitating audit history create additional value. Implementing best practices for compliance protects the organization from risk while streamlining administrative and operational costs. Integrated ECM solutions allow organizations to be proactive in preparing for new or evolving compliance regulations.

Compliance is delivered across all departments within an ECM-driven organization. This chapter outlines how ECM solutions are helping many of the world's leading companies address compliance and governance issues. Innovator stories in this chapter demonstrate how organizations are using ECM solutions to comply with legislation, including the U.S. Government Paperwork Elimination Act (GPEA). In these stories, ECM enables organizations to achieve compliance and improve business operations. Additional

Innovator stories are presented that address email management in the context of corporate governance and overall business improvement.

ECM solutions are playing a major role in helping many of the world's leading companies streamline and accelerate compliance and corporate governance globally.

Corporations in every industry and in all countries face countless government regulations, industry standards and company procedures. How a company manages itself and its compliance efforts has a direct impact on shareholder value. Poor management and/or non-compliance can lead to lost business, financial penalties, and even criminal charges. In some industries, failing an auditor's inspection can lead to a company being closed down until corrective action is taken.

It is critical for any organization to be well managed and compliant, but there is more to compliance than simply following rules. At the heart of each set of industry regulations are basic principles for doing good business—principles derived from the experience of best practices, policies, and procedures for each industry. They are often designed to prevent mistakes from being repeated. To understand how ECM helps organizations manage compliance and governance, it is important to differentiate between the two concepts.

Compliance and Corporate Governance

Today's business environment is more complex and regulated than ever, and for good reason. Corporate issues involving fraudulent accounting, malfeasance and data quality issues frequently dominate news headlines. CEOs and Boards of Directors (BoD) are under public scrutiny and, as a result, regulatory requirements have emerged to address these issues using commonly accepted principals of corporate governance.

Each company has unique corporate governance activities. A company's business units, departments, operations, industry and geographic locations all define the environment in which it operates. These variables combine in a very specific way to determine how the company can and, in the case of regulations, must operate.

Formally, corporate governance has been defined as "...the structure that is intended to make sure that the right questions get asked and that checks and balances are in place to make sure that the answers reflect what is best for the creation of long-term, sustainable value." (Robert A. Monks and Nell Minnow, Corporate Governance, Third Edition, 2004, Blackwell Publishing Ltd.). Informally, corporate governance may be defined as how a company manages itself. A company's environment influences and determines governance activities, which include methods to direct, manage and control the company. These methods must be communicated company-wide and improved over time to drive efficiency and cost savings and to respond to the changing needs of the business.

Figure 3.7: Compliance and Corporate Governance

Compliance may then be defined as conforming to a rule. Types of compliance 'rules' include:

• Government Legislation and Regulation,

• Industry Standards,

• Internal Company Policy and Procedures.

'Rule' implies a consequence for being non-compliant. Government agencies created to enforce legislation, industry standard bodies, and corporate directives are examples of such regulatory bodies. Furthermore, compliance with the rules can be required or voluntary. Figure 3.8 depicts compliance types and typical corresponding consequences for being non-compliant.

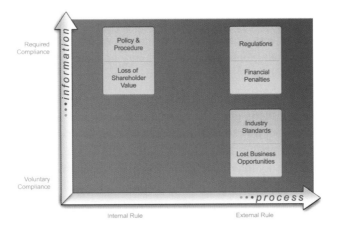

Figure 3.8: Compliance Continuum

In summary, it is important to identify that compliance must happen according to a defined rule (regulation, standard, or policy) to have meaning, and that compliance is only one component of corporate governance.

The Sarbanes-Oxley Act

One of the regulations that has garnered much attention is the Sarbanes-Oxley Act (SOX). The Sarbanes-Oxley Act, administered in 2002 by the Securities and Exchange Commission (SEC), was enacted to prevent scandals (such as the high-profiled ones in the recent past) from reoccurring.

At its highest level, the Sarbanes-Oxley Act is about restoring investor confidence in the integrity of financial reporting. It is a piece of legislation that has caused some confusion with respect to corporate governance. SOX is a regulation that requires compliance; the activities required by the company to be compliant affect a company's procedures and systems.

In short, SOX regulates a component of corporate governance—the procedures and systems regarding internal controls over financial reporting.

The Sarbanes-Oxley legislation impacts the following four main areas:

• Corporate Accountability and Responsibility

• Internal Controls & Procedures

• Audit and Accounting

• Enhanced Disclosure and Reporting Requirements

While Sarbanes-Oxley is complex and broad in scope, there are only three sections that are having significant impact on corporations:

• Section 302: Corporate Responsibility for Financial Reports—The CEO and CFO must prepare a quarterly statement certifying financial statements and disclosures. This has been in effect since August 2002—certifications can found in the 10K and 10Q filed with the SEC.

• Section 404: Management Assessment of Internal Controls—An internal control report must accompany an annual report taking responsibility for and assessing the effectiveness of internal controls. Compliance dates are described in the following section, the earliest being for calendar years ending on or after November 15th, 2004.

• Section 409: Real-Time Issuer Disclosures—Material changes affecting financial disclosures must be reported on a "rapid and current basis." Compliance is effective beginning in August 2004.

Companies need technology solutions that can organize, automate, and make efficient the effort required to comply with these sections. ECM solutions are designed to enable organizations to operate in accordance with SOX and other regulations.

Why Organizations Need Corporate Governance

Two key objectives contribute to why organizations need to address governance: mitigating risk and optimizing operations. The primary goal is to maintain and increase shareholder value. Poor governance exposes a company to unacceptable risks and the threat of disastrous consequences.

In a growing number of industries, organizations must not only achieve regulatory compliance but prove compliance as well—and penalties for non-compliance are severe.

But improved governance goes beyond simply mitigating risk and avoiding penalties. Regulations are based on demands that inherently describe optimal business operations. By meeting regulations, organizations ensure that their business processes adhere to industry-established best practices and procedures.

Corporations across the globe are wisely striving to learn from—rather than react to the enormous governance failures of companies such as Enron and Parmalat. Each industry has its own regulators and regulations, but much can be learned and applied to organizations in any industry.

ECM allows a systemizing of these processes and their underlying data, so that organizations ensure nothing important is omitted, and everyone is aware of who is responsible for doing what, when, how, why, and where. This helps ensure that everyone is not just doing his or her thing, and that time, money and other resources are used efficiently.

Governance is changing business on a global level. A representative sample of various global regulations and regulatory bodies is shown in Figure 3.9:

	USA and Canada	Europe and Rest of the World
Telecommunications	CRTC	CCITT, OfCom, OFTEL
Financial Services	CFTC, FDIC, FRB, FSA NAIC, NASD, OSFI, SEC	Basel 2, BaFin, CCA, FSA FSAP, GICS, IMF
Engineering	APQP, QS	ISO9000, ISO14000
Government	DoD, PIPEDA, RDIMS	DOMEA, EMEA, PRO, SAGA, MoReq, VERS
Pharmaceuticals	FDA, Health Canada, TPD	CPMP, EMEA, MHLW
Healthcare	HIPAA	
Cross-Industry	Bill 198, COCO, OSHA SEC, SOX	King II, KonTraG, Legge 321, LSF, Turnbull,

Figure 3.9: Who Sets the Regulations for Your Business?

A Platform for Compliance and Corporate Governance

Enterprise Content Management platforms play a key role in allowing organizations to provide compliance and corporate governance in a cost-effective and efficient manner. Figure 3.10 provides a framework for how the components of ECM support business requirements to ensure governance and compliance with appropriate laws, regulations and court orders that form part of the environment in which an organization operates.

Although technology alone cannot satisfy compliance requirements, it can play a critical role when integrated into the proper processes and organizational structure.

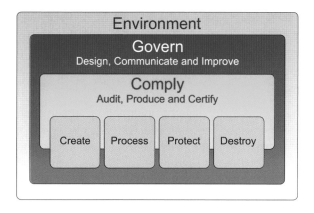

Figure 3.10: DLM Functionality is the Core to Efficient Information Compliance

ECM platforms assist in defining and supporting governance policies by providing capabilities to specify the policies and by allowing the organization to enforce and audit compliance with these policies. The following ECM technologies are key to helping organizations achieve compliance and manage corporate governance:

• Document Lifecycle Management

• Archiving and Records Management

• Enterprise Application Extensions

• Email Management

• Rich Media and Digital Asset Management

• Web Content Management

• Search

Document Lifecycle Management (DLM)

Pertinent corporate information must be identified, captured, and communicated in a manner and timeframe that allows people to carry out their responsibilities. Effective communication must also occur in a broader sense, flowing down and across an organization, as well as to customers, suppliers, regulators, and shareholders. Compliance and governance necessitates the effective capture and dissemination of information as organizations try to achieve compliance. DLM enables companies to capture any type of electronic information and apply retention schedules to it, ensuring that it is archived or deleted and physically destroyed. This capability is essential to organizations pursuing compliance. Permissions and auditing functions provide controlled access to critical information. An audit trail capture ensures that all access and actions are recorded to prevent unnecessary access to information that is subject to privacy regulations.

Email Management

Records management legislation governs information content but not the format in which it is stored, communicated, or conveyed. Records management legislation covers all forms of electronic communication, such as email and instant messaging. However, due to the unprecedented rate at which organizations have adopted email and the sheer volume of communication that occurs through this medium, email represents one of the largest information and risk management problems today. Many organizations have faced large losses because they lacked an effective email management system. A major tobacco manufacturer was fined $2.75 million U.S. in August, 2004, because key executives failed to comply with a court order to retain emails relevant to pending

In response to the new compliance requirements posed by Sections 302 and 906 of the Sarbanes-Oxley Act, UBS, one of the world's leading financial institutions, implemented an internal certification process for financial reports, in which senior executives formally certify their financial figures and processes using a 'sub-confirmation' process.

During the internal certification process, appropriate persons are notified via email when their input is required, and are then granted personalized access to the relevant documents on the UBS intranet. All relevant processes are archived and tracked in a log file. The CEO and Group Controller—generally the CFO— issue a final certification for the Security Exchange Commission only when all internal processes have been completed.

The UBS corporate governance portal enables the company's business managers worldwide to collaborate in developing internal and external business reports. Relevant departments have access to a complete overview and status of the certification processes at all times. All related processes have been automated and simplified, expediting the certification process.

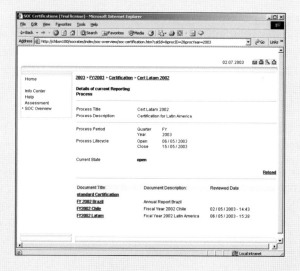

Figure 3.11: Certification Processes at UBS

litigation. ECM platforms reduce risks and maintain compliance with regulations that apply specifically to email.

Regulations such as SEC Rule 17-a4 and NASD 3010 define strict rules on how long emails must be retained. Indexes on emails and attachments allow for auditing and recovery of all content upon request. ECM solutions provide the technical and logistical functionality needed to fulfill these requirements.

Compliance Applications

As part of an integrated system, ECM can provide a powerful and targeted tool for delivering information and training on anti-money laundering policies and procedures to all employees. The system ensures compliance with Sections 312 and 326 of the U.S. Patriot Act by automating the generation and escalation of notifications for account renewals, as well as enabling effective management of archived records when closing accounts. With this solution, ECM reduces the risk associated with non-compliance by making the management of the customer acquisition process more efficient and compliant.

Financial Services: Accreditation and Certification Management

In the financial industry, employees dealing in the sale of financial products (mutual funds, stocks, and other investment products) must be registered with one or more regulatory authorities. Employees are registered with authorities based on where the employee operates and which products they wish to sell. These registrations are term-based (usually annual or multi-year) and are renewed based on criteria established by each authority.

To provide highly effective corporate management and training solutions for the Financial Services sector, ECM enables users provide corporate learning and training programs that meet regulatory objectives.

ECM was designed to address a number of needs: growth in regulatory reporting requirements; leveraging existing investments in training content and programs; maintaining detailed registration and licensing records for compliance management; and the need to manage all detailed records necessary for regulatory compliance.

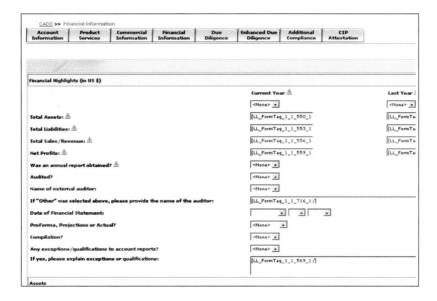

Figure 3.12: Anti-Money Laundering

Financial Services: Anti-Money Laundering

In the wake of the September 11 terrorist attacks in the United States, the focus on money laundering prevention and detection has intensified. Governments around the world have enacted laws requiring banks and other financial institutions to take an active role in preventing and detecting money laundering. Money laundering is a risk that must be managed at the highest levels of any organization.

Financial institutions in particular are vulnerable to money laundering due to the range of customer relationships they manage and the array of products, services, and transaction types they offer. Weaknesses in policies and procedures, regulatory and internal audit compliance functions, and transaction and information systems all compound the financial institution's exposure to money laundering risks.

ECM provides a secure environment for managing customer information, including multilingual forms and workflow that are used to capture and verify information required to authenticate customers.

> HP Singapore

A technology solutions provider, HP Singapore was experiencing rapid growth and an increase in knowledge needs. To establish itself more strongly as an R&D enterprise and increase its leading role in product development, HP Singapore employed ECM technology to facilitate its knowledge strategy and support effective knowledge sharing.

The Web-based solution, named "Konnect" for connecting people with people for knowledge, supports project and program management and departmental workspaces. Deployed in less than six months, the enterprise-wide implementation allows for capturing, sharing, and re-using information and knowledge through workspaces and communities of practice.

Centralizing knowledge has significantly improved project management and collaboration, as access time to information and knowledge has been dramatically reduced from one hour to five minutes. The improvements directly contribute to the organization's goal of operational excellence. Within the first year of implementing the solution, HP Singapore has realized a return on investment (ROI) of approximately 375 percent.

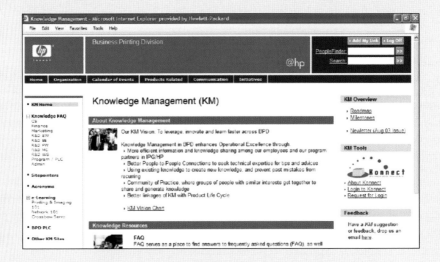

Figure 3.13: HP Singapore's Knowledge Management Vision

Pharmaceutical: Clinical Trials

ECM provides the infrastructure, knowledge management and real-time collaborative workspaces that pharmaceutical employees need to share, manage, and analyze clinical trial data throughout the entire clinical trial process. ECM's combined content management and collaboration functionality helps to reduce costs and improve quality by providing instant access to CRFs, SAEs, queries, patient diaries and inventory reports. ECM extends an organization's ability to share clinical data across organizations and with partnering companies, such as Contract Research Organizations (CROs) and sponsor companies, by providing a secure extranet environment in which researchers can work together.

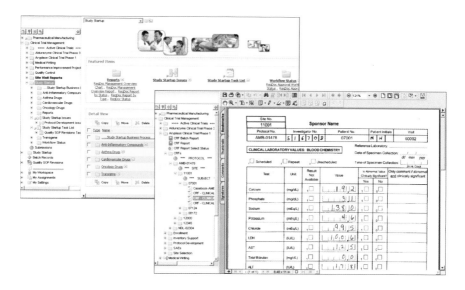

Figure 3.14: Clinical Trials Applications

Government: Email Management

Email messages and attachments represent business records that must be retained and managed securely to support regulatory compliance, avoid legal fines or litigation costs, and satisfy auditing requirements. Regulations like SEC 17-a4, NASD 3010 or DoD 5015.2 define strict rules as to how and for how long emails must be retained. Indexes on emails and attachments allow for auditing and recovery of all content when requested. ECM solutions provide the technical and logistical functionality to fulfill these requirements efficiently.

> Vintage Petroleum

Vintage Petroleum Inc. is a rapidly growing independent oil and gas company. A large organization with facilities across the globe, Vintage operates its satellite offices as independent smaller businesses, while processes such as invoicing remain centralized at the corporate headquarters. The company's U.S. accounting office processes approximately 10,000 invoices per month.

The company chose ECM as a platform for business process improvements to increase productivity, control information, and meet compliance requirements associated with the Sarbanes-Oxley Act. In addition, the solution manages the invoicing process, maintains corporate content and enables employees to access information in a central repository.

Invoicing cycle times have now been shortened with a more controlled process because district offices no longer need to ship or fax paperwork between offices. All invoices are stored in a central location and can be reviewed and processed from various locations. As well, using reporting capabilities, Vintage has improved its forecasting process and audit and revision controls to ensure compliance with regulations such as Sarbanes-Oxley.

Cognos PowerPlay Web Explorer	Vintage					
Invoice Date ▾ Pay Status ▾ Vendor ▾ Engineer ▾ Level 1 Approval ▾ Geography ▾						
Invoice Amount ▾		**NORTH**		**WEST**		**EAST**	
as values ▾		▽ PAID	▽ UNPAID	▽ PAID	▽ UNPAID	▽ PAID	▽ UNPAID
2001	2001 Q 1	$849.00	$6,314.00	$408.00	$.00	$.00	$.00
	2001 Q 2	$2,975.00	$.00	$478.00	$.00	$.00	$.00
	2001 Q 3	$28,490.00	$.00	$4,668.00	$.00	$.00	$.00
	2001 Q 4	$323,870.00	$1,293.00	$75,241.00	$.00	$3,609.00	$.00
	2001	**$356,184.00**	**$7,607.00**	**$80,795.00**	**$.00**	**$3,609.00**	**$.00**
2002	2002 Q 1	$7,964,921.00	$.00	$1,798,193.00	$.00	$254,781.00	$.00
	2002 Q 2	$13,937,544.00	$410,066.00	$2,360,406.00	$1,863.00	$1,057,428.00	$577.00
	2002 Q 3	$4,871,260.00	$1,726,000.00	$1,328,274.00	$363,216.00	$294,349.00	$190,182.00
	2002 Q 4	$12,055.00	$19,915.00	$.00	$108.00	$.00	$.00
	2002	**$26,785,780.00**	**$2,155,981.00**	**$5,486,873.00**	**$365,187.00**	**$1,606,558.00**	**$190,759.00**
Invoice Date ▾	... ▾	**$27,144,029.00**	**$2,172,990.00**	**$5,567,668.00**	**$365,187.00**	**$1,610,193.00**	**$190,759.00**

Figure 3.15: A Data Mart at Vintage Petroleum

ECM: Bringing it All Together

All companies today face the difficult challenge of maintaining performance while operating in an increasingly risky and regulated environment. The key to successful compliance with corporate governance standards is to ensure that consistent processes are rapidly deployed throughout an organization, that all critical information is managed, and that people are fully trained and can work together within the compliance framework.

ECM provides organizations with an enterprise-wide platform that delivers compliance and governance solutions. ECM solutions were designed to address a number of governance needs: growth in regulatory reporting requirements, levering existing investments in training content and programs, maintaining detailed registration and licensing records for compliance management, and managing the records necessary for regulatory compliance.

With a proven history for implementing compliant records management solutions, including ISO 9000, the U.S. Patriot Act, SEC, DOE, and OSHA, ECM delivers the document and process management functionality required, for example, by the Sarbanes-Oxley act in the U.S. It provides a secure environment for managing customer information to capture, track, and authenticate customer information. As part of an integrated system, ECM can provide a powerful, targeted tool for delivering information and training on anti-money laundering policies. The system ensures compliance by automating the generation and escalation of notifications for account renewals, and manages record archiving when customers close accounts. ECM reduces the risks associated with non-compliance by making the control of information and process more efficient, transparent, and compliant.

In the chapters that follow, we'll take a closer look at the solutions that are inherent to effective enterprise content management deployments. Using ECM to implement governance solutions within an organization or across an industry have many similarities.

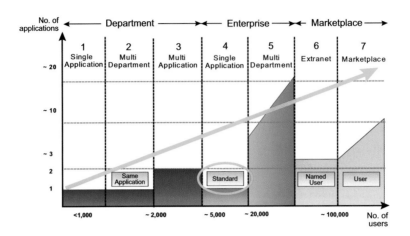

Figure 4.1: The Stages of ECM Adoption

The diagram above, illustrating the stages of ECM adoption within an Enterprise, is organized along two dimensions: users and application deployed. This graph reveals the gradual adoption path of ECM, starting from a simple department application and ending with an online marketplace.

At the Enterprise level, it is important to understand the process by which the organization adopts ECM solutions. Understanding the stages of adoption will lead to more effective results achieved in a more efficient manner. As with other forms of learning and technology adoption, ECM is normally adopted within organizations in a very distinctive, staged manner. While the definition of stages can be arbitrary, the concept of set stages is constant.

CHAPTER 4

ECM ADOPTION WITHIN THE ENTERPRISE

Effectively and securely managing content is good for business. When content is properly managed, it is highly accessible and easy to use. The right information at the fingertips of the right person can make the difference in completing a timely response to the opportunity of a lifetime for an organization. When an entire enterprise can provide effective and timely responses to changing market situations, that is the ultimate in competitive advantage and flexibility.

By improving business processes across the enterprise, organizations stand to recover their investment, decrease time to market and increase overall productivity.

At this very moment, the critical breakthrough or business practice improvement that could sharpen competitive edge exists somewhere in an organization—in the engineer's notepad, in the product manager's briefcase, or embedded in an email. Such seeds of innovation, an organization's intellectual capital, too often go untapped.

Enterprise Content Management (ECM) represents a critical new stage in the advancement of the Information Age. ECM is more than just a product or a solution. It describes both a philosophical approach and the underlying technologies used to help businesses transform content into competitive advantage.

The critical value of ECM solutions at the Enterprise level lies in the fact that they transcend departmental and organizational boundaries, leading to value creation that is greater than the sum of its parts. This is an evolution of ECM that is not easily achieved at the beginning but instead requires a carefully planned adoption process.

For an organization to effectively take advantage of ECM solutions at the enterprise level, it must have the leadership of the executive team. Any inter-departmental use of knowledge will almost always require intervention and direction from the executive team.

Executive Department

The Executive Department is the critical source of information that the organization requires to manage itself. Therefore, this department needs timely management of knowledge and intellectual property (IP). A particular mandate of the executive group is to achieve close co-ordination among departments.

ECM solutions for Executive Departments provide a context in which management practices can be treated as intellectual property that can be created and inventoried for current and future use. Executive Departments have high content challenges that require a variety of ECM solutions. The Executives must share knowledge with colleagues from other departments, customers, partners, and suppliers to manage new programs and proposals and develop effective new products and services. Effective use of ECM will make an executive team more productive. This is critical to achieving competitive advantage.

In many industries, the Executive Department is the most important in the company. In fast-changing environments, co-ordination with just one or two departments such as Marketing or Research and Development can mean the difference between success and failure. The role of ECM with executives covers both collaboration and content require-ments. For the purpose of this discussion, we will define the Executive Department as the Board of Directors, Senior Management and Officers of the company.

The executive group has many operational and strategic duties. Some of these include governance and regulatory obligations. As we discussed in Chapter 3, most major regulations involve at least an overseeing function by the executive group. Legislation such as the Sarbanes-Oxley Act (SOX) is promising to make this involvement even more direct for members of the Executive Department.

Balancing Governance and Productivity

The biggest challenge of an Executive Department is improving the productivity of the organization while meeting quality and governance goals. This is a delicate balancing act for executives, since an over emphasis in one area could cause problems in the other. For example, being overly efficient in the short term can create profits that are then offset by long-term regulatory problems that restrict operations and severely damage the long-term value of the organization. The reverse is also true. Too much adherence to regulatory or litigious concerns can create too much overhead and hurt the bottom line. Achieving and maintaining a balance between these two requirements is the responsibility of the executive team.

Board Management

One of the most common executive management tasks is reporting financial results to the board. The board has a duty to represent shareholders by proper review and discussion of performance and results. This is a critical function of the board and, for public companies, is an area governed by the Sarbanes-Oxley legislation. ECM delivers this information via secure Web access and allows for discussion and deliberation over the Internet. This proves to be advantageous for board members entrusted with governance of the organization. Not only is electronic transition of information beneficial (because of its immediacy), but the information is also recorded and archived for future retrieval. Another benefit is the elimination of travel costs and logistical delays. Using online collaboration tools also permits the capture of decision making for future reference, a critical aspect of Sarbanes-Oxley.

Establishing Company-wide Goals

The most important task of a management team is to create a budget. Without one, organizations lack company-wide goals. Therefore, effective organizations create budget documents that are a result of bottom-up collaboration to achieve buy in. It is critical that this collaboration can be captured for future reference. In today's business environment, maintaining a competitive edge while satisfying the increased scrutiny of industry regulators is the critical balance that the executive team must achieve.

Regulatory compliance is a primary concern of global organizations today. Both financial regulations such as Sarbanes-Oxley and Basel Capital Accord II, as well as industry-specific regulations such as New Drug Approvals (NDAs) for the FDA, are creating new challenges for firms. It is now more important than ever to ensure that all employees understand regulatory requirements, and that the company can prove their compliance.

Capabilities associated with Employee Accreditations provide the infrastructure to support effective employee compliance initiatives by:

- Ensuring that training courses, product information and corporate information are delivered to the right employees at the right time;

- Effectively distributing tests, surveys, questionnaires, courseware and other corporate content;

- Automatically tracking employee progress, analyzing the effectiveness of courses and comparing the performance of individuals taking the same courses;

> British Telecom

Who: Having started as the telephone providers for the UK, BT has become a leading player in the information and communication space. The organization employs approximately one hundred thousand people who are dispersed mainly across the UK and also worldwide.

Business Objective: To successfully support and maintain ECM communities across BT, spanning from pre-launch discovery to post-launch evaluation.

Business Needs: Collaboration was impeded due to geographical dispersion, and document management needed improvement.

Solution Overview: A Coaching & Training program enabled BT to successfully deploy ECM technology and ensure effective use of a Web-based collaboration platform, centralized knowledge and document management, and communities of practice.

Solution Scope: Enterprise wide.

Benefits: Improved collaboration; ability to capture, store, and reuse intellectual assets; direct information access; increased process visibility; enhanced corporate governance; improved productivity and efficiency; cost and time savings.

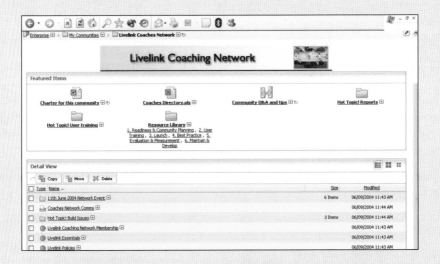

Figure 4.2: ECM Coaching Network at BT

ECM was initially brought into BT in August of 1999 as a knowledge management and communications system for a small, select number of users. In 2002, the organization made the strategic decision to roll out ECM enterprise wide. To do this cost effectively and to ensure full user adoption, BT developed a Coaching & Training program, taking a humanistic approach to the implementation.

BT's Coaching & Training program was created to develop techniques and methodology for ensuring real use of ECM. In other words, the program aimed to enable users to fully understand how they could best use the technology, what the organization was trying to achieve through the implementation, and to encourage information sharing.

This ECM adoption approach included a small, central coaching team who set out the policies, determined the way the technology was rolled out, set up a training program, and then used that program to train select local coaches. This was done through basic Web-based training, film shows, and a coach network zone. Once the local coaches were trained, they received full support from the central team so they could run their community successfully.

Communities at BT may include work teams, project teams, or communities of practice. Each community has its own seven-step journey with a focus on early preparation prior to launch. The journey starts with readiness assessment, planning and coaching training, travels to launches, and user training through post-launch evaluation and maintenance and development. The coaching role is mandatory for the lifecycle of each BT community. As a result, the Training & Coaching program puts an added emphasis on challenging all future coaches and leaders to prove their readiness to create and maintain a successful community. As the size and scope of communities grow, so does the coaching responsibility—BT has seen some coaching roles becoming full-time positions.

Usually distributed across the UK, BT's communities may run anywhere from a few months to a few years, and may encompass several thousand people and involve multi-million dollar projects. The ECM-based communications platform is used for publishing public knowledge libraries, news updates for specific work functions, critical external projects in the Information Communication Technology space, internal projects, and team workspaces.

The Coaching & Training program has reduced costs from up to $18,000 U.S. per community to approximately $600 U.S. and $450 U.S. per coach. User satisfaction with the coach training is at 80 percent. To measure its ECM adoption success, BT looked at the number of auditable actions averaged per user and, at the community level, accounted for logons and contribution rates as reported by coaches.

End users at BT have begun to realize the benefits ECM offers and are motivated to use it and to begin information sharing.

- Building a full suite of exams and questionnaires in a variety of formats, including multiple choice, single answer and short essay;

- Incorporating standard multimedia types, including HTML, Word, PDF, Flash and more;

- Ensuring that these learning initiatives map correctly to employee licensing and certification requirements as they apply to corporate regulations such as Sarbanes-Oxley, Basel II and the U.S. Patriot Act.

Committee Management

A committee can be any group of people working together for a particular task. Typically, committee members work across organizations and geographic boundaries. Most often, their assignment to a committee is in addition to regular duties. The challenge for organizations is to enable disparate committee members to collaborate effectively and efficiently, minimizing time and costs spent on achieving objectives:

- By the time committee initiatives reach consensus, have the results of decisions lost their impact because the issues at hand are not as critical as they were when the committee was founded?

- Do geographic boundaries impair the ability of committee members to collaborate effectively?

- Have the costs of committee initiatives surpassed projected costs?

- Does the impact of committee decisions fall short of its potential scope because committees lack an effective means of publicly communicating their decisions?

With an ECM solution for online committees, organizations can facilitate informal decision making with quick polls and more structured voting requirements with a comprehensive eBalloting system—ensuring that consensus is reached according to the organization's rules. With ECM, organizations can implement tools for managing committees, their structures and their members.

ECM Adoption Stages

This discussion provides one set of stage definitions. These can be adapted to suit the needs of your organization. Stage identification is critical to deployment success. Knowing what stage you are at is a key factor in the readiness identification of the organization to accept change and move on to the next stage. While it is possible to jump stages, this is typically only done by going through a stage in an accelerated manner.

ECM adoption can be defined in seven stages that range from the simple adoption of a single solution in a department to the most complex adoption involving an entire market-place. The difference between the two is substantial, and it is unwise to jump from a solution for 50 users directly to a solution for 1 million users. There are very distinct phases that an organization must go through to evolve from a single departmental deployment to a marketplace deployment.

The table below lists the basic attributes of each stage:

Stage	Description	Organization Level	Users	Applications
1	Application	Department	<1,000	Single solution
2	Multi-Department	Division	2,000+	Single to many departments
3	Multi-Application	Department/Division	2,000+	Multiple applications to one department
4	Application Standard	Enterprise	5,000+	Single application for company
5	Multi-Application	Enterprise	10,000+	Multiple applications for company
6	Extended Applications	Extranet to named users inside the firewall	20,000+	Single external application for a department
7	Multiple Extended Applications	Online Marketplace	100,000+	Multiple applications with guest access in a non-secure market

Figure 4.3: This table shows the gradual learning curve that is followed as applications are first delivered as a single solution and then scaled up to a full marketplace.

A typical ECM deployment begins with Stage 1, which is the adoption of an application that solves a particular departmental problem. This is shown in Figure 4.4. Usually, the deployment consists of fewer than 1,000 people, and it is normally sought and deployed by a department manager who is the business owner of the problem.

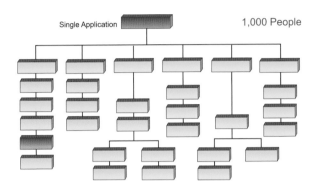

Figure 4.4: Stage 1 – Department Application

Stage 2 involves the adoption of the same solution in other departments. Normally, the IT Department takes an existing and proven ECM solution to other departments that have similar problems. Typically, 2,000 or so people are involved.

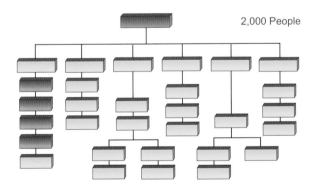

Figure 4.5: Stage 2 – Multiple Departments Deploying the Same Application

> Swiss Air

The Web Content Management (WCM) platform at Swiss Air enables the Sales & Marketing department to maintain a direct channel to the Web. The corresponding Web site offers a set of services including online-bookings, information, frequent flyer management, reservations, and journey planning to the Web community.

One of the major concerns of today's airlines is to keep aircrafts at the highest possible seat load factor. While destination networks, schedules, pricing, and soft factors such as service and image are essential to succeed, clever management of vacant seats also results in a better load factor.

Swiss Air's WCM platform combined with a booking engine empowers Sales & Marketing to release specials offers to vertical markets. The offers can be placed short term, but are integrated with the booking engine and corresponding information management. With this platform, Sales & Marketing not only has a solution to increase seat load, but also an instrument to challenge new markets with almost immediate feedback (for example, terms of booked seats). The gained intelligence from special offers is used to optimize Swiss Air's destination network and pricing strategy.

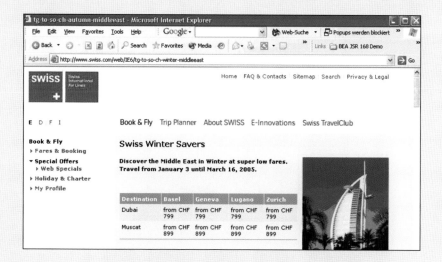

Figure 4.6: Web Content Management at Swiss Air

Stage 3 is the adoption of additional solutions within the same department, as shown in Figure 4.7. Here, the original ECM solution is extended by other ECM components within the same department, typically by the same business owner and possibly by IT.

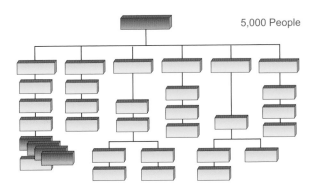

Figure 4.7: Stage 3 – Multiple Applications

The next and most critical stage is Stage 4, which represents the first time that an organization decides on an ECM solution as an enterprise standard. This stage involves not only the IT Department but also the senior-level management team, since the implementation will occur across all departments within the organization, be highly visible, and have a direct impact on operations. Stage 4 typically involves 10,000 or more people in a large organization (shown in the figure below).

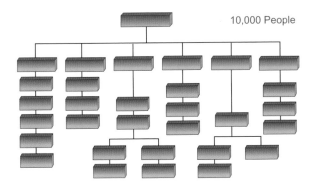

Figure 4.8: Stage 4 – Adoption at the Enterprise Level

It is possible to evolve to Stage 4 quickly, establishing a standard for the organization; however, the jump must be accomplished by going through Stages 1 and 2 at an accelerated rate! In other words, even in attempting to go straight to Stage 4, the organization must pilot a Stage 1 adoption, if only for a short period of time.

Stage 5 represents the proliferation of the standard into multiple different applications throughout the enterprise.

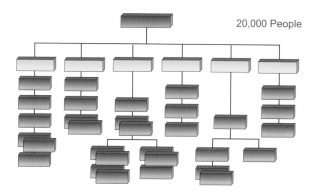

20,000 People

Figure 4.9: Stage 5 – Multi-Application Enterprise

Stage 6, the Extranet Stage, is a natural evolution from an internal collaboration group that wants to extend the definition of "team member" to include someone outside of the organization. It is typically done in limited cases in which the users are named users and well known to the organization. These groups are often built around an existing internal application with a limited number of external users who are granted permission within the firewall.

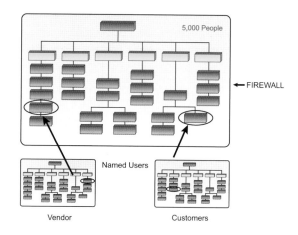

Figure 4.10: Stage 6 – Extranet

The seventh and final stage is the Online Marketplace Stage, as shown in Figure 4.11. In this stage, a series of extranets are extended to include a broad range of market participants, including competitors. An online marketplace functions as the main clearing house for all of the issues of a particular industry. When a marketplace is created around a major organization, that organization then acts as a hub and is responsible for the administration of that marketplace. Chapters 13 and 14 review the different kinds of marketplaces and extranets that exist today.

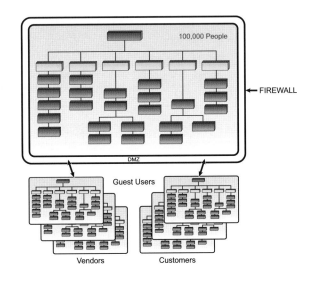

Figure 4.11: Stage 7 – Online Marketplace

Each stage of ECM deployment is built on the previous stages.

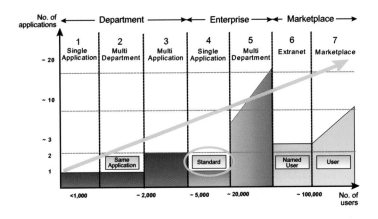

Figure 4.12: The Complete Adoption Cycle of ECM in the Enterprise

From Stage 1 to Stage 7 at Siemens

In the mid 1990s, Siemens began experimenting with ECM technologies within months of the public availability of a Web browser. Initial deployments of basic search and document management technologies managed growing amounts of information in Web-based repositories. At the time, Siemens was experimenting and adopting Web-based search engine technology well before these tools were on the market. With this base of experience, Siemens' IT Department introduced Web-based ECM technologies to various departments throughout the corporation. The following excerpts illustrate the evolution of departmental installs into the enterprise-wide deployment of ECM that occurred at Siemens.

> Siemens is a global powerhouse in electrical engineering and electronics. The company has 434,000 employees working to develop and manufacture products, design and install complex systems and projects, and tailor a wide range of services for individual requirements. With a presence in 190 countries, Siemens has one of the most geographically complex and comprehensive ECM deployments in the world. The organization's global solution will provide the backdrop for effective methodology throughout this book.
>
> Siemens' IT department introduced various ECM technologies to different business areas within the organization in a step-wise fashion. As the departments began realizing significant benefits including time and resource savings as well as improved team efficiency and productivity, the final step in the ECM implementation was the creation of a corporate-wide knowledge strategy led by C-level management.
>
> "As a global company with employees all over the world, it is critical to provide our teams with tools for virtual collaboration and knowledge sharing across geographical and organizational boundaries. The ECM system serves as the backbone of the company-wide Siemens ShareNet and complementary divisional solutions, delivering capabilities that support our ability to work faster, smarter and more efficiently," says Siemens' Corporate Knowledge Officer.

Stage 1: Sales and Marketing

One of the most important early applications of ECM took place in departments related to customers in Sales and Marketing, as illustrated in the example below.

Siemens Industrial Solutions & Services (I&S) is a leading global supplier of electro-technical equipment, drive systems, automation, and IT solutions for the metals, mining, and paper industries, and for oil and gas, infrastructure, marine engineering, airports, and traffic control. To support the lifecycle of offer preparation and tendering, Siemens

I&S created a customized workflow and project template. When users initiate a new offer tendering process, the system automatically creates a project and populates it with the framework for an offer in the form of a compound document. The workflow uses process steps and a dynamically generated address to send email notifications to key people throughout the process.

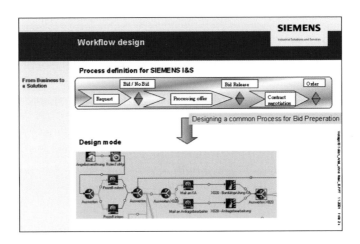

Figure 4.13: Workflow Design Drives the Bid Process at Siemens

Stage 2: Additional Department Applications

Working on cross-divisional projects, Siemens Netherlands sells, manages and executes building projects, adding professional services and consulting value for customers. To reduce the amount of time spent setting up new projects and to ensure that consultants and engineers were all working from the most current version of a document, Siemens Netherlands implemented technology to facilitate collaboration at the departmental level, within user communities, and among cross-divisional project teams. Capturing knowledge gleaned through collaboration means that customers benefit from best practices, project time savings, and improved productivity.

At this stage, Siemens Enterprise Networks was able to develop an application called EZA, an acronym for easy access to contracts and customer engagement information for solutions and services. EZA pulls together all Siemens activities for a single engagement with a customer, from the time a prospect becomes a lead, through installation and final confirmation of the arrangement. As a unique approach to sales and customer engagements, the solution helps the sales force interact with customers, business partners, and internal people.

Stage 3: Multiple Applications in Different Departments

After sales and marketing, Siemens adopted ECM at the production level, specifically in areas where employees required quick and easy access to technical information, both within and outside of the organization. By this time, the sophistication of ECM deployments had increased and applications began to include workflow and business process management elements, closely integrated with document management. Collaboration began to take on a more important role in the deployments, and early versions of knowledge management repositories with advanced search techniques were implemented.

OSRAM, a subsidiary of Siemens AG, is one of the leading lamp manufacturers in the world. As customers grew knowledgeable about the sophisticated materials and technology they were using to develop lighting solutions, access to technical information became increasingly important. Using content management technology, OSRAM's Marketing Department developed a solution to support its sales force with detailed technical information on thousands of lighting products. Today, when a customer asks a technical question, the sales representative has immediate access to product-related documentation that provides the answer.

Research and Development

As the need to produce technical information in electronic format increased within Siemens, the next logical step was to deploy ECM to Research and Development Departments. As this happened, the use of more creative forms of collaboration, such as notification messaging and online meetings became more widespread, increasing the effectiveness of teams as they worked in common document repositories.

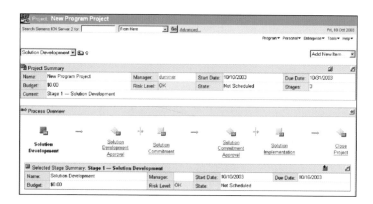

Figure 4.14: Program Management in Research and Development at Siemens

> Capital One

Who: With $75.5 billion in managed loans and $47.2 million managed accounts, Capital One is a leading financial services provider and the sixth largest credit card issuer in the U.S. For two years running a Fortune 500 company, Capital One has locations in 8 U.S. cities, Canada, U.K., France, and South Africa.

Business Objective: To document and tag intellectual capital from across the enterprise to enable easy access for current and new employees.

Business Needs: Facilitation of best practice usage across the enterprise.

Solution Overview: A document and knowledge management system enables efficient document management, search and navigation, and communities of practice facilitate collaboration. Internal user studies were performed to determine how user satisfaction could be increased and best practices usage encouraged.

Benefits: The enhanced ECM-based solution provides a higher degree of accessibility, centralized information, and new document composition and editing functionalities. Support for security requirements, provision of valid records, and improved accessibility standards have enabled Capital One to increase user acceptance and system usage, thus improving performance.

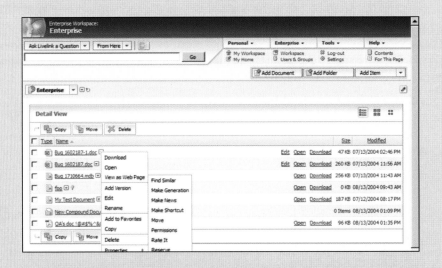

Figure 4.15: An Example of ECM Document Management Functionalities

ECM is the technological foundation for knowledge management—how this foundation will grow and what it will eventually encompass depends on the culture of the organization that implements it. Capital One has a dynamic work culture that requires intellectual capital to be documented and tagged for easy access to reduce the learning curve associated with role fluidity.

Approximately 90 percent of Capital One's end users used their ECM-based document and collaboration management system as a snapshot repository rather than a document and collaboration tool. Capital One's priority was to manage content as a business-critical asset. Although the initial focus had been on nurturing single-source management of policy and project documentation, the organization aimed to improve user satisfaction and encourage single-source publishing beyond policies and project documentation.

To increase user adoption and promote best practices, Capital One, along with external ECM-adoption consultants. Through job shadowing and usability testing, the surveyors aimed to obtain an overview of how nature—how users inherently behave or work—and nurture—how users' behavior and work habits can be developed to align with best practices—have impacted user adoption.

The surveys determined that, at least for the dynamic business culture at Capital One, the best solution would entail directing users' inherent behavior through informal training efforts. For example, users naturally sign on to applications when they need to use them in spite of best practices to sign on at the beginning of the day. By integrating multiple applications into a single sign on, users continue with their inherent behavior but the barriers between nature and nurture are eliminated.

Following the surveys, Capital One determined that usability studies were crucial for clarifying the gaps and providing data to validate the business case for nurturing. Survey results clarified training specifics and confirmed that the more knowledgeable users are about the system, and the longer they use it, the more advanced the usage commitment becomes. This higher level of commitment can be used as a resource to prompt more active usage from novice users.

Some of the design tactics that were developed as a result of the study involved improving user experience when searching and navigating through stored content by implementing a tool to apply a hierarchical taxonomy, designing the taxonomies, and customizing search processes. They also developed alternative navigational structures for standard folders and additional processes for document lifecycle management. Collaboration received a boost through the capture of process requirements and design document review workflows. Overall, on the nature side, enhancing performance, opening the permissions model, and implementing specialized modules for editing and tagging are thought to bridge approximately 60 percent of best practice gaps, whereas nurturing and rewarding document management practices are considered to bridge roughly 30 percent of gaps.

Stage 4: Enterprise Standards Begin at Administration

Administration was the last departmental area at Siemens to adopt an ECM solution. As more divisions and departments came to rely on the Internet for communications, the administration department followed suit and deployed an ECM solution to maximize their reliance on Web-based technology and the Internet. Company wide, the need for compliance-driven documentation extended ECM applications to include records management and document lifecycle management technologies.

Stage 5: Enterprise Collaboration across Departments and Business Units

ShareNet is the global intranet, project, and knowledge management solution for Siemens Financial Services (SFS). Based on ECM technology, ShareNet provides extensive business process support, from selling products and solutions to quickly responding to customer requests and finding experts across the organization. Building efficient processes across business units and regions based on best practices, SFS can set up new projects using predefined templates in minutes.

Replacing 26 document management systems, Siemens Enterprise Networks developed a single, integrated knowledge management and Web publishing application for all of its product documentation, process, and procedure materials—all critical business documents. Keeping its internal people knowledgeable about products and changes in processes, this solution for finding and disseminating key documentation is a critical part of Siemens' Web-based solution for ongoing collaborative communication with partners and customers.

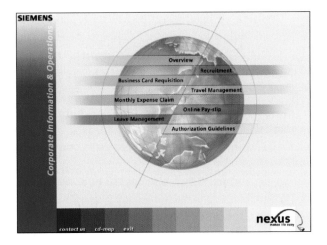

Figure 4.16: Siemens' Screen Capture

Using ECM technology, **Siemens Singapore** hosts a centralized standard solution, called Nexus, for the entire Siemens Asia and Australia region. Nexus is a Web-based, employee self-service solution that automates administrative approval processes, such as signature authority, travel booking, expense claims, leave management, training management, asset management, recruitment, separation, purchase requisition, business card ordering, timesheets, and more. Tightly integrated with its ERP system, Nexus helps ensure adherence to business rules and policies.

A Multi-Departmental, Enterprise-Wide Platform

Stage 5 in the ECM deployment cycle at Siemens began with a corporate-wide inventory and evaluation of ECM technologies and applications, as well as other applications that could be made more efficient with ECM. This evaluation led to the creation of a corporate-wide knowledge strategy at Siemens which was lead by C-Level Management. By this time, virtually all elements of an ECM system were in use at Siemens at various department and division levels. Cost reductions could be achieved by organizing these technologies into common standards across the enterprise.

Motivated by the desire to gain better returns on investment, implementing an enterprise-wide ECM system is key to managing corporate memory. This is a concept that describes a corporation's ability to maintain a memory of all the documents and processes it relies on to function. ECM increases the stability of organizations that rely on intangible assets (people and knowledge) to create value.

Stage 6: Extranet Solutions by Division Application

As the Systems Engineer for total solutions, Siemens Building Technologies (SBT) needed to collaborate and share information with seven locations and six divisions. Turning to an extranet solution, the organization today manages all information related to building and construction projects online. ECM technology has enabled SBT to address productivity and customer satisfaction challenges caused by time consuming searches for documentation, data, and images during building projects.

Stage 7: Online Marketplaces

Siemens Automation and Drives knows that world-class customer care is a critical part of the sales process—the winning and keeping of customers. To that end, the division built a knowledge management system that relieved its Customer Support Hotline staff of supplying daily routine answers to Frequently Asked Questions (FAQ), leaving them free to aid customers with critical issues. The intranet was further designed to host answers in five languages for problem-solving, downloadable software updates, and technical documentation such as end-user or service manuals.

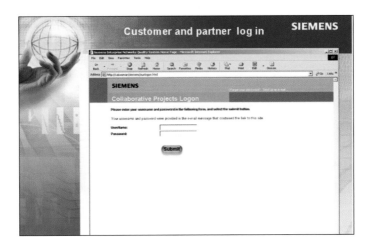

Figure 4.17: Collaboration with Customers and Partners at Siemens

Using the 10 years of online experience at Siemens with ECM, we have illustrated how an initial ECM deployment occurs at the department level and expands to other departments and divisions after six to nine months. After consolidating several applications on a common infrastructure, organizations begin to consider a full enterprise-wide implementation of an ECM solution.

Inter-departmental Benefits

The primary focus of enterprise-level ECM deployments, beyond simply setting a standard for common applications, is the benefits derived from implementing interdepartmental ECM solutions that create competitive advantage. An ECM solution works on existing infrastructure, is accessible from anywhere in the world, and leverages peoples' knowledge of common Web technology. Because it is easy to use and improves the way people work together, it significantly increases overall productivity, employee satisfaction, and the workplace environment.

The inter-departmental benefits of deploying an ECM Solution include but are not limited to harnessing enterprise collective knowledge, making a distributed organization more effective, and breaking down geographical and organizational obstacles. Today's organizations are changing. Traditional management hierarchies have been broken down by the necessity to move further and faster than ever before to stay ahead of the competition.

Communities form across all levels of the hierarchy. Some are traditional, such as the management team that puts the heads of department together once a month to debate corporate policy and direction. 'Project' communities cross departmental boundaries on

> United Nations High Commissioner for Refugees

Detailed and accurate records management is essential for the United Nations High Commissioner for Refugees (UNHCR), an organization dedicated to leading and coordinating international action to protect refugees around the world. Meeting their objectives involves electronic correspondence among their over 6000 employees in 116 countries.

In order to meet legal, regulatory, and compliance policies, UNHCR needed a solution to archive and record this email communication. Expanding on their current Enterprise Document Management Strategies (EDMS), UNHCR implemented an email management solution to help preserve, track, search, and retrieve valuable information from their email communications.

This solution allows UNHCR to manage email and email attachments, and save the information to their EDMS applications. Email metadata is automatically captured and recorded, facilitating archiving and retrieval while maintaining the email structure. Email retention is automated to provide complete and accurate records and meet with compliance requirements.

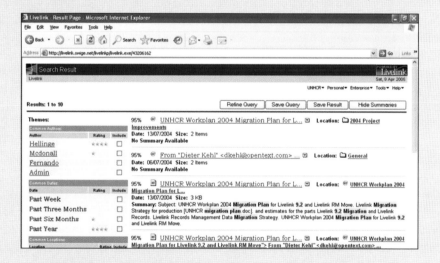

Figure 4.18: Screen Shot Showing Capture of Email Metadata

many levels. For instance, imagine a project to install a new computer network in your office. Information Technology will be involved with engineering, logistics, administration and finance. In fact, just about every department in the enterprise will be affected in some way and will need to play a role in the project community. And even a simple business process such as raising a purchase order will touch a virtual community of employees within the business.

Internet technology enabled companies to overcome the geographical barriers that prevented collaboration among different office locations. In a hyperlinked enterprise, individuals can collaborate with peers and work in virtual communities that span the globe.

Combining People, Processes and Information

Organizations generate vast amounts of information that they must control, from invoices, records, and contracts to emails, spreadsheets, design specifications, marketing materials, and Web pages. For global organizations, productivity can suffer without a system that helps people find information and work together to deliver results. To succeed, individuals need to work as teams that can cross geographical and departmental boundaries. They must be able to access best practices and information from previous projects, share documents, and collaborate throughout the development process to rapidly supply team members with the information they need to get their jobs done. An effective ECM solution needs to bring together people, processes, and information. The software must seamlessly combine collaboration with content management, transforming information into knowledge, providing the foundation for innovation, compliance, and accelerated growth.

Measuring Productivity at the Enterprise Level

Measuring ECM productivity at the enterprise level is not unlike measuring any other process change within a business at the department level. The scale and scope of an enterprise ROI calculation is much larger since it involves longer time periods and several inter-related activities in different departments. To determine ROI, organizations must benchmark enterprise-level performance before and after implementing an ECM solution. In many cases, this is tangible and easy to calculate. The reduction of costs associated with the physical storage of records can be easily seen on a comparative statement of expenses. Improvement in time to market can often be easily benchmarked and measured as well.

You can measure an ECM solution's effectiveness by assessing the difference between the value created by the business with the solution in place versus the value without it. The traditional metrics include return visits, referrals, cycle times, retention rate, and satisfaction. Overall profitability, profits as a percentage of revenue, and sales generated per employee are other metrics.

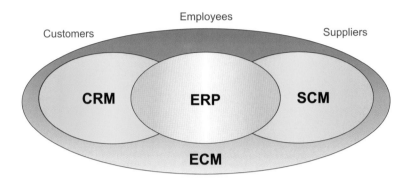

Figure 5.1: ECM Software in the Enterprise Ecosystem

One natural question to consider before beginning any ECM implementation is how it relates to the existing applications in the organization. These applications deliver the core business functions of the organization: Customer Relationship Management (CRM), Supply Chain Management (SCM), and Enterprise Resource Planning (ERP).

These applications are naturally used when there is something specific to do, or some real transaction has been executed and must be recorded. An example in SCM might be, "deliver this widget at this time;" in CRM: "change that status and process the customer's claim;" in ERP: "run the payroll." ERP systems, whether internally developed or provided as an integrated suite by a vendor, exist to run the daily operations of the business.

Clearly there are now three independent but related **lifecycles** that can occur depending on whether the primary interaction is with a **customer**, **supplier**, or **employee**. Each of these lifecycles involves a different spectrum of collaboration interactions. But in a well designed enterprise, all of these lifecycles will interact through a common **content** model that addresses the business goals of the organization.

So ECM applications extend the reach of an organization's ERP systems. This extension results from the **collaboration** component of ECM, which delivers user coordination ahead of the transactions captured by ERP systems, and from the **content** component, which extends the information store across workspaces.

This chapter discusses the issues involved with integrating ECM software with other data and software applications throughout the enterprise. This can be a critical step in establishing a working governance system that provides a bridge between information that is computer generated and that which is human generated.

CHAPTER 5

INTEGRATING ECM INTO THE ENTERPRISE IT ECOSYSTEM

When deploying an enterprise software application such as ECM, it is important to understand the environment within which the applications will operate. Key to this environment are the three major components of the IT ecosystem that an ECM application must operate in:

• Enterprise Platforms

• Enterprise Applications

• Enterprise Information

Of course, these components can take on many forms throughout the enterprise and understanding the form that various IT components have is key to a successful deployment of any ECM application, regardless of the stage of deployment.

Enterprise Platforms

In larger organizations, there are generally two major platforms within most IT enterprise-wide architectures—desktop platforms and server platforms. Most of the time, the desktop platform is based on some release of Microsoft software, while the Server platform is a based on Oracle, IBM or SAP software or a combination of them.

Enterprise Applications

There are many different kinds of applications within an organization. They generally belong to one of four groups—desktop personal productivity (Office), server-based transaction process (ERP), server-based content storage (ECM), or server-based collaboration (ECM).

There are a variety of applications that run across the enterprise or within mission-critical departments that belong to the ERP family of applications on the server side and personal productivity software on the desktop side. Most ERP applications are made by SAP and Oracle, while most desktop applications are made by Microsoft. Archive applications are made by mass storage vendors such as EMC, Hitachi, and IBM.

Enterprise Information

Most enterprise information is maintained on mass storage servers. This information is generally long term in nature, while all of the short-term memory resides on the applications previously described. Connecting enterprise information into the ECM repository is a critical part of any successful ECM deployment. With the rise of governance requirements regarding information management, this connection will be bi-directional, with requirements for audit trail and security around the destruction or modification of records. This content integration is much more complicated than previous systems such as portals.

ECM Solutions Framework for a Modern IT Ecosystem

If we consider all of these components as an ecosystem, we can begin to understand the architecture and integration needs of an ECM deployment. Consider the following architecture in Figure 5.2, which is based on the ECM Solutions Framework model.

The two primary points of integration for all of the components of the IT ecosystem are based on either information (content integration) or people (collaboration integration). The primary points of integration are typically at the end points of the enterprise system. These end points are described for each type of integration and application in the following sections.

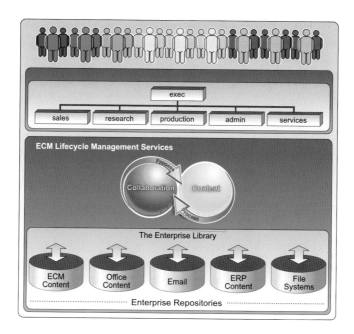

Figure 5.2: ECM Solutions Framework for Enterprise Content Integration

Integration of ECM with the Desktop

The dominant applications on the desktop today are Microsoft® Office, Microsoft Outlook®/Exchange and Lotus Notes®. This set of personal productivity tools lets you create content and store it in a filing system as well as collaborate from the desktop through email or instant messaging. Recent extensions to the desktop include Microsoft SharePoint®, which enables desktop file sharing among small groups and Microsoft LiveMeeting, which provides online meeting tools from the desktop environment.

The end point of these tools is at the desktop hard drive or just beyond at the server level for common file directory storage. ECM applications that work with desktop information must integrate with these content creation and people collaboration tools by extending them to the entire enterprise, while creating an ECM lifecycle of content and people archiving within a set of business rules administered through a business process. The entire lifecycle is described in Chapter 2 of this book.

The key point to understand about desktop integration with enterprise ECM tools is that the desktop tools are more effective the closer they are to the client location of the data and the application software. As this content is stored farther away, a comprehensive ECM platform is required to manage the complexity of the huge amounts of file directories that are created in email systems and basic office systems. The key points of content integration are best completed through SharePoint at the basic server level. The second area of integration is the people side. Email collaboration and instant messaging must be stored and managed through a records management system, and the most common point of integration is the metadata about the collaboration content.

The Role of ECM with ERP in the Enterprise

The dominant environment in enterprise software today is the Enterprise Resource Planning (ERP) system. This software resides at the back end of the software environment and is typically managed at the server level. In most modern systems, it is delivered via the Internet to a Web-based client of some form, depending on whether the client side is embedded or dedicated or the Web, as shown in Figure 5.2.

The essential difference between ECM and ERP is that ECM is based on words, while ERP is based on numbers. Information consists of words and numbers. We treat these data types quite differently.

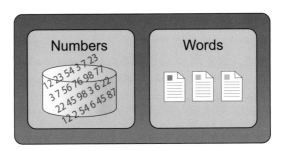

Figure 5.3: Two Types of Information

Let's first consider how we use this information in our daily lives. We use numbers and words very differently. If we consider personal productivity tools such as Microsoft Office, we would never consider writing a long memo in Excel, for example, nor would we consider calculating a large budget spreadsheet in a Word document. In business, numbers mean transactions such as price of a product, while words mean collaboration such as email or Web sites which act as catalogs.

ERP - Database   ECM - Word Index

Structured Data = Prices   Unstructured Data = Email/Web

Figure 5.4: ECM versus ERP

The reason why words or unstructured data matter is because of the sheer size of this information and its recent growth rate. It is estimated that some 10 percent of the information in organizations is numbers in a database. Normally this information is very important and it relates to the transactions that the organization is involved in.

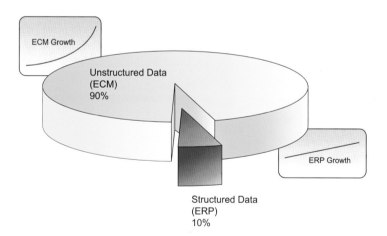

Figure 5.5: Structured versus Unstructured Data

However, 90 percent of information is unstructured data, or words. Or, put another way, there are 10 words for every number in the organization today. This means that the dominant source of information in an organization is in word form. Not surprisingly, this is how people collaborate with one another. We use numbers to describe transactions, not how things and people interact and collaborate.

> T-Systems

Who: T-Systems is one of Europe's leading providers of information and communications technology (ICT). A part of the Deutsche Telekom group, the organization has locations in more than 50 countries with over 2,000 access points.

Business Objective: To provide T-Systems employees with one of the most advanced collaboration tools possible.

Business Needs: The rise of numerous small intranets led to increasing costs and lacked the necessary collaboration support.

Solution Overview: A central project repository with document management capabilities and a search engine, myWorkroom is a collaborative environment integrated with the T-Systems portal for easy and direct single sign-on access.

Solution Scope: Enterprise wide.

Benefits: The organization and end users are benefiting from the solution, which has increased efficiency, improved the quality of collaborative work, enabled quicker project completion, and sped information retrieval and processing. As a result, T-Systems has been enjoying considerable cost and time savings.

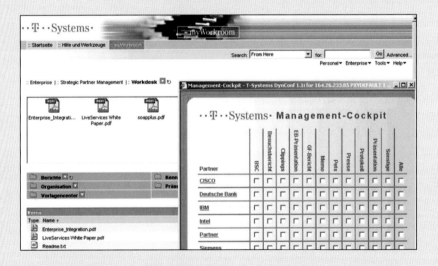

Figure 5.6: Partner Management Work Area at T-Systems

T-Systems has acquired considerable experience in the deployment of various ECM solutions for client organizations and holds an established competence in the area of knowledge and records management. Based on this experience, its own knowledge management approach recognized that a successful ECM strategy is an integral part of an organization's philosophy and culture. Therefore, T-Systems established a strategy that focuses on a marriage of technology with culture, while integrating three equally vital components: people, processes and content.

Only four months after T-Systems began its ECM technology implementation, the implementation was completed and a pilot phase was launched to deploy the solution to end users. T-Systems then began to organize training programs for administrative and key end users and, 4 months later, welcomed the kick-off of the T-Systems communications platform rollout.

Integrated with the enterprise portal, myWorkroom is a universally applicable communications platform at T-systems. Collaboration support on an international scale has been effectively developed based on a 'workroom-doorway' concept: virtual project rooms and team forums create the enclosed workrooms, while role-based access opens doorways in between. Document management provides powerful functionalities such as search, versioning, and notification, and thus enables knowledge to be effectively gathered, classified, applied, and exchanged.

The solution was received with a high user acceptance and myWorkroom became the standard system for 20,000 users. Both the organization and the users are benefiting from the solution, which has increased efficiency, improved the quality of collaborative work, enabled quicker project completion, and sped information retrieval and processing.

The implementation has allowed T-Systems to learn first hand many valuable lessons that were further enhanced by experiences with client projects: successful ECM projects begin with a concrete establishment of project requirements; effective bottom-up knowledge management crosses three phases: the pilot phase, the implementation phase and the penetration phase; and, finally, successful ECM projects are more than just technology.

T-Systems attributes the successful ECM deployment to its central framework and self-organization roll-out strategy. A clear division of roles and responsibilities set the framework basis and enabled a seamless end-user support structure. A central roll-out team was created to assume the responsibility for standard workrooms, the deployment strategy, as well as training and coaching programs. Local roll-out teams were created and trained by the central team to initiate and coordinate the roll-out to specific areas. These teams were responsible for introducing end users to the solution and supplementing deployment guidelines based on the specifics of their area. Once end users were familiar with the system, they assumed ownership of their areas and provided feedback to the central roll-out team. Throughout the deployment, the central roll-out team was available for support. In addition, a user hotline and Web-based end-user training were established.

While this is important, what makes unstructured data the focus of IT for the future is the astounding growth rates of digital content that are being reported with main stream adoption of the Internet. It is estimated that large corporations are doubling their unstructured data every two months. Even if this rate slowed to every six months, it represents an enormous change in the location of information that is available for use within an organization.

Think about this rate for a minute. Consider all of the digital information created by mankind since the start of computing, and then consider that the same amount of information will be created again within the next few months!

Our every-day experience suggests that this is happening when we consider the incredible growth in the size of our email inboxes and the scope and scale of the public Internet.

As a comparison, consider that ERP information tracks transactions, and that tracks the economy. Our economy grows by an average of four percent per year and ERP growth is commensurate with that, probably in the 10 percent range as shown.

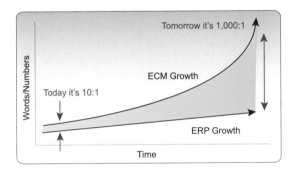

Figure 5.7: Estimate of the Relative Growth Rate of Unstructured Data and Structured Data

Now consider the two growth rates together. Today ECM-based data is probably about 10 times the amount of ERP data, but consider the impact of even a few years of hyper growth by ECM and steady growth by ERP—ECM will be 1,000 times the size of ERP. This means that there will be 1,000 words for every number that we use in our Enterprise Ecosystem. Clearly, the ECM repository of Web sites and email will dominate the future and the strategic management of these repositories is a top priority for any organization.

Words are known as unstructured data and numbers are known as structured data. The best way to think of the difference is to consider your desktop software. Think of a spread-sheet application like Excel or a writing application like Word. The two applications are not combined since Excel is optimized for handling data in a structured way while Word is optimized for writing letters such as email.

ERP software is based on a database of numbers. ECM software is based on an index of words. The table in Figure 5.8 provides a simple comparison of common ERP terms and their equivalent term in ECM.

ERP Term	ECM Term	Comment
Database schema structure	Word index content, Index directory	Database schemas define ERP access paths. ECM systems use a similar approach but house the paths to content within documents and unstructured content for example found on Web sites.
Tables	Metadata (XML)	Metadata viewed as sets of attributes.
Rows	Objects, Documents	Component pieces of both approaches.
Columns (fields)	Attributes	Component pieces of both approaches.
Data Models	Taxonomies	Data models may be relational, E-R, object etc. Taxonomies may be Flat, Hierarchical, Faceted or Network.
Database Structured Query	Search unstructured Query	ECM Search queries may be Boolean Natural Language, full text, or a combination of all of these. Semantics and context are considered when search is initiated. Relevance rankings are used. ERP is flat operator logic based.
Weekly, Month End, etc. Reports based on fixed assets, inventory etc.	Reports based on digital assets. Risk, location, tenure, relevance, age, in addition to Search Result Lists.	Most ECM platforms also provide reporting tools similar to databases.
History, Rollback	Versioning	Versioning history is fundamental to ECM. For example, entire Web sites and all the content is time stamped and versioned for rollback history. Just like ERP.
Archiving	Records Management	ERP systems use DB reorganization to reclaim space and unload deleted records. Some use third party products to archive record history. Records management and retention are built in features for an ECM system. Databases do not generally provide standard information lifecycle management tools analogous to RM.

Figure 5.8: Common ERP and ECM Terms Compared

The ERP environment was initially composed of transaction-based software designed to support the basic operations of a company. All organizations have customers and suppliers. They take raw materials and combine them with employee labor to produce products and services for customers. This flow is the essence of an organization. This is shown in Figure 5.9 in which suppliers provide raw materials to the company that transforms them into products for sale to customers.

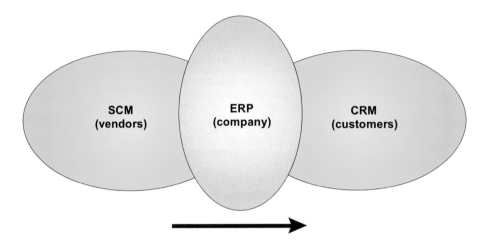

Figure 5.9: The Basic Flow of Transactions in an Organization

There are three main types of software that are used within the enterprise software market to facilitate this process as shown in Figure 5.10. With suppliers, there is Supply Chain Management or SCM software which makes the integration of suppliers with company operations fast and efficient. This has lead to reduction of inventories and an entirely new way to manage the demand for components within a finished product. With customers, there is CRM or Customer Relationship Management software which provides the interface for the company with its customers. CRM ranges from simple online service support to full marketing information for prospective new customers. In the middle, within the company, there is ERP and ERP manages all of the transactions from the date employees will take action to the status of an inventory of products within the accounting system.

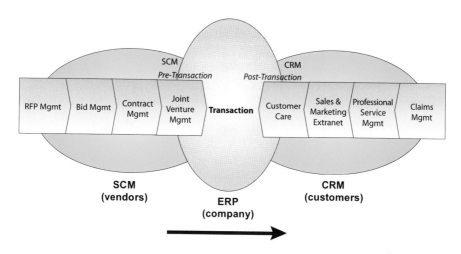

Figure 5.10: The Major Types of Enterprise Software

The challenge for ECM systems is that the collaboration and content aspects of ECM must integrate not only the unstructured or word data, but also must understand and inter operate with numerical content such as that found in ERP, SCM and CRM.

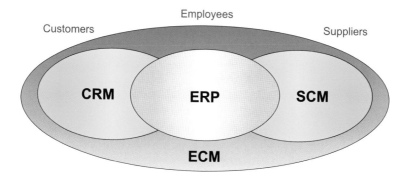

Figure 5.11: ECM Software in the Enterprise Ecosystem

> Sasol

Who: An innovative and competitive global energy company, Sasol is a world leader in the commercial production and marketing of liquid fuels and chemicals. Headquartered in Johannesburg, South Africa, the organization is a global market player with corporate entities across six continents.

Business Objective: To streamline document management processes across the enterprise while enabling improved capture of tacit knowledge.

Business Needs: A common platform was needed to connect separate enterprise systems through a single point of access.

Solution Overview: A SAP Enterprise Portal was established as the primary user interface for all enterprise applications such as ECM and SAP as well as information streams and collaboration initiatives within Sasol. The ECM solution provides document management capabilities, including advanced search, versioning and notification functions, and support for capital project management. Establishment of communities of practice enabled improved collaboration on a global scale.

Solution Scope: Enterprise wide.

Benefits: Thanks to the integration of the enterprise systems at Sasol, users require only one password to access all functions necessary for effective job performance. As a result, knowledge management has become easier and productivity has increased. The consolidation of systems has reduced costs and overhead at Sasol.

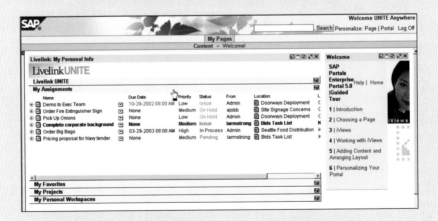

Figure 5.12: The SAP Enterprise Portal to ECM,
SAP and Other Functionalities at Sasol

Corporate knowledge is most often captured in documents and for this reason, organizations establish incentive schemes for employees to utilize knowledge libraries. This type of knowledge is also referred to as explicit knowledge. A debate surrounds the determination of how to capture tacit knowledge, or the knowledge rooted in individual experience that encompasses personal beliefs, perspectives, and values. One possible solution is to capture and organize the relationships between documents and the work employees do, the discussions they have, and the material they read.

Most enterprises have a number of document libraries. Although organizations usually strive to deploy a single repository for documents, the reality of corporate life makes this task virtually impossible. Due to financial constraints, geographical limitations, or historical values, a number of legacy document bases will most likely always exist, which limits the value of a corporate knowledge library.

At Sasol, group governance has positioned both ECM and SAP technology in the document management space. The ECM system supports collaborative work, while SAP technology caters more to documents that directly relate to business processes, including invoices, contracts, and receipts. The separation of these systems gave rise to a number of grey areas at Sasol. For example, should contracts be stored in the contract management system like SAP, or should they be stored in the ECM system with the project manager who is responsible for the expenditure of the project against such a contract? In many cases, both scenarios were followed, causing duplication and often a lack of synchronization between systems. Another challenge was the capture and extraction of tacit information. In order to do so effectively, a common platform was needed to search for content; rate, review, and discuss selected information; and recommend items to colleagues.

To address the challenges that stemmed from the separation of systems, a single enterprise portal—the SAP Enterprise Portal—was established as the primary user interface for all significant applications, information streams, and collaboration initiatives within Sasol. The ability to connect to ECM and other document repositories like SAP and Microsoft file systems has positioned the portal as Sasol's knowledge management platform.

Sasol's implementation methodology was founded upon the notion that modern management and administration require process-centric presentation of information to address a variety of diverse business needs. Once all information sources are presented through a single point of access, content management becomes easier, making it simpler for employees to do their jobs. Content is published, managed, and consumed on the same platform and search becomes centralized and more intelligent. Advanced search engines can draw relationships between objects across systems and experts can be located based on the work they publish. A single point of access to all enterprise applications has streamlined processes and productivity has increased at Sasol.

ECM is the integration of enterprise applications. In the ERP world, the solutions thus far have been known as CRM, or customer relationship management and SCM, or supply chain management. At the center of the corporation is ERP, or enterprise resource planning. ERP has been creating transactions that interact with all three of these applications. As the Web evolves, industry analysts have identified the process of making all of the collaboration pieces work together with ERP transactions as ECM. So, going forward, one can imagine deployments where Oracle or SAP is used for ERP, Siebel for CRM, and IBM for SCM.

When we look at the e-business model, it consists of three functional steps—pre-transaction processes, point of transaction, and post-transaction processes. It may be delineated along two value chains. First, the manufacturing value chain (from SCM and e-procurement) and second, the resource planning value chain (from ERP and CRM). However, ERP is not just about transactions, it is about interactions. For every order matching event, there are about 10 to 15 discrete interactions that support it, such as purchase approval and routing, product design, promotions and campaigns, contractual negotiations, warranty, regulatory compliance, and customer support. This is where ECM plays a role.

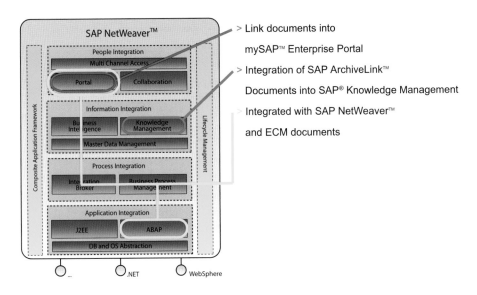

Figure 5.13: Content Integration with SAP NetWeaver

One of the simplest ways to achieve content integration is by choosing points with which to integrate ECM components with enterprise middleware. Shown in the Figure 5.13 is the potential integration of documents with SAP NetWeaver. Also shown is the integration from portals to knowledge management to the ABAP platform. The same type of integration to other middleware such as .NET and WebSphere is similar.

ERP becomes ECM

So far, we have looked at the distinction between ERP and ECM in terms of the type of content (numbers or words) that these solution platforms are best at handling. This is information architecture and modeling approach that looks at what is stored. Another way of viewing the distinction between them is an "action oriented" approach based on what is done with the information and the lifecycle over which it is managed. A common example of this approach to ECM in many organizations today is the demand for records management solutions, often driven by compliance and regulatory risk requirements. In particular, the need to bind records management to the use of the variety of messaging tools (instant messaging, email, Blackberry™, and so on) now available is driving a need to be able to identify the actionable intelligence derived from content and integrate it with ERP and ECM platforms. ERP Systems record what actually happens in an organization; ECM systems manage the decision structures to support that.

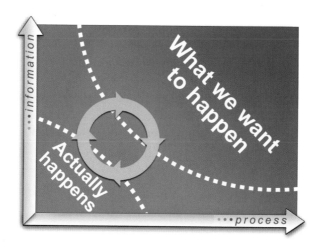

Figure 5.14: Best Practices Make Things Happen

An interesting example of this view of ERP and ECM can be seen in the evolution of trading platforms in the securities markets. Traders' desktops have long been ECM environments with very strong ERP support. They expect to receive continuous streams of quantitative (market prices) and qualitative (news, research opinions) information in order to make effective decisions. Trading desktops are designed to deliver images, words, and numbers as an integrated view of the market so that decisions can be taken quickly and acted upon immediately through the trading [ERP] platform. ECM components support decision making on human timelines, from seconds to minutes; ERP components deliver information handling on faster time scales. This has been a fairly stable approach

for a decade or more, but in the past several years has started to change with the introduction of "algorithmic trading." In modern electronic markets, with much reduced price
spreads, the market reacts so quickly to new transactions that the traditional trader's
decision time is too slow to obtain the best price and order placing becomes automated
and integrated into the ERP system. The function of the ECM Solution changes to strategy
setting, "what we want to happen," and the space occupied by the ERP Solution ("what
actually happens") expands towards the top right in the diagram.

Does ERP become ECM or ECM become ERP? The example above and the actionable
intelligence approach to these issues suggest that the question is not that important.
It depends on the perspective from which the issue is formulated. When approached
from the quantitative, transactional side of the boundary, an ERP system can be thought
of as eventually subsuming ECM platforms, as they have the Business Intelligence
applications. If approached from the collaboration and rich content side of the boundary,
we can regard ERP applications as the (potentially smart) systems to which the final
business execution is delegated, as in our algorithmic trading example. Both viewpoints
have validity; reality probably lies somewhere in between the two. Because ERP solutions
are already so familiar to most practitioners in business and information technology, we
take the ECM and collaboration viewpoint in this book.

Many ECM initiatives are established with great fanfare and optimism but then
wither. In a decentralized company like Siemens, it can be especially difficult to
standardize the use of ECM. To encourage adoption, Siemens appointed a Chief
Knowledge Officer who encourages best practices and knowledge sharing and
establishes standards for ECM platforms throughout the company.

One of the primary goals was to draw a roadmap outlining an overall corporate
ECM strategy and guidelines for establishing communities of practice. Every
organization within Siemens is provided with an ECM implementation guide—a
best practices guide that aids with implementation. The guide contains information
for building communities and covers topics such as creating incentive systems,
assessing the health of a community, and shutting down a community while
preserving content.

What Does ECM Do, and When Does it Get Done?

There are two ways of organizing the rich set of tools that make up ECM environments
in a way that makes them manageable. In this section, we consider another way of thinking about ECM that develops the lifecycle approach identified in the introduction to this
chapter. How is ECM activity organized in time, and what are the appropriate timescales
to consider when assessing ECM lifecycles?

The diagram in Figure 5.15 shows, above the diagonal, the essential ECM processes used to assemble the business solutions of Book 1 and the timescale on which they are typically used. In the viewpoint taken here, ECM solutions are essentially tools to facilitate interactions between people (collaboration) or between people and information repositories (content management). There are only a few basic processes used to do this, but they take place over a huge range of timescales—from the seconds of active collaboration it takes to create and retrieve content to the years it takes to create a reference library or archive. Full range ECM Solutions, shown below the diagonal, manage content and information over a range of greater than 200 million to one in time.

ERP Solutions, focused as they are on the execution and recording of transactions, do not generally share these characteristics. Though business intelligence applications do require maintenance of significant databases over time, the issues of whether these have any usefulness for more than short time statistical prediction are well known. Business climates change rapidly and transactional information more than a few years old is not considered to have much value. In contrast, "persistence" and management of information over the long term is often considered a key attribute of an ECM Solution.

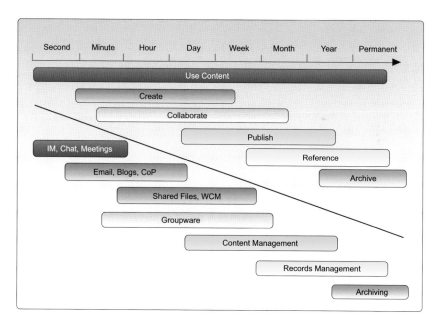

Figure 5.15: ECM Processes, Tools, and Timescales

This huge range of timescales and lifecycles poses many challenging problems in architecting ECM deployments. Perhaps the best way to get a sense of what is involved is to consider how media businesses are structured to manage the delivery of content in the real world. Radio stations, TV networks, newspapers, magazines, book publishers, lending libraries, and reference libraries span similar timescales but are managed as independent business lines, corporations, or public services. Few, if any, single organizations attempt to deal with the full range of timescales for interaction and collaboration, yet ECM Solutions are expected to address this.

Summary

In this chapter, we have examined the relationship between ECM and ERP solutions. We considered what determines which kind of solution should be adopted to deliver the desired business value, and how those solutions can be integrated into the enterprise infrastructure. We also considered the differences between ERP and ECM, including:

• Words and Numbers

• Structure of information, relational tables or classification schemes and taxonomies

• Lifecycle of information, when the content is relevant and how is it used

• Framing strategy, or facilitating and recording execution

The next section of the book considers the methods needed to deliver each of the stages of ECM adoption.

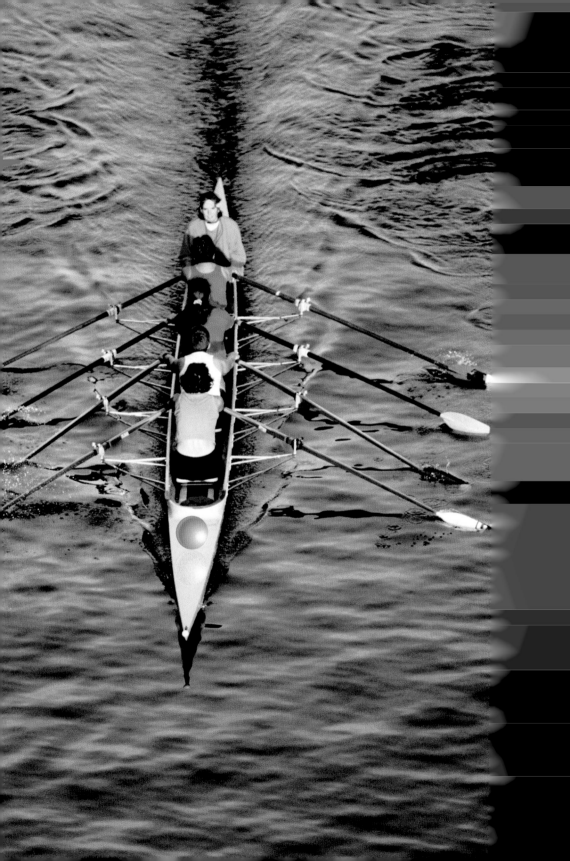

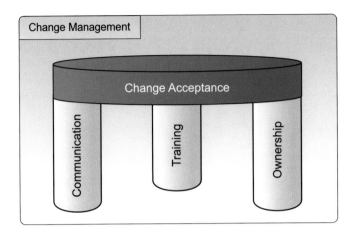

Figure 6.1: The Three Pillars of Change Management

It has been said that one of the few certainties in life is change. This is absolutely true in the business world. Roles change, pay changes, teams change. Companies go through mergers, grow dramatically, or close their doors altogether. The question that business people must ask themselves isn't "How well do I handle change?" but "How can I handle change successfully?"

To handle change, organizations need a Change Management Strategy. A comprehensive Change Management Strategy is composed of communication, training, and ownership pillars. The communication pillar is very important to the overall success and adoption of the change initiative. The training pillar is also a critical supporting pillar for user adoption. The IT and implementation teams must be well trained on the ECM application, as well as the end users. The third pillar, ownership, is defined as "belonging to oneself" and is a critical factor during the initial deployment of an ECM application.

This chapter will explore in greater detail each of the three pillars of change management as well as how to develop a Change Management Strategy.

CHAPTER 6

CHANGE MANAGEMENT WITH ECM

Deploying ECM challenges an organization in unforeseen ways. The major IT deployments of the past—databases, office productivity tools, and ERP all followed one primary goal: saving time and money by using information technology. There was no choice for the user— the customer's address was no longer in a file cabinet, the typewriter had gone, and the ledger had stopped being a book with many rows and columns. So the user adopted the new tools.

For ECM however, this is only half of the truth. The double bubble not only distinguishes technologies, it becomes crucial when an organization must decide how to deploy these technologies successfully.

Figure 6.2: ECM Value Proposition

The "content" side of ECM, driven by compliance and ROI, has much in common with the traditional way of implementing a new technology in an organization.

With the "collaboration" side of ECM, the old paradigms fail. Organizations must rethink the way they deploy this unique piece of technology. Bringing the virtues of collaboration into the structured, hierarchical universe of a profit-driven company is a cultural challenge.

This chapter is divided into three sections. The first reviews the key principles of change management. The second applies them to the people aspect in the "content" part of ECM and gives you the necessary tools to integrate the people aspect in your project plan. The last section discusses our vision of a new corporate world, where people are proud to contribute to current and future successes, where the best idea always wins, and where knowledge is no longer an attribute of power.

Change Management with ECM

Deploying the "content" side of ECM is another example of such a change process. The better we anticipate employee reactions and the better our project plan covers the people aspects, the smoother the ride towards the new process and the faster we will achieve our compliance and ROI targets.

Consider two classic ECM examples: the rollout of a company-wide master file plan to eliminate a multitude of personal or departmental file servers, and the implementation of a paperless, workflow-based claims process in the insurance industry.

In the master file plan case, denial will be strong. "This will never allow me to do my work," and, "our department is special; it can't fit into a general structure" are just two examples of the remarks you will get in an initial user meeting. During the rollout, people will complain about functionality or user interfaces.

In the claims process case, the result will be a compliance officer's nightmare. All employees have a copy of the well defined, Standard Operating Procedure (SOP) at their desk, and the department head will claim that they are complying. However, the staff has developed a set of shortcuts or extensions in the process, which have never found their way back into the SOP. If you map the SOP with your ECM project, you will face mutiny and your business continuity will be at risk.

Having the proper IT design and staying within budget does not guarantee success. To be successful in deploying the content side of ECM, no matter the level, you must ensure that your end users are committed. This is especially important for the first small project, because it will set the expectations for subsequent larger projects.

The next section provides a set of tools to manage the ECM implementation process well. It is an evolutionary process, a part of your organization's ongoing drive to run its business better.

We all witnessed the rise and fall of Knowledge Management (KM) in the nineties; how can we do better this time? Now, the technology is more advanced. KM in the nineties was a way to teach databases to work with words instead of numbers. Now, we are talking about integrated ECM platforms that cover all aspects of collaboration: virtual meeting rooms, interactive discussions, immediate capturing of results, and indexing and search functionality across platforms and languages.

Furthermore, organizations are realizing that they cannot deploy KM and ECM solutions successfully by applying project and people management principles alone; they must do more.

Why did the Internet spread in its early days? Because scientists all over the world wanted to share results and have a better way of communication. Why is LINUX so stable? Because thousands of programmers around the world brought forward their best ideas and felt proud to contribute to a better world of operating systems. Why can you find accurate information about almost everything on this planet (and beyond) in a dozen of languages on wikipedia.org? Because experts from all areas are dreaming of a world where the freedom of information is a key element in ensuring human rights.

This is what ECM can do for your organization if you are not afraid to appeal to your employees' real values: their wish to make a real contribution, their pride in sharing what they have learned, and their desire to openly discuss new ideas.

It is not by accident that all examples mentioned above are coming from the non-corporate world. Cultural change is one of the most difficult aspects of change management in the world of business, and today's climate of SOX-mania may not necessarily be the best ground for starting such an initiative. However, if you implement change correctly, the payoff will be worth it.

Applying its own business service methodology internally, Siemens instilled various incentives and other measures to overcome potential cultural barriers that people have when introduced to an ECM system for the first time:

- the solution was marketed internally through promotional materials that highlighted the benefits of the system;

- an incentive program provided users with "frequent user points" for uploading, downloading, participating in communities of practice, rating documents in the knowledge base – points can be redeemed for PDAs, books, and other prizes;

- the adoption of certain ECM skills and use of the solution was incorporated in some job objectives and tied to salary.

Change Management Strategies for ECM Deployments

A study completed by the Standish Group in 1994 found that nearly 33 percent of all Information Technology projects fail and only 16 percent are completed on time and on budget. In organizations with revenue greater than 500 million, only nine percent of the IT projects were successful.

Implementing an ECM platform can have a significant impact on an organization's culture and business processes. The changes it brings impact the way in which people perform their jobs and are often met with resistance. If these changes are not addressed before you deploy an ECM platform, user adoption will suffer.

To increase user adoption, a comprehensive change management strategy should be implemented before the ECM application is deployed. One of the many misconceptions with ECM deployments, or any enterprise software application, is that if training is delivered that teaches employees how to use the system; they will begin to use it. As some organizations have experienced, this is not necessarily true—just because employees understand how to use an application, it does not mean they will. Most employees will want to understand why they should use the application, and telling them "because it's your job" is not sufficient. Training is never the only solution to effect change; it is only part of the solution.

An error that many organizations make when managing change is assuming that the change management strategy should be delivered by consultants who are not employees of the organization. For a change management strategy to be successful, it must be owned, managed, and delivered by the organization. This sends a message to the employees that the organization takes the change seriously. This does not imply that consultants should not be used in developing the strategy—they should guide the organization in developing it and coach the Change Advocates (employees within the organization who promote the change) on the delivery.

A comprehensive change management strategy includes three pillars of change: communication, training, and ownership.

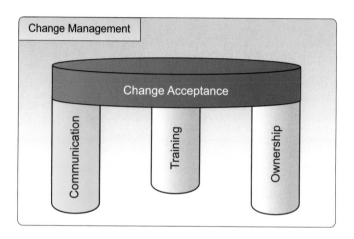

Figure 6.3: Three Pillars of Change

The Communication Pillar

The communication pillar is very important to the overall success and adoption of the change initiative. Just as with the other two pillars, this pillar alone is not sufficient to support the overall change acceptance. A comprehensive communication plan should be developed that includes the vision statement for the change initiative and that uses a variety of delivery methods (such as emails, posters, video conferencing, and so on). The communications will also include the "how, what, why, and when" of change, as well as a number of success stories of the ECM application within the organization. As discussed in the book "Fast Forward Organizational Change in 100 Days" by Elspeth J. Murray and Peter R. Richardson, the communication plan should ensure that the organization has a shared understanding of why the change is necessary and what the system is going to do to help resolve these issues. The objective of the communication pillar is to build a sense of urgency within the organization. Urgency builds the momentum required to help propel the change initiative at a fast pace.

> CARE International

Who: CARE International is a non-profit, non-governmental organization dedicated to ending poverty and providing humanitarian relief in response to violent conflict and natural disaster. CARE has member organizations across five continents and operates more than 800 projects in over 80 developing countries worldwide.

Business Objective: To share critical information and best practices in order to coordinate relief efforts and save lives.

Business Needs: An innovative solution to capture, share, and retrieve data and make it accessible across the organization.

Solution Overview: Integrated with the e-glue initiative, the ECM system at CARE is the basis for libraries of crucial documents that can be accessed by member agencies from anywhere in the world using specialized portals.

Solution Scope: Enterprise wide, including CARE members, partner organizations, and researchers worldwide.

Benefits: Projects, development, and relief efforts can be implemented faster and coordinated on a massive scale as a result of increased access to critical information and greater collaboration among agencies worldwide. Significant cost and time savings have been realized as a result of information re-use.

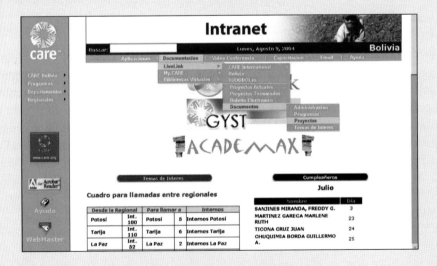

Figure 6.4: Intranet at CARE Bolivia

"One piece of information could literally mean saving more lives or being able to implement a critical service or program in a shorter time frame or at a lower cost"—this statement by the Managing Director of the i2K Group (CARE Canada's information technology arm) sums up how vital effective information sharing is at CARE International.

The i2K Group is responsible for building and providing intranet-based knowledge management solutions for CARE and relief agencies around the world. In 1998, i2K first implemented an ECM solution, called LINK, to bridge the information gaps within CARE International and across partner organizations. With CARE's success in administering relief to victims of Hurricane Mitch using the LINK system, the i2K Group is leading the way in leveraging technology to improve global relief efforts. A bold new initiative enables globally dispersed development and disaster relief organizations to share ideas, collaborate on projects, and improve overall response time to crisis situations. E-glue (Global Linkages, Universal Empowerment) is a program jointly developed by i2K, CARE Canada, its global partners, and visionary private sector companies that enables relief workers around the world to collaborate over a secure Internet e-community.

The deployment team for the ECM solution at CARE had to overcome one major obstacle: not all users had the same access to essential technology resources, such as Internet access or telephone lines. The organization overcame this challenge by integrating ECM technology with the e-glue initiative. Users can now access a secure, Web-based workspace from remote and underdeveloped areas. E-glue also provides emergency services, including a Rapid Deployment Communication Team, to establish and maintain Internet communications in areas struck by disaster. Teams can leverage precious information resources during emergencies when quick access and response are critical.

Access to training across the organization was also problematic for CARE. As part of its implementation strategy, the organization developed creative long-distance learning techniques to train new users on location.

CARE found the evolutionary, needs-based approach to system development and deployment to be best practice for its needs. Users felt more ownership of a system that was tailored to their needs, which, ensured adoption of the technology. Another best practice that resulted from the deployment was CARE's knowledge management strategies. The organization found that indexing all content related to collaborative projects helped them focus on the 'big picture' by providing context and relevant information surrounding successful strategies and projects.

CARE International's ECM solution has significantly changed how the organization carries out international relief efforts. Agencies can collaborate to reach common goals rather than focusing on individual projects, while the system facilitates co-operation and co-ordination within CARE and beyond to its partner organizations. Valuable information can be accessed by researchers and academics investigating third-world development and other crucial topics.

In the past, organizations would implement a crisis model to help build a sense of urgency, however, this is not necessarily the best way to go about this task. The problem with using a crisis model is that most employees will look for a quick fix to quell the crisis. These quick fixes tend to be short lived and do not help with the long-term adoption of the change. Initially, we may see a behavior change from employees in response to the crisis, but as time passes, they often revert to their previous patterns. Old habits die hard. Furthermore, this methodology puts the organization into a reactive mode, which can be even more problematic for the adoption of the change and for the overall health of the organization.

A healthier communication plan increases urgency proactively. This is accomplished by initiating the communication plan well in advance of the ECM application deployment. The objective is to educate people in small increments, and not to overwhelm them with large chunks of information. These messages include describing what the change is, why it is needed, how it will be deployed, and when it will happen. This allows employees to absorb the information and ask questions about how the change will affect their jobs. When employees do not understand this, they are more likely to assume it will have a negative impact, which will cause them to resist the change completely.

In addition to the "how, what, why, and when" of change, the communication plan should include success stories of the ECM deployment throughout the organization. Success stories help increase the sense of urgency within the organization. As the departments begin to adopt the new ECM application, a change advocate must communicate the ECM deployment success stories to the rest of the organization. These stories typically include how the ECM application has helped the department or enterprise become more successful. Whenever possible, these messages should articulate how the ECM application saved the department time and/or money. These messages resonate well with other department managers, increasing the likelihood that they will begin using the ECM application as soon as they can.

In order for a communication plan to work, executives and managers must trust the individuals that are communicating the success stories as well as the deployment team. Many change management methodologies encourage you to communicate success stories and stop short there; this can hurt user adoption in the long run, especially if a failure occurs. For a change management strategy to work, failures must also be communicated to executives and managers. However, for this to work, you must first get over the idea that failure is something negative. Failure is only negative if nothing is learned from it and, subsequently, the same mistake is made a second or third time. When failure occurs it should be communicated to the executives and managers within the context of what lessons were learned and what adjustments were made to the deployment and change management strategy. This builds a sense of trust with the managers and executives. Ownership, the third pillar of change, which is discussed later in this chapter, can never be achieved if trust does not exist among managers, executives and the implementation and change management team.

When a large Pharmaceutical company decided to deploy their ECM application, the first step they took was an internal mass marketing campaign. Their initial message announced that a change was coming, but did not disclose what the change was. They used comical posters and emails to communicate this to the organization. As time passed, they released more information about the change and its importance to the organization. As time grew near for the deployment of the application, they released more information in small chunks so that employees could absorb the material. They also conducted lunch meetings to allow employees to ask questions about the change and how it would impact them. By doing this, they were able to reduce resistance to the change and keep urgency high.

The Training Pillar

The second pillar, training, is also a critical supporting pillar for user adoption. The IT and implementation teams must be well trained on the ECM application, as well as the end users. End users are the ones who use the system daily. A successful ECM application deployment is not measured by whether it is up and running or whether the implementation team understands the application. It is measured by the number of end users actively using the system daily.

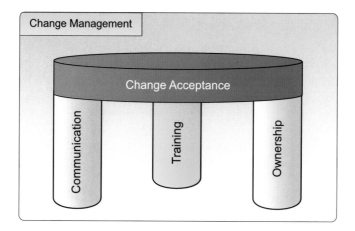

Figure 6.5: The Second Pillar of Change Management

When training your end users, ensure it is done in an environment that reflects the one that they will be working in. This increases the likelihood that the training material will be retained. If this doesn't occur, employees become frustrated, which negatively impacts user adoption. To increase retention and user adoption, you should develop a comprehensive training plan that captures the unique way that the organization plans to deploy their ECM application. Doing this gives the end users the skills that they will use in performing their daily job activities.

A mistake that organizations can make in training their staff has to do with timing. Training should be delivered to the end users after the ECM application is up and running. If you deliver it two or three weeks before the application is available, the users will forget what they have learned by the time the system becomes available. If, on the other hand, the system is made available to end users before training is available, they might try to learn how to use the system on their own. This is a potential problem, as they may become frustrated with trying to understand the application, increasing the chances they will resist the change.

A preferred timeline for training delivery is just before you give users access to the new ECM system. In most cases, it should be a pre-requisite to receiving their system log-in credentials. When they leave the training session, give them immediate access to the application. With well designed training systems, end users should be excited about using the new application by the end of the session. Not having access to the application can stifle the user acceptance.

When an oil and gas exploration company began to deploy their ECM application, they immediately identified that they would need to create custom training material to capture the unique way they would be using their ECM application. The existing training material was not sufficient for their needs. To ensure that their employees understood how to use the application, they developed custom training material that instructed employees on how to use the application, within the context of their unique deployment. The training material communicated the organizational policies about when and how to use the application and also included examples of other successful deployments within their organization.

The Ownership Pillar

The third pillar, ownership, is defined as "belonging to oneself" and is a critical factor during the initial deployment of an ECM application. Although we can define ownership, it is difficult to measure, but you will know it when you see it. When executives and middle management take ownership of the deployment, there tends to be a higher user adoption rate. For ownership to occur across the organization, it must be addressed at the top. The first step in increasing ownership is to meet with the organizations' executives and get their buy-in. It is not enough to have them say they will take ownership; they must show their commitment through their behavior. This is best accomplished by having executives regularly use the ECM application themselves. To get their buy-in, the ECM sponsors should meet with the executive team one-on-one, armed with data that supports the importance of adopting the ECM application. This data should consist of real-world examples and financial data whenever possible.

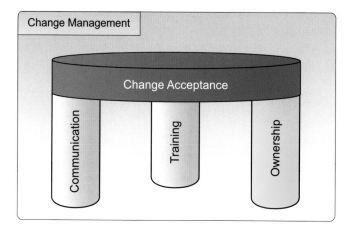

Figure 6.6: The Third Pillar of Change Management

> Booz Allen Hamilton

Who: An industry leader in strategy and technology consulting, Booz Allen Hamilton has been providing business solutions to major corporations and government clients for over 90 years. With over 16,000 employees across six continents, Booz Allen Hamilton now handles over $3 billion in sales annually.

Business Objective: To improve user adoption and address the security concerns of the existing enterprise-wide ECM system.

Solution Overview: A firm-wide, global collaborative tool, ECM provides a basis for business process automation to protect, organize and categorize information and users in an automated and extendable fashion. System evolution has led to improved user adoption and increasingly effective and specialized usage.

Solution Scope: Enterprise wide; extranet.

Benefits: Capture and sharing of knowledge assets across organizational and regional boundaries have been streamlined, while security modeling differentiates between users and protects intellectual capital. Improved collaboration among employees, contractors, and clients across 18 time zones has enabled a performance increase of 50 percent.

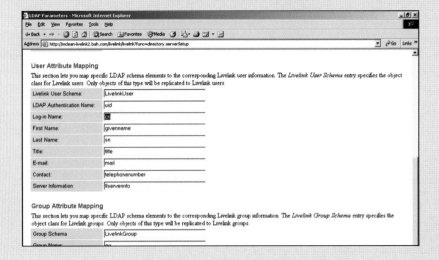

Figure 6.7: User Attribute Mapping at Booz Allen Hamilton

Deployed as a monolithic instance, the ECM system at Booz Allen Hamliton has since evolved to an enterprise-wide solution used by both internal employees and external users, including clients and contractors.

Three years after the initial stand-alone implementation, the system was upgraded and deployed on a global, enterprise-wide scale. After another three years, the solution was integrated with ERP technology and upgraded. After replacing the hardware for the front-end system instances and scaling the solution by adding two more front-end instances and moving them to a dedicated server, the system performance increased by 50 percent.

Although the solution was running smoothly and system performance had improved significantly, the flat organization of the enterprise and certain processes caused some concerns. Booz Allen Hamilton turned to the system provider who conducted an operational modeling study to determine possible development areas. The company formed an implementation team to target these development areas, which included the user interface, the authentication process, security, and cost savings. Enhancements resulted in the development of a new interface for internal and external users—to better meet the demands of employees, clients, and partners. The new system is more intuitive and easier to navigate, which has streamlined the capture and sharing of knowledge assets across organizational and regional boundaries. Thanks to the enhanced user interface, system usage has significantly increased.

They addressed security concerns by designing a tailored permission and group structure that restricted public access to information at the enterprise level. The new security model differentiates between internal and external users and accordingly protects and leverages the intellectual capital of Booz Allen Hamilton.

Integration with ERP technology has revised the employee authentication process, suppressing proprietary employee information according to policy. Creating user profiles in the ERP application allows the company to track and maintain employee information, while an authentication process suppresses confidential employee numbers.

The manual maintenance of creating internal accounts was replaced with a robust, automated process, which has improved overall services within the organization. They reduced costs for group maintenance by synchronizing end users into groups based on four attributes in the employee profile: geographic location, employee level, team role, and organizational segment—attributes retrieved from the human resources ERP application.

The system evolution at Booz Allen Hamilton has not only enabled direct and in-direct cost savings, but has also resulted in a maintainable, extendable, and flexible strategic solution. The organization is already considering future developments and extensions to the system, including increased storage capacity planning, and integration with additional applications to eliminate nightly jobs and allow an easily maintainable real-time synchronization environment for accounts management, attributes, and passwords.

When the executive team has taken ownership of the ECM deployment, the next step is to meet with several department managers to get their buy-in. The ECM sponsors should arm themselves with data supporting the advantages of adopting the application; in particular, how it will help the department financially and with overall performance. Sponsors should provide examples of how the executive team is using the application, which will increase the chances that the department managers take ownership themselves. If a manager refuses to use the application, end users will follow suit for fear of retaliation.

Once your organization has a few well documented, successful deployments, the next step is to communicate their stories to other departments. Using these success stories will build a sense of urgency throughout the organization. Ongoing communication of success stories to executives should continue regularly to ensure that they maintain their commitment to the deployment and adoption of the application. A common mistake made by organizations is that once they see user adoption begin to climb, they discontinue communications to the organization as a whole. Communication must continue throughout the deployment lifecycle; without it, employees will revert to their previous behavior and user adoption will suffer.

The three pillars of change are interdependent. For example, failure to have a communication plan in place has a direct impact on the ownership pillar. If we do not communicate the organizational need to deploy ECM, or the benefit it will have at a department and personal level, high user adoption can never be achieved. Similarly, if we do not train users properly, user adoption will suffer.

One might think these pillars must be rigid, but this is a misconception. The three pillars must be flexible or the change strategy will fail. During the deployment process, unforeseen problems may arise. If the change management strategy is too rigid to allow for these problems, it will fail. For the strategy to be successful, it must be reviewed regularly and compared with the overall ECM deployment strategy. A good change management strategy is developed in conjunction with the ECM deployment strategy.

The best solution for any organization undergoing an ECM deployment is to complete a comprehensive user adoption analysis. This analysis is the first step in identifying the unique training needs of the organization, and identifies potential deficiencies in the change management plan your organization is deploying. If your organization has not addressed change management issues, the user adoption analysis will guide you in developing an appropriate change management plan.

Developing the Change Management Strategy

The three pillars have been reviewed, but how do we develop and deploy the change management strategy? An effective change management strategy is one that is developed collaboratively by a change management consultant and a representative of the organization. However, as mentioned above, the delivery and ownership of the strategy must belong to the organization that is implementing the change. The change management consultant can offer guidance in the delivery, but they should never be used in the execution of the strategy. Remember that no two change management strategies are alike; each is unique to the organization that is undergoing the change.

The key to an effective ECM change management strategy is to tie it into the overall ECM deployment strategy. The deployment strategy typically includes a list of the functions that will be deployed and the timeline for their deployment. As well, it usually includes the groups that have been identified as the first users of the new deployment. Once this information has been gathered, the next step is to develop a communication plan.

Developing a communication plan is an ongoing process that evolves over time. The first step is to develop generic internal marketing material that can be distributed to the whole organization. Keep the messages short and simple. Humor is a useful tool that can be used when appropriate. A good time to start to distribute the material is three to six months before the ECM application is ready for use. At this point, an organizational change advocate should meet with the executives to get their buy-in to the ECM application. It is imperative that the executives take ownership of the changes and that they demonstrate this through their behaviors.

Once the ECM application goes online, the change advocate and ECM stakeholders should deliver one-on-one training to the executive team to encourage them to start using the application. Once they are using it, the communication material can be updated to broadcast this and include examples of how it helps with their daily activities. Using direct quotes or video testimonials are excellent tools for delivering these messages. At this point, you should create communication material that explains the importance of the change to the organization and that the executives are committed to the change.

When the previously discussed oil and gas exploration company deployed their ECM solution, they started with one group and ensured that their deployment went smoothly. Next, they recorded video-based testimonials about the ECM solution from this group. They also recorded executives discussing the value that the ECM application brought to the organization. These testimonials were posted on the home page of the company intranet for everyone to see.

Once additional communications have been distributed, the stakeholders and change advocate should to meet with the department managers to introduce them to the ECM application. The target group that is the first to use the new solution should meet regularly with the change advocates to discuss any concerns they may have. This will help reduce anxiety and any change management barriers.

When the ECM application is at the 75 percent build phase, you should start developing the training solution. The first step is to gather information about how the application is going to be used at the organization, including any policies or procedures that employees should be aware of. The training material should be built around the application that is being deployed. This will help users retain the learning and reduce frustration. The training material should be delivered just before users are given access to their ECM application.

Training should be delivered by internal trainers whenever possible. Developing the training material, however, should be done in a collaborative effort with consultants who have a strong background in the ECM application and a representative from the organization that is deploying the application. This ensures that the material will cover not only the functionality of the ECM application, but also will be developed within the context of that organization's unique deployment.

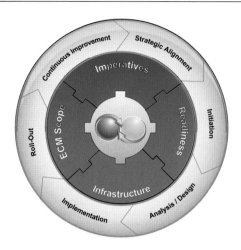

Figure 7.1: ECM Deployment Framework

For many years now, ECM experts have assisted users in deploying ECM applications. They have recognized that successful ECM deployment is about business and process change first, technology second. Recent market developments have pushed this truism into the foreground. As ECM deployments expand in scope, this is even truer.

Business change is about people behaving differently, and many ECM functions require a 'self-service' model. A business change program of the scale and power that ECM demands requires much more than technology implementation skills. Even visionary, business minded IT managers and thoughtful knowledge managers can be incomplete in their deployment planning. Planning change requires the consideration of many aspects.

As shown in Figure 7.1, the six deployment steps encircle the four deployment corner-stones, showing the continual evolution of the ECM platform. These steps are strategic alignment, initiation, analysis and design, implementation, roll-out, and continuous improvement.

CHAPTER 7

ECM DEPLOYMENT

The process of deploying ECM must be taken as seriously as ERP. ECM is not just an upgrade or a platform change—it is an evolution in the way that an organization does business. All aspects of deployment must be carefully considered and executed in order to achieve buy in at all levels of the organization.

The Enterprise Content Management (ECM) technology platform covers a wide range of functionality that can sometimes be overwhelming to those who are implementing it for the first time. Expansion of an ECM solution to address additional business imperatives can be daunting as well. Implementing proven deployment methods becomes vital in introducing organizational change as enterprises adopt ECM and eventually migrate from simple shared-drive replacement to more advanced solutions involving team collaboration, process management, corporate governance, and compliance.

The breadth and depth of ECM and its potential to transform business is growing rapidly. Visionary managers identify not just a wider range of departmental and process applications, but also the enormous potential of enterprise-wide deployments where inter-departmental collaboration can yield distinct competitive advantages. The organization that effectively leverages ECM to create, manage, search, store, and retire information in a full audit trail will have a distinct advantage over its competitors.

Deployment Aspects

There are four cornerstones of an ECM deployment required to successfully manage an ECM platform. These aspects make up the Deployment Framework and provide the foundation for the ECM deployment.

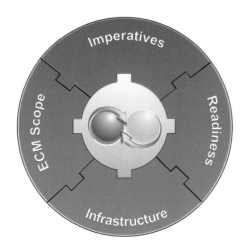

Figure 7.2: The Four Cornerstones of an ECM Deployment

Imperatives – The key business drivers that justify an ECM solution.

ECM Scope – The ECM application services that address the business imperatives.

Readiness – Guidelines, policies, procedures, and organizational structures to properly support the on-going development, maintenance, expansion, integrity, and evolution of the ECM solutions.

Infrastructure – The system components and architecture that constitute the ECM platform.

ECM Scope

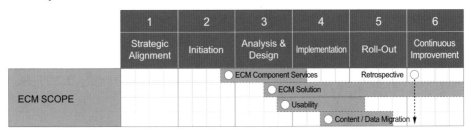

	1	2	3	4	5	6
	Strategic Alignment	Initiation	Analysis & Design	Implementation	Roll-Out	Continuous Improvement

Figure 7.3: ECM Scope

The ECM platform consists of a broad set of functionality that can sometimes be daunting to those who are deploying the technology for the first time. ECM Scope maps the ECM platform services and solutions that best satisfy the business imperatives.

Deployment Steps

There are six steps in the Deployment Framework that show the basic sequencing of events for the four cornerstones. These steps promote an understanding of the business need before deployment. As shown in Figure 7.4, the six deployment steps encircle the four deployment cornerstones, showing the continual evolution of the ECM platform. These steps are:

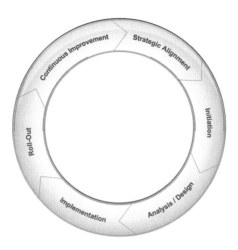

Figure 7.4: The Six Deployment Steps

Strategic Alignment – Focuses on strategy, visioning and identification of core requirements.

Initiation – Focuses on planning and confirmation of business and functional requirements.

Analysis and Design – Focuses on solution analysis and design activities.

Implementation – Focuses on solution development and test activities.

Roll-out – Focuses on tasks that bring the solution into production.

Continuous Improvement – Focuses on monitoring adoption, quantifying success, documenting lessons learned, and performing infrastructure health check activities. Organizations often overlook this step without realizing the importance it plays for the long-term vitality of an ECM platform.

Strategic Approach to ECM Deployment

Deploying ECM in stages by building on a series of incremental successes and implementing the corresponding organizational changes in parallel is a fundamental principle of ECM deployment. ECM adoption generally starts from a single-point solution at a departmental level and can evolve to multiple solutions that extend outside the enterprise to the marketplace. Each stage of adoption is built on the shoulders of the previous stage.

A staged approach to deployment offers many advantages. Lessons learned are captured from each stage and re-used for subsequent stages. ECM expansion can be targeted at solutions that achieve the greatest ROI. Momentum is built through word of mouth. Deployments can happen more quickly, allowing you to realize ROI sooner.

Deployment Framework Work Streams

The Deployment Framework shown in Figure 7.1 demonstrates the evolving nature of the ECM platform. In Figure 7.5 we unwrap the cycle of Figure 7.1 and consider the work streams associated with the intersection between the deployment cornerstones and deployment lifecycle. Together, these create the blueprint for a typical ECM deployment.

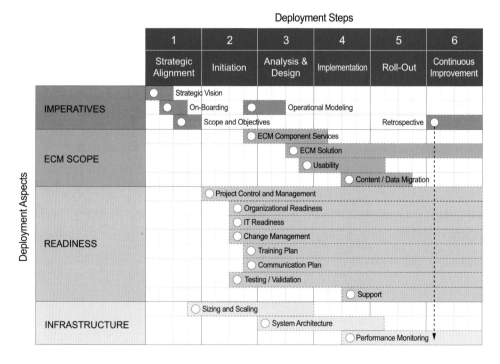

Figure 7.5: Deployment Work Streams

Strategic Alignment Work Stream

One of the most important activities within the Strategic Alignment work stream is defining a strategic vision and identifying the key business drivers that justify the ECM solution. This requires examining business problems and ECM opportunities. Think about how you would finish this sentence:

"Everything in my business would be great if we could only..."

In other words, figure out what you are trying to solve. Then address the problem.

Sample business drivers might include reducing cost by reusing content, reducing repetition, and reducing training and travel expenses. Time can be saved by preventing the redundancy of rework, allowing quick access to experts, knowledge assets, and content as well as establishing formal, optimized modes of communication and collaboration for all employees, customers, and partners. Improving quality through leveraging global competencies and using collaboration to create "think tanks" can be another business driver. Increasing business value by using ECM to solve business problems faster, decrease cycle times such as go-to-market, and to facilitate cross-selling through a high customer satisfaction is another good example.

Without a clear understanding of the business problems you are trying to solve, it becomes difficult to measure whether an ECM solution is meeting your objectives. A sure way of achieving deployment success is to quantify your success.

Recognizing the value that can be derived from the interoperability between ECM and ERP systems, Siemens incorporated this concept into one of its most successful application deployments. Nexus is a completely Web-based employee self-service solution that automates administrative approval processes such as signature authority, travel booking, expense claims, leave management, training management, asset management, recruitment, separation, purchase requisition, business card ordering, pay slip, timesheet, and so on.

All these ECM processes are seamlessly integrated with Siemens' ERP system at the backend and connected to global travel systems externally to ensure a completely paperless workflow. Employee master data and process transactional data are maintained in the ERP system, while business rules and approval structures are maintained in the ECM database.

On-boarding Work Stream

As an organization expands or introduces new ECM initiatives, there must be a process to manage the prioritization of this expansion. The absence of such a process can lead to uncontrolled growth, end-user dissatisfaction, and delays in the deployment of mission-critical applications. "On-boarding" is used to describe processes involving:

• The prioritization of groups, operational areas, and departments wishing to access existing ECM solutions.

• The prioritization and assessment of new ECM initiatives to be developed for the organization.

The on-boarding process involves evaluating three key metrics that can be used to prioritize—benefits, complexity, and investment size.

Benefits

Hard benefits that are directly reflected in the financial performance of the organization factor heavily in prioritization. Ongoing cost reductions, costs avoided, headcount reductions and additional margin secured through new sales are prime examples of hard benefits. Soft benefits could include the creation of spare capacity, added value in the marketplace, improved process efficiency, lead time, or an improvement in a metric that is important to a key customer. Soft benefits are often indirectly related to financial performance. Intangible benefits are those that are not directly linked to the organization's financials. Improved security, compliance, employee satisfaction, and customer satisfaction are difficult to see on an income statement or balance sheet but are important to most organizations.

Complexity

Assessing the difficulty of implementing a particular ECM initiative is key to prioritizing deployment. Organizational and process change must be measured. New skills, new ways of doing business, and overcoming organizational inertia are good examples. While measuring this change, it is also possible to assess legal or regulatory hurdles that may exist while implementing the initiative. One question to be considered is whether the resources needed (such as people, money, etc.) are commensurate with the system complexity.

Assessing the technical complexity of a deployment initiative is critical. Understanding the number of systems involved, how difficult the technology is to work with, and the availability of skilled resources to implement solutions is important in prioritizing. Tied in with this is the assessment of the project scale of the project, for example, numbers of documents concerned, complexity of a workflow, integrations with other systems, and use by third parties.

Investment Size

Assessing investment size involves estimating the total cost of time and resources to implement the initiative. This includes the cost of IT resources, but not software, hardware, or business resources. These metrics can be used to drive a prioritization model which can, for example, be used by executive management to make more informed decisions on the ECM initiatives targeted for on-boarding. A similar approach could be used for on-boarding groups, operational areas, and departments in the use of existing ECM solutions.

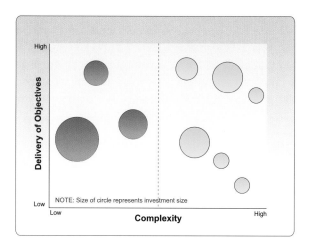

Figure 7.6: Prioritization of ECM Initiatives

Operational Modeling Work Stream

Once a targeted group or operational area has been targeted for On-boarding, Operational Modeling (OM) helps an organization optimize and prioritize their use of ECM. This involves applying a "business first" approach in identifying how an organizational group or department operates on a daily basis, and is used to accelerate the identification and design of core functional requirements.

An organization's Operational Model is a construct that defines how an operational group or department operates on a daily basis.

Figure 7.7: Operational Modeling Flow Diagram

The OM methodology can be used as an accelerator tool in identifying the way in which an operational role creates, consumes, controls, and contributes content within their organization. The OM consists of the synthesis of five categories that provide a view of how the business and the respective roles operate on a daily basis.

Information Assets – Documents used on an daily basis to operate the business,

Business Processes – Both structured and ad-hoc operational procedures,

Operational Events – Any operational event either internal or external for which individuals within the organization require action,

Operational Reviews – Regular reviews of operational information undertaken within the organization,

Collaboration Points – Teams formed within the organization to collectively produce a specific work product.

The resulting Operational Model refines the business requirements used to drive ECM platform design. The Operational Modeling process has the additional benefit of engaging business owners into the deployment process by gathering their issues, concerns, and requirements prior to ECM solution design.

Scope and Objectives – Project Charter

Business goals and success factors must be determined for a specific ECM initiative once it has been selected for deployment. Developing a project charter is a key activity that must occur prior to the initiation step. We recommend that a project charter be defined no matter how small or complex a project might be. Doing this increases the likelihood that the project will achieve its desired result.

Charter components include project vision, mission statements, and clear, measurable project objectives. Critical success factors must be identified and documented. Such factors as Executive Sponsorship and ensuring fulfillment of the business vision, mission, and objectives are important to establish. These will guide the project team and its leadership in setting priorities and evaluating issues. Identifying stakeholders as well as the resources required or assigned is important. Assessing the project complexity and defining the assumptions, constraints, issues, and risks are also key to success.

Retrospect Work Stream

It is important to review and assess lessons learned with the deployment team after completion of a work phase. The objective of a retrospective is to capture the new knowledge from the Deployment Team and incorporate the lessons learned for re-use for future projects.

The longer-term significance of incorporating a retrospective is monitoring and evaluating the metrics identified during On-boarding process. It is extremely important to track and, if possible, quantify whether the ECM solution is meeting the business imperatives. Doing this will motivate executive management to reinforce why the decision was made to on-board the solution to the business.

To execute an effective retrospective, you must revisit the project objectives, deliverables, and metrics. You must identify what you set out to do and determine what you have achieved. Next, you can establish what went well in the context of reaching the objectives. Assessing aspects that could have gone better is important as well. Understanding why certain aspects of the project went well or poorly and expressing this as learning advice for future projects is the real goal of a retrospective.

> Novo Nordisk

Who: A global market leader in diabetes care, Novo Nordisk has an overall market share of 20 percent and produces more than half of the world's insulin. More than 179 countries carry Novo Nordisk's products and the organization has 20,725 employees in 78 countries.

Business Objective: To support more active ECM system usage.

Business Needs: Improved system performance on a global scale.

Solution Overview: The rollout of a distributed document caching solution for remote sites that have low bandwidth connections with the central ECM server. Overall, 18 remote cache servers have been installed to date.

Solution Scope: Novo Nordisk Region Europe, Novo Nordisk Region International Operations and parts of Novo Nordisk HQ in Denmark.

Benefits: The solution had been crucial in driving increased user adoption of the ECM system. As performance improved considerably, system usage has almost doubled every year. Users no longer have to perform lengthy information searches and information loss has decreased. As a result of the solution, Novo Nordisk has experienced a lower total cost of ownership.

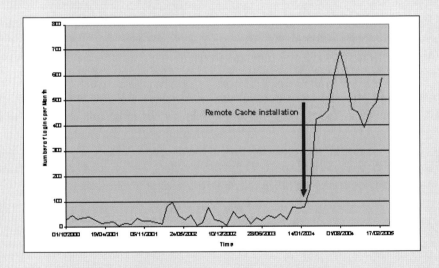

*Figure 7.8: Correlation Between Remote Cache Installation
and Number of Logins at Novo Nordisk*

Since the pilot implementation of an ECM system at Novo Nordisk, system usage has almost doubled every year. This number is true for all the usual measures of usage: number of documents, number of logins, number of unique active users and number of events. Novo Nordisk expects these usage statistics to continue growing at a considerable rate in next years.

The rollout of a remote cache server was a crucial component in driving the increased adoption of the ECM system at Novo Nordisk. A remote cache is a distributed document caching solution for remote sites that have low bandwidth connections with the central ECM server. As a remote cache stores local copies of recently requested documents, HTML renditions of documents as well as embedded images, users at remote sites have much faster access to local information. Once a remote cache server was in place in a Novo Nordisk office, performance improved so much that end-users began logging on to the system on a daily basis.

Figure 7.8 illustrates the change in usage pattern at Novo Nordisk after the installation of a remote cache server. Before the implementation, usage was low, as users typically logged on to the system for retrieving local information or for administrative purposes only. After the installation, the ECM system could be set up as the default browser home page and users began using it for their daily work.

With users dispersed across 67 countries, the system currently supports more than 35,000 logins per month and provides storage for approximately 100,000 documents, which amounts to 120 GB. Content is available in various languages including English, Hebrew, Turkish and Russian.

The remote cache installation was performed in three stages: analysis, deployment and follow-up. During the analysis stage, the organization size, the bandwidth limits and replication areas had been determined. In order to be effective, the deployment phase required local support at each installation site as well as process standardization including standard templates and setup: server names, drives, folders and services. The last stage, follow-up, represents an ongoing process during which the administrators monitor the server and the usage rates, and actively record their observations.

The primary ECM servers are hosted in Zurich, Switzerland. The remote cache has been rolled out to the regional offices in Europe and International Operations, together with selected strategic countries. 18 remote cache servers have been installed to date, with 30 servers expected to be installed by the end of 2005.

Advantages of this centralized solution at Novo Nordisk include built-in sharing and simple administration with one ECM system installation, one database server and one system administrator. Overall total cost of ownership of the system has also been lowered.

ECM Component Services Work Stream

ECM component services are the key functional components that must be incorporated into the ECM platform to meet the business imperatives. Application services include Document Management, Web Content Management, Digital Asset Management, Enterprise Application Extensions, Messaging and Email Archiving, Records Management, Knowledge Management, Business Process Service, and Repository Bridge Service.

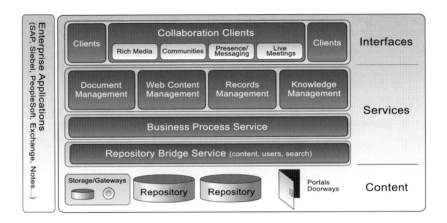

Figure 7.9: ECM Architecture Diagram

Understanding the mix of application services required to support the overall ECM platform is based on clearly defined business objectives and requirements.

Collaborative Structures

ECM collaborative structures involve interaction among three main constructs. The Library is tightly managed for explicit organizational knowledge and intellectual property. Incubation refers to Communities of Practice and/or collaborative working group areas used to incubate new ideas and draft documents not yet ready for release. Process can be either ad-hoc or structured, and is used to manage the interactions that take place between people and process (both internal and external) that are more formal in nature. To take full advantage of an advanced ECM platform, it is a good practice to think of these collaborative structures interacting in three primary ways.

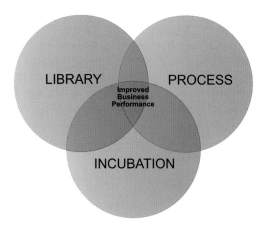

Figure 7.10: Collaborative Structures

Viewing these collaborative structures in this way enables organizations to manage, control, and share their knowledge assets more coherently.

ECM Solutions Work Stream

The ECM Solutions Layer involves combining and extending ECM Application Services to address business and/or industry specific imperatives, often mission critical in nature. These solutions often advance the capabilities of the ECM platform.

As an example, regulated industries such as life sciences, financial services, energy, and utilities need to make compliance with regulations an integral part of their document management and control processes to reduce risk and gain competitive advantage by bringing new products to market faster. Other solutions layers include invoice data capture and automated invoice routing. These layers seamlessly integrate processes with accounts payable and email archiving applications that manage the exponential growth of corporate email.

Usability Work Stream

Usability involves enhancing the end user experience to achieve greater adoption and satisfaction in the way information is accessed and consumed. Branding and using corporate design standards is one usability element, along with personalizing the content based on a user's daily responsibilities. Integrating data from existing systems and other sources is also part of usability. For example, you may want to integrate ERP systems with a back-end ECM platform to manage the invoices or other data generated from your ERP system. Modifying the graphical user interface to make common tasks easier to accomplish is also a key usability consideration.

Content/Data Migration Work Stream

The method and process for migrating data and content into the ECM repository must be planned and coordinated with great care. You must define your migration strategy, including the short and long-term objectives. Having a solid migration strategy minimizes the risk of including old, unused, or duplicate documents. Along with migrating content, you must decide what type of meta-data tags that you want to associate with the content.

Organizational Readiness Work Stream

Readiness involves defining the methods and practices required to successfully manage ECM projects and initiatives.

There is a direct correlation between the successful deployment of ECM solutions and project managers that use proven project management methods. Many organizations overlook the importance an experienced project manager plays in successful deployments. Project management methodologies play a key role in successful deployments, but having an experienced project manager with the requisite skills and temperament is even more important.

Project Management

Most proven project management methodologies emphasize the importance of the charter as well as detailed project planning, project monitoring and control, risk management, and teamwork.

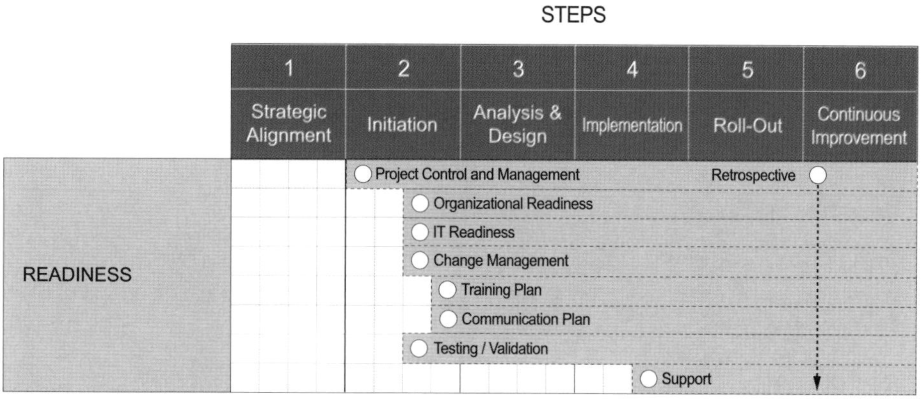

STEPS

	1	2	3	4	5	6
	Strategic Alignment	Initiation	Analysis & Design	Implementation	Roll-Out	Continuous Improvement
READINESS			○ Project Control and Management		Retrospective ○	
			○ Organizational Readiness			
			○ IT Readiness			
			○ Change Management			
			○ Training Plan			
			○ Communication Plan			
		○ Testing / Validation				
				○ Support		

Figure 7.11: Project Control and Management Work Stream

Program Management Office (PMO)

If an organization is deploying multiple projects, it may become necessary to develop a Program Management Office (PMO). A PMO centralizes multiple initiatives by managing budgets, schedules, and resources to create a competency center for ECM enterprise deployments. The PMO also serves as a repository for best practices and methodologies. It creates the guidelines, fact sheets, and checklists that are used to manage projects.

Guidelines

Guidelines provide the project team members with the basic requirements for tasks within the PMO methodology. Typical guidelines include defining a project, assigning costs to projects, developing backup strategies, disaster recovery tests, and guidelines for long-term production support. Guidelines also usually cover topics such as problem resolution processes, quality management planning, validation protocols, volume tests, stress tests, and system administration.

Fact Sheets

Fact Sheets provide instructions for completing the project templates provided by the PMO. Typical fact sheets include baseline scope templates, change request templates, issues management templates, weekly/monthly report templates, project request form templates, and project work sheet templates.

Checklists

Checklists provide task lists associated within a particular project phase. Typical checklists include task lists for the baseline scope, system cut-over, initial project estimating, PMO review per stage, project team preparation, training, and technical failure testing phases.

Organizational Readiness Work Stream

Organizational Readiness focuses on the policies, procedures, and organizational structures that are geared to the on-going management of the ECM platform from a business perspective.

Processes and Controls

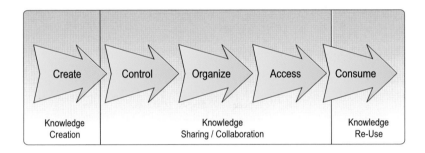

Figure 7.12: Managing Knowledge Process Flow

The first step in understanding Organizational Readiness is identifying the key processes and controls that must be established to manage the information assets, explicit knowledge, and unstructured content of the ECM platform. The five steps in managing knowledge within the context of an ECM platform are: create, control, organize, access, and consume. Create involves activities that result in new knowledge or new assemblies of existing knowledge. Control refers to activities that make the knowledge explicit. To organize is to classify and categorize knowledge for navigation, storage, retrieval, and maintenance. Access refers to activities that disseminate knowledge to users. Consume is defined as activities that apply knowledge to business decisions or opportunities.

From these five steps are derived the key processes and controls that you must consider when managing knowledge (see Figure 7.12). They are: capture, knowledge maintenance, knowledge retirement, feedback processes, knowledge access, and knowledge organization.

Figure 7.13: Knowledge Management Lifecycle

Once the processes are defined, you must define the roles and activities that are necessary to sustain them (see Figure 7.14).

	Functional Unit			ECM Support Team	
	Subject Matter Expert	Knowledge Manager	Knowledge Users	ECM Platform Administrator	Solution Consultant
Create	Creator	Controller	Consumer	Controller	
Create new knowledge object	•		•		
Create documents	•	•	•		
Review existing documents	•		•		
Advise to retire documents	•				
Decide to update / revise documents	•				
Update / revise documents	•				
Capture					
Submit documents / knowledge	•	•		•	•
Regulate the processes for content inclusion		•		•	•
Monitor the business processes for compliance with KM requirements		•		•	•
Maintain the relationship with knowledge owners		•		•	•
Maintain relationships with knowledge users		•		•	•
Maintain relationships with other LOBs		•		•	•
Organize					
Establish the KM Process Framework		•		•	
Maintain the KM Process Framework		•		•	
Initiate document review		•		•	
Maintain knowledge library-technical aspects		•		•	
Add submitted documents to Library		•		•	
Delete retired documents from repository		•		•	
Add updated documents to repository		•		•	
Access					
Access the knowledge			•		
Consume					
Apply knowledge to assignments			•		

Figure 7.14: Example – Knowledge Management Role and Activity Matrix

> LVA

Who: With more than 4300 employees and over 6.6 million insurance holders, LVA, or Landesversicherungsanstalt Rheinprovinz, is one of the largest German federal state pension funds. The organization provides insurance services in the administrative districts of Düsseldorf and Cologne.

Business Objective: To optimize business processes by enabling faster and easier access to pension dossiers.

Business Needs: Over a million paper files needed to be scanned and stored electronically, while ensuring confidentiality, integrity, and availability.

Solution Overview: A Web-based solution for production document management facilitates scanning, indexing, and electronic archiving of business records and enables electronic transaction processing. Secure long-term storage and the use of digital signatures ensure compliance with statutory regulations for tamper-proof archiving.

Solution Scope: Administration

Benefits: LVA has been able to optimize business processes as files can be accessed within seconds and related transactions can be processed electronically. The user-friendly interface has ensured high end-user acceptance, and the organization has been able to realize cost savings due to eliminated floor space, filing department resources, and paper handling.

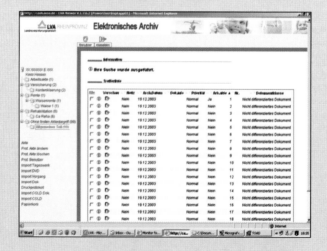

Figure 7.15: Electronic archiving at LVA

Prior to implementing archiving technology to manage its enterprise content, LVA stored approximately 1.3 million business records for seven million insurance policies in paper format in a central archive building. When an administrator requested a file, it took an average of five to ten days to process the request. As a result, LVA management decided to transfer the paper-based pension files to an electronic archive which would also help the organization meet the statutory regulations for revision-proof archiving through the use of a qualified electronic signature.

Within a year of implementing the solution, approximately 125 million documents, representing some 1.7 million files, had been transferred to an electronic archive with full consideration for confidentiality, integrity and availability. The volume of processed files measured over 15 miles long. The core element of the solution, an ECM platform, contributed significantly to the project's success through its ability to integrate with storage systems like HSM (Hierarchical Storage Management). The in-depth integration of fully qualified signatures plays another important role in the in the scanning and validity-checking stages. One of the archive server's unique features is the ability to renew signatures in long-term archiving.

Preparation for this new electronic archive involved scanning 600,000 paper documents every day and adding a qualified electronic mass signature before burning them on to DVD. After the SecCommerce signature server checked the electronic signatures against a black list supplied by the participating trust center, the documents were transferred via an import pipeline and stored in the archive server in a revision-proof condition. The entire import process was recorded in logs according to the ID of each DVD, including the number of images, delivery date, and documents to be archived for an insurance number. This process enabled the departmental administrators to check the import for accuracy and completeness. This carefully thought-out process ensured that all of LVA's 2,000 administrators were able to access the files in the electronic archive after six days at the most.

Users can now quickly and easily access files from an Internet browser. Instead of taking several days to process a request, a maximum of two seconds elapses between the request for the electronic documents in the archive and their display on screen. The appearance and functionality of the front end have been customized to the needs and requests of users in order to make their work as simple and convenient as possible.

The pensions insurer now archives pension files for LVA Landshut, and for some time has also been testing digital transaction processing in a pilot project. The electronic files already stored are now being used as the information base. Even incoming mail is now scanned and supplied to administrators as digital documents.

IT Readiness Work Stream

IT Readiness focuses on those policies, procedures, and organizational structures that are geared to the on-going management of the ECM system from a technical perspective and are usually managed and controlled within the Information Technology (IT) group.

The IT group manages key system management processes that must be defined and adhered to. This is especially important for industries that are under strict regulatory control. IT Readiness Plans include a back-up recovery plan, business continuity plan, and disaster recovery plan.

Procedures that must be clearly defined in an IT Readiness Plan include application performance monitoring, redundancy fail over, system upgrade, system data conversion, password rules, procedure (enforcement auditing), security policy, server security, RDBMS security, firewall placement/rules, and accounts (local and domain).

Change Management Work Stream

Change management is a formal methodology through which an organization governs change. For a discussion of change management, refer to Chapter 6.

Support Work Stream

Support is vital to the long-term success of the ECM platform and provides the foundation for continuous improvement. It typically involves a Support Desk, a service level agreement, and support procedures. A well planned support organization increases operational efficiency and end user confidence.

Establish Support Levels

Categorize your support into levels, with each level reflecting an increase in the technical involvement of the Support Desk personnel. Determine whether the organization needs extended support, which may include emergency support outside of standard operating hours, telephone access to a Product Specialist 24x7, a one-hour response time for critical issues, or a dedicated line that connects directly to a voicemail-activated pager.

Along with establishing support levels, you must establish escalation times (see Figure 7.16).

Escalation Level	Critical	Normal
Priority 1	Hours	Days
Priority 2	1 Day	Days
Priority 3	Days	Days

Figure 7.16: Support Escalation Times

Support Resources

You should consider three key support resources when a developing a Support Desk.

Solution Consultants are usually from within the business unit, typically an expert user who knows the business. A Senior Technician (Product Specialist) is assigned to handle all technical support issues for the organization. A Support Manager is the dedicated point of contact for all questions, status reporting, issue escalations, and inter-departmental contact.

Procedures

Establishing Support Desk guidelines require you to develop Standard Operating Procedures (SOPs) that must be followed unless changes are formally introduced through a change management process.

In configuring users and groups on the ECM system, SOPs are required for creating new groups, leading a group, editing and deleting groups, creating reports to assist with administering users and groups, and so on. SOPs required to administer users and groups must include restricting a user's ability to access certain administrative functions, administering tasks for a new system, and administering large user populations.

Administering access control requires SOPs that control how permissions are applied to items, how the ECM platform maps permissions from the repository to daily work items, and how it maps them from the repository to the collaboration work areas. SOPs must also be in place to manage how permissions change when moving and copying items and editing item permissions.

Issue Tracking

You must have a robust process in place to track issues and get back to the end user with status and resolution. Some issue tracking programs suggest developing a process to report back to end users regularly and grouping similar issues together.

Marketing the Support Desk

Raising the profile of your Support Service Desk is critical to the success of the Support work stream. The Service Desk must attain its own identify to instill confidence and strengthen the customer relationship. You can achieve this by inviting customers to visit the Support Desk, and using advertising vehicles such as mouse mats, screen savers, bulletin boards, seminars, and Support Desk stationery.

Sizing and Scaling Work Stream

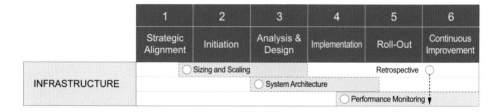

Figure 7.17: Sizing and Scaling Work Stream

Sizing and scaling involves the technical analysis of how a system is going to be used. The sizing and scaling stream involves gathering information about your current infrastructure, future usage projections, hardware requirements, and system design issues.

Request Type	Profile Percentage
Library / Project browsing	60%
Document Fetch	15%
Document View	15%
Other	10%

Figure 7.18: Library-Centric Usage Pattern

Usage Profile

A usage profile shows what the users will do on the ECM system. Figure 7.18 provides an example of a generic "Library-Centric" profile of using ECM's document management function.

Systems Architecture Work Stream

The System Architecture work stream drives and is driven by many things. From corporate standards to security and performance requirements, system architecture is much more than simply a machine or set of machines. An ECM platform is capable of operating in a variety of architectures, from monolithic installations to mixed-system, clustered, multi-tier environments. It is not always apparent which approach is best for each system.

A number of factors should be considered when choosing a systems architecture approach. You should consider functionality, reliability, availability, maintainability, performance, and security when determining what type of architecture to use with an ECM solution.

Functionality

Functionality considerations are determined by your business imperatives. For example, you may require the use of remote caches, certain modules, and add-ons which may have specific software or hardware prerequisites.

Reliability

Reliability is the measure of a system to function continuously without interruptions. Each component of the system architecture must be considered.

Availability

Availability of the architecture is its ability to recover or handle problems such that end users experience little to no interruption of service. To determine availability requirements, you must account for the cost of downtime and whether redundancy is required.

The goals of a system are typically measured in "percentage of uptime," represented by x-nines. For example, a five-nines solution would measure 99.999 percent uptime, which amounts to approximately 315 seconds (or 5 minutes) of downtime per year.

System availability is not any single application's or person's responsibility. It is the combination of many separate, uncoordinated components, and only policies and procedures provide this coordination.

Maintainability

As the availability goals of a solution become more aggressive, the maintainability of the solution becomes more important. Maintainability is defined as the ease with which the solution can be reconfigured to meet changing requirements, and be fixed when hardware or software issues arise. System maintainability may vary largely depending on the platform setup.

Performance

Performance of an ECM platform is key for users to embrace it. The operating system is the main consideration for performance. Each operating system has its own strengths, weaknesses, and performance capabilities, and has an impact on ECM platform scaling.

Security

Security is a key concern for most organizations that implement ECM solutions. Although ECM solutions maintain as much security as they can within the platform, external factors such as encrypted data transmission and Web browser caching are implemented through the overall systems architecture. Security policies may influence certain system architecture decisions.

Performance Measuring and Monitoring Work Stream

Monitoring is an integral aspect of an ECM deployment. Effective monitoring keeps the system administrator aware of what is happening with the machines, helps avoid potential problems, and improves system performance.

To fully understand the health, performance, and stability of an ECM solution, it is imperative that comprehensive measurements are taken from each of the major system components, including the ECM core application, the ECM system database, the ECM Web-server, the supporting operating system(s), the supporting network infrastructure, and the end users.

All information collected as part of an ongoing measurement activity should be collated and archived so that over time, a complete historical picture of the system can be developed. When investigating recurrent problems on a specific system, using a body of historical system data can be an invaluable resource.

Inference Monitoring is the practice of inferring a sub-system's status by relying on the successful completion of a different service that relies on that sub-system. For example, successfully logging into an ECM solution lets you infer that the Web server, the ECM platform server, and the database are functioning.

Direct Monitoring is the practice of monitoring a specific service or sub-systems directly using monitoring tools.

Deployment Roles and Responsibilities

Each person involved in an ECM deployment plays an important part in ensuring its success. Political, geographical, and cultural issues are involved with each role, so careful consideration must be given to selecting the right person for a role.

The **Executive Sponsor** retains overall responsibility for the program costs and strategy. They identify and outline the program ROI from a business perspective. The Executive Sponsor is the main authority that can alter the company practices in support of the project.

The **Business Owner** provides guidance and representation to ensure that business benefits will be realized. They champion business process improvements or alterations due to the functionality of the solution. Business Owners also communicate potential project impacts to the organization.

The **Programs and Project Manager** develops and maintains the overall program plan, and provides leadership to drive the initiative. They control, monitor, and report on program initiatives, and manage the program budget and risk, as well as overall program issues. They are responsible for staffing, rewards and recognition, organizational readiness, data migration, and technology. They execute the overall program communications plan, update the executive steering committee on project status, and resolve the majority of business issues, identifying and escalating critical one where necessary.

The **Steering Committee** approves the direction of all work streams within the program. They have the authority to stop, delay, and prioritize projects, as well as assign additional resources to the program. They resolve critical business issues, review budgets, and review the achievement of projects against budgets. This committee supports the Program Management Office and changes policies and procedures to support the program.

The **Program Management Office** reviews the progress and status of each project. It makes proposals on how to handle identified issues and escalates as needed. The Program Management Office procures resources and resolves roadblocks.

The **Subject Matter Expert (SME)** is the knowledgeable business unit resource that participates in the requirements gathering, testing, training, and implementations. The SME works under the guidance of the Business Owners and is the liaison to the Business Owners in introducing new functionality within the organization. The SME can serve as the "power user" that trains the users.

The **Application Architect** is the senior technical associate from the Architecture Group that specifies the system architecture. They work closely with the project associates to ensure that an infrastructure plan is in place to support the system architecture. The Application Architect solicits input from appropriate SMEs to make sure that the technical architecture will meet the business goals.

The **Business Analyst** is the liaison between the technical resources and the Business Unit SMEs with whom they work to collect and document business requirements. They ensure that these requirements are accurate, complete, and approved by the Business Owners. They develop the procedures to support project objectives. The Business Analyst reports to the Project Manager and the Business Owner.

Quality Assurance works closely with the Business Analysts and Business Owners to understand the business model requirements. They prepare test scripts based on the business requirements and perform unit / integration testing and regression testing.

The **Technical Lead / Application Developer** designs, installs and supports the infrastructure requirements for the ECM system, including UNIX Server, Networking, Windows Server, and Security and Desktop requirements. They design, install, monitor, and support the databases required by the ECM system and the application server. They provide system access requirements for users to support the ECM system.

Summary

A successful ECM deployment can dramatically improve the speed at which an organization does business. Using ECM to control processes increases accuracy. Working faster and more effectively means improvements to the bottom line of an organization and its ability to compete in today's marketplace. These are enticing statements, but in order for them to come true, we must ask people to change the way they work. They must fully embrace this new technology and work to leverage its vast potential.

The ECM Deployment Framework (illustrated at the beginning of this chapter in Figure 7.1) is a structured, wide-angle view of successful planning for major ECM deployments. It highlights the thinking, planning, activity sequence, and range of skills required across the business to fully leverage ECM. By following a deployment framework (and the associated deployment aspects and stages), organizations can successfully deploy ECM applications.

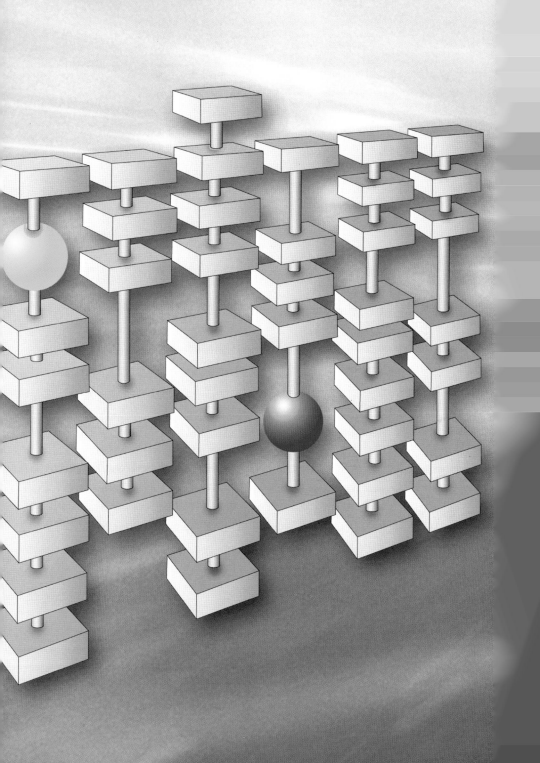

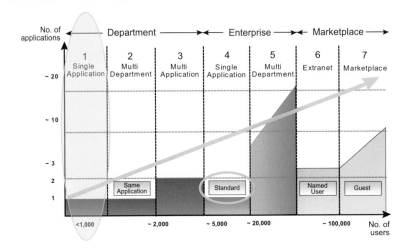

Figure 8.1: Stage 1 of ECM Adoption

ECM deployments usually begin with the adoption of an application that solves a particular departmental problem, shown in Figure 8.1 above.

Typically, the deployment is made to less than 1,000 people, and is sought by a department or operational manager who is the business owner of the problem. A Stage 1 deployment could involve almost any application from the full suite of ECM solutions. A solution may be narrowly targeted—for example, an Accounts Payable department might implement an imaging and workflow ECM solution to better manage its invoice flow processing. Or a solution might be a broad-based initiative—for example, an architecture and strategy group in IT may initiate a collaboration and knowledge sharing platform to support their work in coordinating the technology foundation of the organization.

Both of these are departmental solutions, and both have connections to the rest of the enterprise, yet they are very different ECM implementations serving very different communities. This chapter discusses how to use the deployment framework of Chapter 6 to establish the initial ECM deployment.

CHAPTER 8

DEPARTMENT DEPLOYMENTS STAGE 1

This chapter explores the characteristics of deploying a solution during ECM Stage 1, Adoption. We'll use the Deployment Framework as our blueprint to highlight the deployment steps that must be considered to mitigate risk and increase success for each stage of adoption. Adoption and expansion of ECM within an organization occurs iteratively by building on a series of incremental successes. To proceed to the next stage of adoption, you must make sure you have achieved success in the previous stage.

The Deployment Framework demonstrates the sequencing of tasks and resources involved in each work stream. Although each work stream plays an important part in the long-term success of the ECM program, certain streams take on a higher priority depending on which stage of adoption you are in. As illustrated in Figure 8.2, each work stream in the Deployment Framework has been prioritized as either high (yellow), medium (blue), or low (green) based on Stage 1 adoption. We'll explore this prioritization for each stage of adoption in this and subsequent chapters.

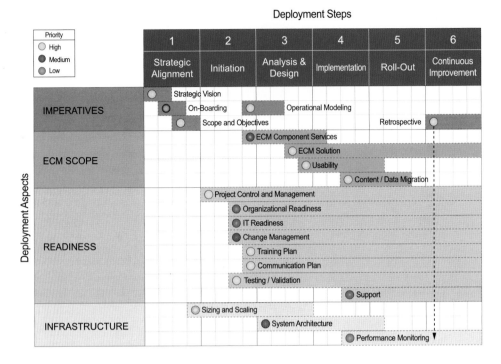

Figure 8.2: Deployment Framework for ECM Adoption Stage 1

Enterprise Application Extensions (EAE)

Enterprise applications such as Enterprise Resource Planning (ERP) and Customer Relationship Management (CRM) perform transaction-based processing. However, data residing in these applications is the result of work that has been completed and, in many cases, cannot effectively support other business processes. Many processes, like contract creation, still require collaborative efforts of employees in multiple departments. To maximize content's effectiveness, organizations must connect content to the appropriate business processes and make it accessible to people participating in the process. Enterprise Application Extensions provide the underlying business structure that supports these business processes. Allocating unstructured content to business processes puts the information that people need at their fingertips without having to search across many systems for content.

ECM extends enterprise applications by providing links between key processes and transactional information as illustrated in Figure 8.3. Making this information secure and accessible across a variety of processes helps companies lower costs and the risks associated with meeting data retention and disposal requirements.

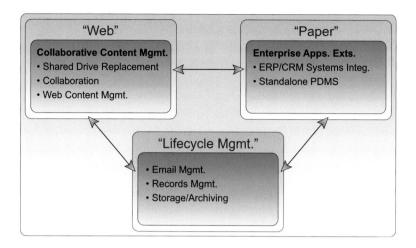

Figure 8.3: ECM Solution Segments

Lifecycle Management

The core of content lifecycle management is records management, the discipline of managing records to meet operational needs, accountability requirements and community expectations. Records management software works by allowing you to attach rules to electronic documents. These rules tell the system when it is okay to delete documents or move them to a data archive, either physically in boxes or electronically on storage devices such as CD-ROMs.

Government offices are superb at record keeping. When we are born, when we are married, when we have children, when we get divorced, and when we die, a record is created at a government office. The rules that determine when those records can be archived and deleted are stipulated in government regulations and policies. Records management systems enforce these policies for government organizations, and for the equivalent form of vital records in an organization.

With daily pressure to comply with regulations and with changes to legislation, managing records and the lifecycle of documents have become crucial components of ECM.

Teams and Collaboration

We have quickly grown accustomed to being able to phone each other anywhere at any time and in a matter of seconds. Cell phones and mobile telephony are so entrenched in our daily lives that it is hard to imagine life before they existed. The Internet has also revolutionized our ability to connect with others. We send documents over the Web and drum our finger impatiently awaiting their delivery. Being able to connect so easily with our colleagues over the Internet has made it possible to work effectively in virtual teams, with geography no longer a concern.

The Human Genome Project began in 1990 as a collaborative effort by research establishments around the globe to identify the 30,000 genes in human DNA. The project required the collaboration of scientists from many fields, including molecular biologists, engineers, physicists, chemists and mathematicians at the U.S. Department of Energy. Technology had a huge role in the project; the Genome Data Base (GDB) is the worldwide repository for genome mapping data. Researchers around the world used the Internet to share research and answer questions. The project successfully concluded in April, 2003 and would not have been possible before the creation of the World Wide Web.

Global organizations are now able to capitalize on Web-based collaboration facilities to empower their workforces, working as virtual project teams to bring expertise from different areas and office locations to tackle business-critical problems. ECM systems include collaboration tools that enable the best minds within organizations to work together more efficiently—sharing information, capturing and preserving knowledge, managing collaborative processes and projects, and resolving issues.

Stage 1 of the ECM Deployment Framework

First let's confirm the characteristics of a Stage 1 Adoption:

- Single application solving a specific departmental business problem that has been clearly understood and articulated

- Usually less than 1,000 end users involved

- Department manager is the business owner

- Highly homogeneous culture and organizational structures

- The change to the business is primarily operational and tactical versus cultural or a major paradigm shift in the business.

Imperatives

All ECM stages require, at a minimum, a clear understanding of the business drivers that justify the ECM solution being deployed. There is a significant risk that the solution will not be recognized as successful if the business motivation is not defined and agreed upon prior to project initiation.

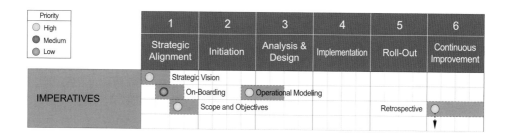

Figure 8.4: ECM Deployment Framework Stage 1 Imperatives

Strategic Vision

The stronger the alignment with the corporate strategic vision, the more likely it is that the ECM solution will be adopted. This isn't always essential to a stage one deployment, where executive management may not be directly engaged. As well, the type of ECM application being deployed makes a difference. The more strategic the sponsoring department, the more important strategic alignment becomes. When ECM solutions are new to the organization and do not have the history to showcase their long-term benefits, being able to show alignment with the organization's strategic, operational, and technology directions will help overcome initial skepticism.

Scope and Objectives

It is a truism in systems implementation that the way to success is to show a "quick win." This is especially true when the implementation is envisaged as the first of many that will follow in the adoption of a new technology. The ideal stage 1 project will have a limited and practical set of goals and clearly identifiable success factors: reductions in processing cost, measurable increase in the use of common architectural elements and documentation, reduction in shared file server space and usage, and so on.

> South East Water

Who: South East Water is one of three retail water companies that provide water and sewerage solutions for Melbourne, Australia. Encompassing a square footage of 3,640 kilometres and with more than 1.3 million customers, South East Water manages infrastructure and assets valued in excess of AUD $1 billion.

Business Needs: An innovative and extensible solution to measure and improve customer service in response to increased service quality regulations.

Business Objective: To implement a single repository for unstructured documents and automate business processes.

Solution Overview: Electronic workflow enables process automation in the Customer Services Division, and a Quality Management System allows all employees to read and update policies, procedures, and work instructions. An electronic repository facilitates management of scanned customer correspondence; plans, drawings and photos; quality procedures; executive and board correspondence; and 650,000 property plans.

Solution Scope: Enterprise wide.

Benefits: Significantly diminished paper usage; document status and audit trail; centralized storage and search; improved collaboration and project management; productivity and efficiency; and enhanced customer services.

Figure 8.5: A Corporate Image Library at South East Water

In response to the introduction of further regulations in the Victorian Water industry, South East Water implemented an ECM solution to measure and improve its customer service in relation to paper-based requests. Although an intranet existed, most of the organization's documents were stored on a shared drive. The system limited document searching to within departments, and documents were duplicated and difficult to access.

South East Water used its project management methodology to identify the business problems, system and business requirements, and potential solutions. Potential ECM projects were prioritized according to their business value, ability to deliver, and the impact on the overall knowledge management strategy. This detailed analysis of potential ideas identified close to 40 projects that were prioritized, scheduled, and resourced.

Taking a staged approach to the implementation, South East Water first integrated scanned customer correspondence in an electronic repository in the Customer Services Division. Phase two involved adding 650,000 property plans to the repository, and subsequent stages included adding a Quality Management System, IT Project management methodology documents, executive and board documents, and a corporate image library. With the introduction of the Quality Management System, all divisions within the organization began to use ECM to read and update policies, procedures, and work instructions.

While there was initially some resistance to the changes introduced by ECM, subsequent internal training and promotion of its benefits has made the system highly popular with staff who continue to embrace and extend the kinds of content to be stored. ECM is now considered a critical system to the business success by both staff and management. A staff survey of ECM has indicated very positive results. The solution end users are mostly staff and internal contractors; however, the Customer Contact e-business solution enables customers to upload plans and submissions that are automatically uploaded into the ECM repository.

The system plays a key role in automating and streamlining the customer correspondence process. Incoming letters and forms are visible and auditable for all customer service staff and management. ECM has been integrated with the Customer Billing System, Customer Contact System, Contract Management System, GIS/Mapping system, Asset Register, and MS Office. 98.5 percent of customer correspondence is now answered within five days—a result that far exceeds the service requirement for a ten-day turn-around. Tracking the status of incoming correspondence has significantly reduced the risk of non-compliance with federal regulations.

South East Water is now recognized as a leader in collaborative document management in Australia's water industry—enhancing the organization's reputation of Excellence, Innovation, and Leadership in Water. South East Water's ECM solution has become a strategic platform for information management, increasing corporate communications and reducing support costs. The company is now embarking on adding a Records Management module and automating further complex paper-based business processes with electronic workflow.

Operational Modeling

Some degree of analysis that uncovers how a business operates on a day-to-day basis is essential to define the implementation. It is particularly important for any stage 1 customer that is introducing a new ECM solution to get the business involved in the early steps of the project. In particular, identifying the roles of the ECM solution users is critical; the number of possible stage 1 applications is so large that there is no standard definition. For example, with invoice processing, roles might include approvers, reviewers, supervisors, workflow managers, and so on. With Architecture Knowledge Management, roles might include authors and content contributors, reviewers, content consumers, and managers, Or the solution may operate as a peer-to-peer flexible collaboration community; it depends on the culture and needs of the organization.

Retrospect

Once the solution has been rolled out, you must monitor to determine whether it is meeting the original business objectives.

ECM Scope

All ECM Stages must select the appropriate ECM component services to address the business solution targeted for deployment. The functionality of an ECM platform is extensive, so conducting the proper analysis and design (Stage 3) to determine the best combination of component services to address the business problem is essential.

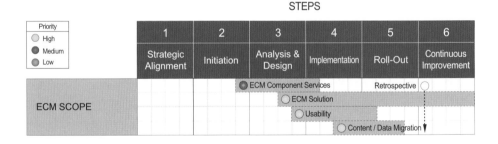

Figure 8.6: ECM Deployment Framework Stage 1 ECM Scope

Other important factors when developing organizing schemes for information collaboration and knowledge retrieval solutions are:

- Plan for growth—a taxonomy that is appropriate for a Stage 1 solution with 1,000 users and 20,000 items in the repository will not be adequate for 10,000 users and 200,000 items.

- The "long-tail" nature of classification schemes—most user retrievals are concentrated on relatively few search terms. This means there is a complex trade-off in the scheme design between the up-front indexing effort and the retrieval time in the search.

Siemens in Johannesburg, South Africa was one of the first groups to address a complex ECM requirement from its business units. To comply with government regulations, Siemens developed Internal Control Sheets to serve as an auditable tracking system for quality care of its internal and external customer bases. Siemens identified specific ECM functionality directory services, caching servers, and Secure Socket Layers (SSL) to satisfy the compliance requirements its Internal Control Sheets were designed to address.

Replacing twenty-six different document management systems, Siemens deployed a single content management and Web publishing application for all of its product documentation, process and procedure material—essentially all critical business documents. Keeping its internal people knowledgeable about the products and about changes in processes and procedures in the organization, this solution for finding and disseminating key documentation is a critical part of Siemens' Web-based efforts for ongoing collaborative communication with partners and customers.

An application call EZA—an acronym for easy access—provides access to contracts and customer engagement information for solutions and services. EZA pulls together all Siemens activities for a single engagement with a customer, from the time a prospect becomes a lead, through installation and final confirmation of the arrangement. A unique approach to sales and customer engagements, the solution aids the sales force in their ability to interact with people internally, customers and business partners.

ECM Solution

Once the appropriate combination of component services has been selected to address a business problem, it becomes an ECM solution. For Stage 1 solutions this is usually straightforward, as many ECM components are designed or packaged to be aligned with specific solution applications. Some solutions might require a single primary service such as Document Management, Workflow, or Web Content Management. Others, often in a specific industry or business unit, might use a standard package, for example a regulated document solution for Life Sciences.

During Stage 1 adoption, this solution establishes a standard which requires documenting configuration details, procedures, guidelines, and organizational structures.

Usability

A solution can succeed or fail based on how the end user interfaces with the application. The greater the transparency of the application into the user's daily tasks, the more likely it is that users will embrace it and the solution will succeed. Key elements of usability to consider for Stage 1 are:

- Can the solution be delivered through the user's standard desktop tools? This is important when the solution impacts intensively used tools, for example email mailbox archiving.

- If a new interface is needed because the solution introduces a new job function, can it be made simple and consistent? An example here might be a Discovery Search interface for email. The objective is to improve the legal department's ability to search, determine relevant responses, package them, and deliver them to counsel with the minimum intervention of IT. A simple but powerful search tool with the ability to select results and then perform actions such as holds or downloads should be provided.

Data Migration

A thorough analysis of the data that is to be managed within an ECM repository must be done to properly control, organize, access, and consume the information. Developing an appropriate data model from scratch is a considerable undertaking, and for most Stage 1 solutions, should not be necessary, especially if they are aimed at common business processes such as invoice management. The models can be significantly more complex and time consuming to develop for compliance solutions, especially if records management and retention strategies are needed. In such situations, even a Stage 1 departmental deployment may require an enterprise view, which can increase the cost and time to define the deployment strategy considerably.

Readiness

Readiness may be the most important and overlooked of the four aspects of deployment. It broadly covers the work streams that manage, control, organize, and sustain the ECM program. We assume that good project management methodologies will be used regardless of which ECM adoption stage you are in. In this section, only those aspects of readiness that are particularly relevant to Stage 1 applications will be discussed; other elements of readiness are covered in later chapters.

Figure 8.7: ECM Deployment Stage 1 – Readiness

The degree of effort that will be put into Readiness depends on the nature of the ECM Solution and whether it is expected to continue as a departmental solution or be the starting point for extended adoption throughout the enterprise. Adding ECM support to a departmental ERP application such as invoice processing is not much different from any other IT project and requires little special treatment beyond good project management and user training.

Organizational Readiness

All Stage 1 applications require, at minimum, the definition of roles and responsibilities necessary to manage and evolve the solution. Defining these will help set the standards as the application migrates from one department to multiple departments. This is especially important when deploying compliance-centric applications. Content and collaboration applications may also require models to be developed of the social networks that are operational in the organization. Figure 8.9, for example, shows email flows among a large project team (Valdis Krebs, 2003, http://www.orgnet.com/email.html).

> Transport Research Laboratory

Who: A globally recognized centre of excellence, TRL (Transport Research Laboratory) provides world-class research, advice, and solutions for all issues relating to land transport. The center employs 550 staff, including 400 scientists, and its work provides innovative solutions for a range of clients from the public and private sectors.

Business Objective: To implement and maintain an information strategy that would incorporate a long-term IT plan, and to employ an information architecture with tools and processes that would allow knowledge, information, and data to be managed efficiently and fully utilized.

Business Needs: Diminish heavy reliance on paper-based processes, reduce physical storage space required, retain capitalized knowledge, and enhance information access.

Solution Overview: Implementation of an electronic document management and retrieval system (EDRMS) enabled electronic document scanning, filing, and retrieval, and facilitated the conversion of paper-files to electronic format.

Benefits: Improved and more effective document access; improved cross-divisional co-operation, which produced better work results and increased productivity; greater consistency in customer-facing and corporate activities; increased accuracy in business decision making; and improved document and records tracking with full audit trails.

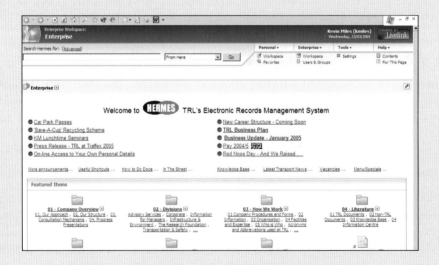

Figure 8.8: Welcome Page of the EDRMS at TRL

An office premises move required TRL to re-examine its document and information management practices. Insufficient physical space in the new building prevented the organization from continuing its paper-based business processes and localized document storage lacked structure.

The decision to implement an Electronic Document Records Management System (EDRMS) had created a daunting challenge. Paper records and artifacts were stored in just about any available space at TRL—offices, stairwells, corridors, laboratories. A survey revealed shelf space of 10 kilometers of physical records, but only four percent of them were managed in registered files. More than 90 percent of data, project files, and documents were locally stored and backed up by users individually. All this data had to be sorted before the move into the new building, ensuring that business-critical documents were retained while unwanted files were weeded out—all without interrupting normal business activities or the move schedule.

All staff participated in 'Records Management Weeks'. More than 125 tons of paper and 15 tons of confidential material were shredded and recycled. Over 500 filing cabinets were emptied and recycled, 109 garbage bins removed and 8,300 books donated out. The clean-up stage was followed by a phase of restructuring and scanning the remaining 300,000 documents into a file plan that was seamlessly migrated to ECM. The complete migration took place over three consecutive weekends, and throughout the migration, existing access permissions were fully maintained.

Prior to the move, TRL believed it possessed approximately 3,000 formal scientific reports and a similar number of confidential client reports, but most staff only had access to documents they had created themselves or to those written by immediate predecessors. However, the records clearance program identified more than 8,000 scientific and over 7,500 client reports. As part of the 'Moving Ahead Project' these reports have been scanned to PDF files, indexed, and made text-searchable within the ECM system, ensuring that researchers can find the most relevant information.

The growing use of structured procedures using templates and workflows is resulting in a more uniform approach to business management at TRL. Project decisions reflect greater and more effective access to supporting documentation, while decision record keeping is supported by full audit trails. Before the transformation, only four percent of documents were in registered files, as opposed to today, when all project documents are kept in their ECM project folders.

The 'Moving Ahead Project' fundamentally changed the information culture at TRL. Within just four months, TRL had transformed its information environment by converting paper records collected over 40 years to electronic files. The completed project told a story of information management in its most comprehensive form—from preparing the organization and documents for the EDRMS to managing the cultural transformation as staff moved to an open information environment.

Figure 8.9: Data Mining Email to Discover Social Networks and Emergent Communities

IT Readiness

It is important to set the precedent by codifying your guidelines and procedures from a technical perspective. Most IT organizations can leverage existing procedures like backup and maintenance, continuity planning, and disaster recovery. Establishing these procedures early in the ECM Adoption lifecycle will better prepare the organization for the growth of ECM program.

Testing / Validation

All applications must go through rigorous testing and validation protocols before they can go into production. While extensive testing of solution functionality and performance is essential, the nature of the test procedures will depend on the type of ECM Solution being deployed.

Enterprise Application Extension (EAE) – Enterprise Application Extension (EAE) solutions can be tested with simulated or real datasets derived from the core operational and transactional applications that the ECM Solution will support. These solutions generally involve standardized business processes and workflows, providing a convenient and appropriate framework for structuring the testing.

Records Management and Email (RME) – Records Management and Email (RME) solutions must be tested for compliance with regulatory mandates and industry standards. This provides an external objective basis from which to develop the test procedures and plan.

Collaboration and Content Management (CCM) – Collaboration and Content Management (CCM) solutions are, in general, the most difficult and complex in terms of developing validation tests. The adaptive content management approaches required to support flexible collaboration applications mean that each user's approach to the ECM solution may be very different. Test procedures and plans should be role based and cover the interaction effects of collaboration as well as the basic information addition and retrieval functionality.

Change Management

During Stage 1 adoption, most of the focus of change management is on Training and Communication Planning. A good choice for a Stage 1 application deployment is one for which the department and culture are generally homogeneous and no major paradigm shift in the organization is sought. This will decrease resistance to change and deployment risk significantly.

Training Plan – As a subset of Change Management, developing a good training plan will become essential for end-user adoption. The complexity of the application will determine the level of effort required in training your end users. In many instances, the new solution is replacing a process that was done manually or on old technology. It is often necessary to look at incentives and rewards program to encourage people to adopt the new system.

Communication Plan – Along with training, a good communication plan will go a long way in convincing the end users of why the new business solution is necessary. Their question is always, "What's in it for me?" The plan should leverage the strategy and visioning developed during the Imperatives phase in communicating the reasons why the department is implementing the new system.

Support

It is vitally important to have a support infrastructure in place to answer questions and investigate and resolve issues that arise during the use of the application. The type and depth of support, and how it is delivered, depends on the class of ECM solution being deployed. For EAE solutions, such as the Accounts Payable example, support should be delivered through the same channels used for the underlying operational application.

Similarly, first-line support for email solutions should come through the existing enter-prise support infrastructure, although specialized second-tier support must be readily available for records management and compliance issues.

ECM solutions will likely need new support services and approaches. Especially when the collaboration solution involves changing working patterns, it is essential that users do not feel that they are being left "out there" to figure it out for themselves. The most important attribute of support for a collaboration initiative is speed of response. It is essential to get the user back into the collaborative environment as quickly as possible so that the new working habit is reinforced. This approach is also one of the most effec-tive tools in word-of-mouth marketing of the new solution.

Infrastructure

All ECM Stages require a hardware and software platform that will support the ECM application. Developing an infrastructure plan is a standard function of IT capacity plan-ning units. However, ECM solutions can pose particular problems depending on the technology and application being deployed.

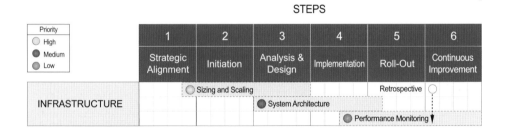

Figure 8.10: ECM Deployment Stage 1 – Infrastructure

Characteristics of ECM Solutions that affect the design of the IT infrastructure include the following:

Document Object Size

ECM, which focuses on words, pictures, and sound, inevitably deals with much larger document and file sizes than ERP applications. This impacts both storage and network bandwidth requirements. It is especially important to handle these loads efficiently in

ECM solutions that support existing ERP applications. Introducing delays or latency through the ECM solution can have unpredictable and often adverse effects on the performance of the established ERP application.

Indexing and Search

Introducing large-scale ECM Search into a working environment (especially for a solution such as email) may require careful planning of the index design to ensure efficient backup and recovery, and to minimize the impact of a rebuild should the index become corrupted. Modern search engines require specialized design and deployment to make the best use of the hardware and infrastructure investment.

Workload Patterns

Most collaborative and content management solutions show very wide variations in activity during the working day. Peak activity exceeding ten times the average is common in these environments and users are intolerant of response slowdowns.

ECM Vendors have developed considerable experience with these and other infrastructure issues and have extensive packages of monitoring, analysis, and modeling tools to support the design process.

Follow-On Steps

The main reason to monitor the solution after deployment is to confirm and demonstrate that the original business objectives of the project have been met. Examples of metrics for this measurement were identified earlier in the Imperatives work stream description. Once this is established, monitoring should focus on metrics that will help characterize the ECM Solution as one that is suited for further deployment and which can help build the business case to support the future stages of adoption. Solution performance, cost of operation, user satisfaction, and so on are all metrics that add value.

The solutions that are most likely to need fine tuning after deployment are those in the collaboration and content management group. This is partly because the initial success criteria for these classes of application tend to be softer and less well defined. Another reason is the adaptive nature of the applications—they often evolve in unexpected ways, and the stable use configuration and working patterns may be very different from those initially envisaged. Good tracking and documentation of this adaptive change process not only improves planning for Stage 2 adoption and beyond, but also supports the business case by showing how the ECM solution is impacting the organization.

> Unilever

Who: Unilever is one of the largest international manufacturers of leading brands in foods, home care and personal care—brands that are known and trusted by millions of consumers around the world. Best known for carrying brands such as Knorr, Becel, and Conimex, Unilever Bestfoods Netherlands (UBF NL) is organized into business units, sourcing units and a number of corporate departments.

Business Objective: To promote internal branding values and to align the daily business processes of Unilever's units and departments.

Business Needs: An unfriendly user interface of the corporate intranet needed to be redesigned in order to increase usage and expand communications methods.

Solution Overview: A single digital platform has been implemented across the enterprise for general document and knowledge management. Internal usage and system adoption have been facilitated though a custom-made look and feel for the corporate intranet including an improved user interface, news channels for individual departments and dynamic content publishing.

Solution Scope: Enterprise wide.

Benefits: Creation of a standard, consistent intranet look with improved functionality has increased usage and enhanced internal communication, while enabling successful internal branding values promotion and increased usage of standard ECM functionalities.

Figure 8.11: Recipe Management at Unilever

Unilever

In order to align the daily business processes of its units with IT, Unilever Bestfoods (UBF) NL decided to implement a single digital platform across the organization. The solution was supposed to enhance internal communications and promote branding values to all employees—but this could only be achieved if all employees actually adopted and used the system. As a result, once ECM was identified as the sole platform for all digital content, three parallel developments were required to address the following issues: simplification of the user interface specifics; an intranet-based display of new branding identities and their communication to all employees; and a variety of options for corporate communication, including both formal and informal messaging methods.

With the help of external consultants and the solution provider, Unilever Bestfoods developed a tailored user interface for the ECM system. By assigning specific request parameters, XML data is dynamically exported from within an ECM application and applied to a specified XSL style sheet to create an HTML page—the 'skin'. ECM modules were specifically developed to provide user-maintainable skin control and some extended XML export to support the custom XSL style sheets, software and documentation. This solution enables UBF to publish ECM content, including documents, news items and discussions, in a Web site-like interface that fully reflects the organization's internal branding efforts.

The developed UBF news pages were automatically launched by every employee's Web browser, bringing together the functionality of the ECM enterprise workspace and the power of the news channels. Every department in UBF NL maintains a unique news channel supported by a designated news channel manager. The news page displays all corporate news and select articles, improving the visibility of activities across the enterprise. An intranet home page serves as a template for all UBF departments—every business area can set up a localized information structure that completely addresses the distinctive needs of each department. Each home page displays hyperlinks to categorized content stored in the ECM.

UBF's tailored solution leverages the functionality and XML architecture features of ECM to apply a familiar and consistent user interface across the organization and support a standard corporate look and feel, which enables internal promotion of branding values across the enterprise. The ECM implementation includes key applications for brand/image management, recipe management, recipe marketing and a news-feed. These key applications are designed to generate user-awareness and draw increased traffic to the intranet—a 'pull' strategy that has been instrumental in encouraging users to utilize the ECM system for document and knowledge management.

Future maintenance of the site pages can be fully administered by UBF, eliminating costly and time-consuming necessity of further development. This level of internal control will enable UBF to continually update and tailor content based on current needs.

Stage 1 Summary

The essential step in ensuring a successful Stage 1 Adoption is to be clear about the type of ECM Solution that is being deployed, whether Enterprise Application Extension, Records Management and Email, or Collaboration and Content Management. Once this is determined, the design approach, success metrics, user support, and training strategy are easily defined.

• Stage 1 Adoption will quickly enter Stages 2 and 3 when the application is perceived as a tangible and measurable success by executive management, and when those in the department recognize its benefits and communicate the results to others within the organization.

Figure 8.12: ECM Solution Structures

As the future deployments from Stage 2 through Stage 7 occur, the initial ECM solutions, implemented for just one of the ECM Types we discussed, will develop into a more sophisticated architecture in which an Enterprise Content Management platform provides integrated content lifecycle management services to the collaborative content, and enterprise applications are used to manage the business. As this occurs, the ECM Solution Segmentation shown in Figure 8.2 at the beginning of this chapter matures into the ECM Solution Structure shown in Figure 8.12.

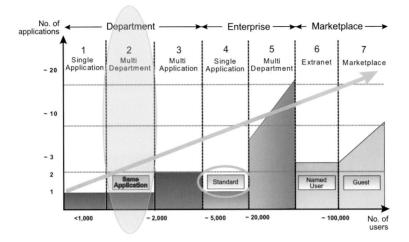

Figure 9.1: Stage 2 of ECM Adoption

Stage 2 is the adoption of the same ECM solution that was deployed to one group in Stage 1 to other departments. Normally, the IT department takes an existing and proven ECM solution to other departments that have similar problems. Typically, 2,000 or so users are involved.

CHAPTER 9

DEPARTMENT DEPLOYMENTS STAGE 2

This chapter explores the characteristics of deploying a solution during ECM Stage 2, Adoption. We'll use the Deployment Framework as our blueprint to highlight the steps of deployment you must consider to mitigate risk and increase success for each stage of adoption. Adoption and expansion of ECM within an organization occurs iteratively by building upon on a series of incremental successes. To proceed to the next stage of adoption, you must make sure you have achieved success in the previous stage.

The Deployment Framework provides a wide-angle view of the sequencing of tasks and resources involved in each work stream. Although each work stream identified in the Framework plays an important part in the success of the ECM program, certain work streams assume a higher priority depending on the stage of adoption you are in. As illustrated in Figure 9.2, each work stream in the Framework has been prioritized as either high (yellow), medium (blue), or low (green) based on Stage 1 adoption.

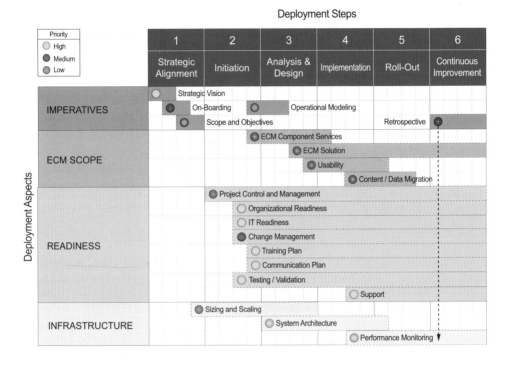

Figure 9.2: Deployment Framework for ECM Adoption Stage 2

Stage 2 Characteristics

The characteristics of a Stage 2 adoption are very similar to the Stage 1 characteristics discussed in Chapter 8. The common characteristics are:

• A single application that solves a specific departmental business problem has been successfully deployed.

• A second (or more) department is being considered for the same application.

• Fewer than 5,000 end users are involved.

• The change to the business is primarily operational and tactical, and does not represent a cultural change or major paradigm shift in the business.

At some point in Stage 2, several characteristics start to change as additional complexity is introduced through the extended rollout. For example, the project ownership moves to a steering committee, meaning that the initial department manager from Stage 1 must give up some control. The highly homogeneous culture and organizational structures that were good for Stage 1 deployments become less prevalent in Stage 2. Especially for collaborative solutions, these structures cannot be maintained as user numbers pass the 2,000 level.

Siemens Financial ShareNet—the intranet and project management network for the Siemens Global Financial Services community—was specifically designed to make available financial market information, customer data, risk management taxonomy, financial engineering methodology, industrial knowledge and guidelines in one place.

The decision made by one Siemens business unit to centralize its European back-office functions set the stage for the Financial Services ECM solution to be extended to the Siemens Global Tax Community. A business unit login located at the intranet homepage ensures secure access to the ECM solution which is also integrated with the financial services ERP system. As the solution was rolled out to the Global Tax Community, employees needed only one day of training to make effective use of its content.

Scoping

For Stage 2 deployments, scoping is straightforward; the solution has already been proven in a single department, so you should have clear expectations as to the impact of an extended rollout. Similarly, you will be able to reuse the Stage 1 scope analysis for any new departmental applications (Stage 3) that are from the same ECM solution class as the Stage 1 solutions.

This perspective on which aspects of the deployment are most strongly influenced by the earlier (or later) stages of adoption is shown for Stage 2 solutions in Figure 9.4.

> Federated Investors

Who: With over 135 different domestic and international equity, fixed-income, and money market mutual funds, as well as a variety of separate account options, Federated Investors is one the nation's largest investment management organizations with assets under management of approximately $184 billion.

Business Objective: To streamline a manually intensive and time consuming marketing and regulatory material production process.

Solution Overview: An expanded document management solution offers workflow functionality and a standard set of rules to govern content management and production within the marketing and regulatory departments. A central content repository includes approximately 55,000 documents, including marketing collateral, regulatory reports, and internal information.

Solution Scope: Intranet and extranet.

Benefits: Business processes have been automated and standardized and the process time required to publish content has decreased significantly. Automated and comprehensive audits can be created and kept for every workflow—there are up to 2,000 concurrent workflows at any time. Monetary savings and an improved work environment have created a good return on investment.

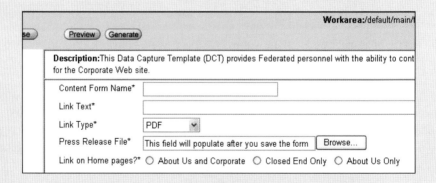

Figure 9.3: Dynamic Content Publication at Federated Investors

Early in its deployment, Federated Investors' ECM solution soon evolved from document management into a storage solution for marketing literature and similar documents. As the company grew, so did the number of content authors and business processes, resulting in a scattered and confusing content publishing process. In particular, Federated Investors was burdened with a manually intensive and time-consuming marketing and regulatory material production process.

A quick analysis showed that a solution was already close at hand. "We already had a product on site that could solve the publishing process. We had previously used the work-flow functionality offered by the [ECM system], but now we needed to extend it for more business-critical processes," explained the Business Analyst and Project Manager at Federated Investors.

With the help of the system provider, Federated Investors upgraded its existing solution to include an integration with a Web content management system and the implementation of new workflow functionality. The project team deployed the system on a departmental level in two stages; first in the marketing, then, eight months later, in the regulatory department.

"The biggest challenge to the development and implementation of [an ECM] workflow project is not the development of the workflow itself. Rather, it is the cultural change that is involved when an automation tool is implemented to handle everyday business processes." The regulatory department, being very deadline and compliance driven, adapted promptly to the change, while the marketing department required a longer adaptation period.

The new solution meant applying a standard set of business rules to govern business processes. To address adaptation challenges throughout the organization, Federated Investors applied a methodology whereby the existing business processes are analyzed and documented. Following that, a second analysis is conducted to determine and document a proposed improvement to the process. The proposed process is sent for appropriate approvals and then the workflow(s) is built, tested and implemented. This approach has resulted in a speedier and more satisfactory deployment for the organization.

Following a successful implementation, a new intranet, called Internal Federated, and an extranet, named External Federated, were created. Employees can easily move documents between the two Web instances. All content is stored in a central content repository that includes approximately 55,000 documents, including marketing collateral, regulatory reports, and internal information.

Federated Investors developed a number of steps to govern workflow management, which significantly and visibly changed employee work habits. The company has observed an increase in the volume of projects being worked on simultaneously, having transitioned from linear fashion work habits to as many as 2,000 workflows at a time. After the initial adaptation period, marketing has fully embraced the new solution. "Both regulatory and marketing departments are very satisfied."

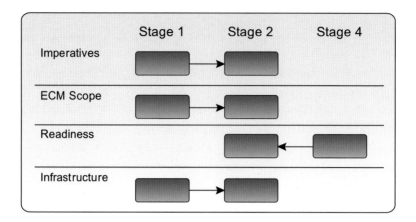

Figure 9.4: Stage 2 Perspective

ECM in Stage 2

Stage 2 of an ECM deployment involves expanding an ECM Solution from a single departmental solution into a common resource that delivers multiple solutions to multiple teams. If just getting a new solution deployed to one department is the most difficult part of the work, then this phase perhaps carries the most risk. Often, resources are limited in Stage 2, and the full range of the benefits of ECM is not yet apparent. At the same time, the complexity of deployment starts to rise rapidly compared to Stage 1, especially as more departments begin wanting to share in the success of the initial solution—particularly if this appears to be a "free ride."

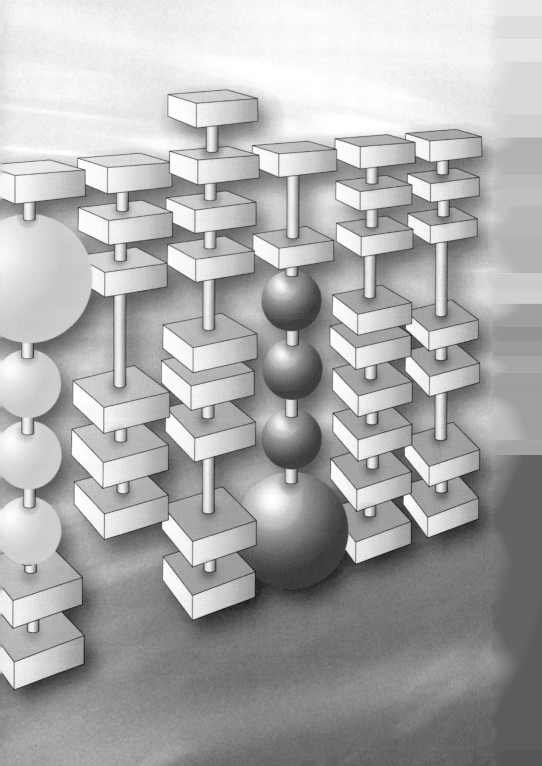

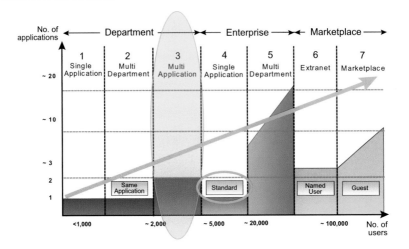

Figure 10.1: Stage 3 of ECM Adoption

Stage 3 is the adoption of multiple solutions within the same department, as shown in Figure 10.1. Here, the original ECM solution is extended by other ECM components within the same department, typically by the same business owner and possibly by IT.

CHAPTER 10

DEPARTMENT DEPLOYMENTS STAGE 3

This chapter explores the characteristics of deploying a solution during ECM Stage 3. Stage 3 involves deploying multiple ECM applications within a single department. This stage can be considerably more complex than Stage 2, depending on whether the applications you are deploying are from the same ECM solutions class as those you deployed in Stage 2. This chapter reviews the characteristics of a Stage 3 deployment, the Scoping and Readiness considerations of this stage, and the follow-on steps necessary to take you successfully to the next stages of deployment.

Stage 3 Characteristics

A Stage 3 deployment is based on the characteristics of Stages 1 and 2. In this stage, multiple ECM applications are deployed within the same department.

The critical factor that may change the deployment approach in this stage is the class of the ECM solution. If the second (or later) solution is of the same class type (Enterprise Application Extension, Records Management and Email, or Collaboration and Content Management) as for the Stage 2 deployment, then you can reuse the processes used in Stage 2. In a Stage 3 deployment, the IT infrastructure is already substantially in place and users are already familiar with the solution platform.

If the new Stage 3 solutions are of a different ECM class than in the Stage 2 deployment, then matters become more complex. A different solution strategy may be needed, and you may need to account for the risk of crossover effects between the two ECM Solutions. This occurs at the technical and the business user level. For example, users who have been trained for standardized processes (such as accounts payable) in Stages 1 and 2 may find adapting to a less structured collaborative working solution in Stage 3 more difficult.

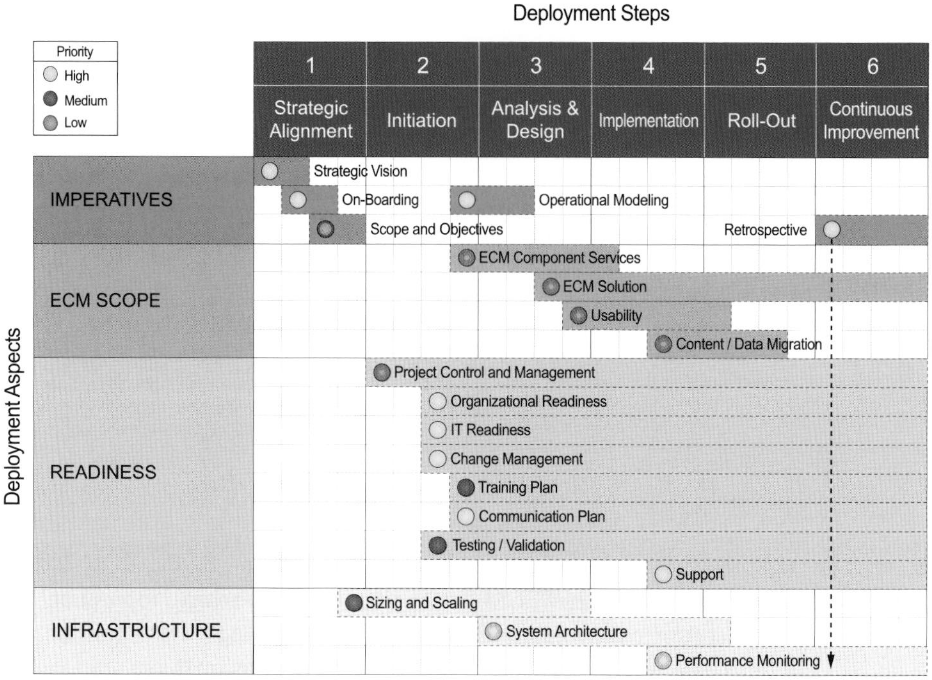

Deployment Steps

Figure 10.2: Deployment Framework for ECM Adoption Stage 3

Siemens I&S tenders more than 100K offers a year—each one requiring the coordination of 10 employee roles, a minimum of 18 signoff steps, approximately 40 templates and sets of instructions, and more. A customized ECM workflow automates the business process for review and approval. However, Siemens also conducted a careful analysis to determine user requirements and information taxonomies that would address the more collaborative components of the tendering process.

Their ECM solution was extended to address document management, quality management, auditing processes, and collaboration on projects. When users initiate a new offer tendering process, the ECM solution automatically creates a project and populates it with the framework for an offer, in the form of a compound document. The workflow uses process steps to send email notification to key people throughout the process—and a customized process step allows the email address to be dynamically assigned. The deployment provides relevant and up-to-date information to all users and it is anticipated that it will include customers and partners in the future.

Scoping

A Stage 3 solution that is from a different ECM class than in Stages 1 and 2 (for example, a collaboration solution following on from an Enterprise Application Extension, one such as invoice processing) will require a complete rework of the ECM scope.

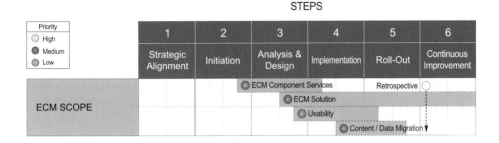

Figure 10.3: ECM Deployment Imperatives

Readiness

In Stage 3 of ECM deployment, two work streams assume greater importance—on-boarding and operational modeling.

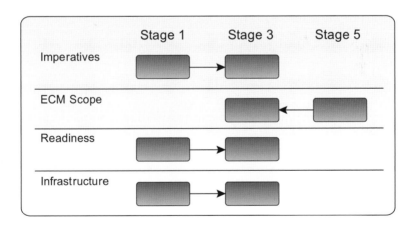

Figure 10.4: Stage 3 Perspective

> Giant Eagle

Who: A pioneer of the modern supermarket, Giant Eagle Inc. was originally founded in 1931 and has grown to operate 138 corporate and 81 independently owned and operated stores throughout the mid-west United States.

Business Objective: To develop a plan to expand the company's presence and its revenue base by doubling its top and bottom lines.

Business Needs: Tremendous growth brought about a need to disseminate a massive volume of information across an ever-expanding network of stores, while promoting knowledge sharing across the chain.

Solution Overview: Giant Eagle's Standard Operating Procedures (SOPs) are managed entirely online. Manuals, departmental procedures, product information, and best practices are accessible to employees right on the grocery store floor. Version control capabilities and auditing functionality enable Giant Eagle to monitor compliance processes and manage all compliance records online, ensuring quality processes and absolute compliance with FDA regulations and guidelines.

Solution Scope: Enterprise wide, covering 21 lines of business and 220 stores.

Benefits: Giant Eagle reached its five-year business objective in only one year. Best practices can now be shared across all stores and Giant Eagle has realized a return on investment and increased revenue generated as a result of improved operations and sales by all its stores.

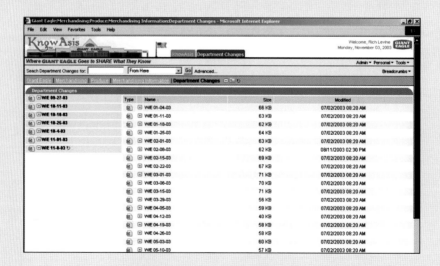

Figure 10.5: ECM at Giant Eagle

Conceptualized as a three-legged stool, Giant Eagle's ECM strategy consists of three key supporting structures: Collaboration, Content Management, and Culture. The organization's goal was to directly address the first and second legs of the stool (Collaboration and Content Management) through technology, while indirectly influencing the organization's internal knowledge sharing practices—the third leg of the stool (Culture). Although each leg operates independently and is equally important to the system's stability, the three legs combine to create an ECM strategy that encompasses both human and information management processes, as well as the interaction between the two types of processes.

Unlike the traditional office environment, content and knowledge management in a busy grocery store poses several unique challenges. The technology skill level of most employees is, on average, basic, even at many corporate locations. Turnover for sales floor staff is also quite high, requiring training to be as quick and easy as possible. Having established the need for a minimum technology learning curve, Giant Eagle determined that contribution of content to its solution should be technically easy to accomplish, but must follow corporate methodology regarding ease of use, as well as consistency of content and appearance.

Prototyped to two key lines of business—meat and produce—Giant Eagle developed a role-based gateway to add a level of simplicity to its content management solution. The gateway provides each employee with a tailored view of rich content, according to the business area that the employee deals with daily. The need for fast access to information among managers throughout Giant Eagle stores led to a solution that could provide a 'rifle shot' to explicit knowledge—the ability to point and click for answers to customer questions.

On the sales floor, grocers traditionally have a high employee turnover rate. To prevent inexperience from impacting customer service, Giant Eagle deployed ECM right to the sales floor. A computer placed strategically in every department provides sales associates with access to the company's ECM solution, arming them with the knowledge they need to answer customers' questions about every product the store carries.

As knowledge management, collaboration, and content management began to catch on at Giant Eagle, individual groups, such as meat and produce, found a home online. These communities regularly use discussion groups to share advice and best practices about things like the best ways to stock a shelf; special offers for drawing customers into the store; and how best to serve customers during peak times and long weekend holidays.

Giant Eagle manages all its compliance records and documents online to ensure absolute compliance with FDA regulations and guidelines, while ECM version control and auditing capabilities enable the company to monitor compliance processes and ensure the quality and consistency of content.

On-Boarding

Prioritizing and identifying the criteria for scheduling is important. Even if the Stage 2 ECM deployment was successful, you will still need to conduct prototyping and adaptation for Stage 3.

Operational Modeling

For Stage 3 deployments, operational modeling must account for the additional complexity caused by the rollout of multiple solutions. Good operational models are essential to minimize the impact the deployment will have on the existing ECM implementation and to ensure smooth adoption by the new users.

Follow-On Steps

Stage 3 is transitional to the full ECM solutions described in the next chapters. It should be regarded as a functional proving ground for the prospect of an enterprise-wide ECM deployment. Monitoring should focus on developing the materials needed to support the business case for an ECM deployment and a rapid transition to Stages 4 and 5.

Performance and user satisfaction metrics are important, but most important is validating the return on investment (ROI) for scaling the Stage 1 solution. It is essential that the benefits of Stages 2 and 3 are closely monitored and reported in order for you to proceed to the next stages of ECM deployment.

Summary

Successful ECM adoptions seek to transition from Stage 1 to Stages 2 and 3 from approximately 1,000 users to around 5,000 as quickly as possible. An organization should aim to do this within 12 to 18 months after the Stage 1 deployment.

The necessary steps in planning and managing Stage 3 of deployment are:

- Understand clearly the ECM applications that are being deployed.
- Make sure that the criteria of success for extending a Stage 3 solution to multiple departments are well understood.
- Identify where planning and execution can be based on the successful Stage 1 and 2 implementations.
- Choose carefully which work streams to upgrade to the enterprise level of Stages 4 and 5 in order to position the solution for the next phase of ECM growth.
- Apply the Operational Modeling and Scoping tools of Stage 5.

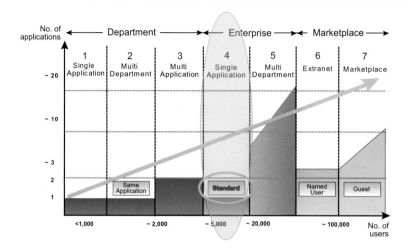

Figure 11.1: Stage 4 of ECM Adoption

The next and most critical stage in the adoption cycle is Stage 4, when the organization decides on an ECM solution as an enterprise standard. It involves not only the IT Department but also the senior management team, since the deployment will occur across all departments, be highly visible, and have a direct impact on operations. Stage 4 typically, but not necessarily, involves 10,000 or more people in a large organization, as shown in Figure 11.1.

It is possible to evolve to Stage 4 quickly, establishing a standard for the organization. However, the jump must be accomplished by going through Stages 1 and 2 at an accelerated rate. In other words, even in attempting to go straight to Stage 4, the organization must pilot a Stage 1 adoption if only for a short period of time. However, some key thinking about enterprise information (not IT) infrastructure and system use policies can begin to take shape in parallel with small-scale beginnings.

CHAPTER 11

ENTERPRISE DEPLOYMENTS STAGE 4

The inspiration for enterprise ECM deployment can come from a variety of sources, such as a CEO's frustration with limited information sharing across the organization or with pushback from operational managers confronted with the workloads of compliance in a "non-ECM" organization. A CIO might be aware of ECM technologies and be able to communicate their benefit to the board, or recognize individual operational requests as susceptible to an enterprise platform approach, or see success in an individual ECM application as replicable enterprise wide.

The defining decision is "We want our whole organization to benefit from ECM." It's vital the reason for this is clear, because it makes a fundamental difference to the deployment program. If there is a desire for genuine, enterprise-wide information sharing and collaboration crossing organizational boundaries, an information infrastructure in a common "language of the business" is likely needed. If the desire is rather for a common platform that individual departments or divisions can use, such an infrastructure is less likely to be needed.

Whatever the origins of the decision, a clear deployment vision is vital—what imperatives will ECM address? The more quantified the benefits—cost savings, process acceleration, demonstrable time-to-market benefits—the more powerful the case for deployment.

On-boarding - "It's enterprise first, deployment second"

Enterprise ECM deployment is first of all a business change program and secondly an IT project. Therefore, an organization must do its thinking and planning in that order.

ECM is not inherently complex nor is deployment inherently difficult, but large organizations are complex, so truly effective collaboration and information leverage across and within them has the potential to be equally complex.

The challenge is clear and addressable: boil down the complexity of the organization and the information needs of its people into simple user experiences that match what users see today.

Making a start and seeing how things develop is rarely the best option. The more painstaking the deployment, the less painful the user experience.

The foundation for successful enterprise deployment of ECM is "on-boarding," visibly aligning organizational and program priorities to secure operational sponsorship and involvement. It involves networking into the organization and ensuring ongoing communication:

Engage the enterprise – the worst thing an ECM sponsor can do is assume they know what the true needs of the enterprise are. Key managers must be engaged.

Create the right engagement model – The needs of the organization as expressed by senior managers (the imperatives) must drive the deployment, but be funneled into viable methodologies for ECM deployment. This requires a model for engagement that captures vital business needs input and secures committed sponsorship.

Operational Modeling

Operational modeling explores the business assets, processes, operational events, collaboration points, and operational reviews of a business and maps them into the ECM platform so that it is a reflection of and enabler for the business.

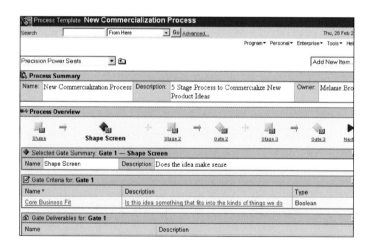

Figure 11.2: Modeling a New Product Development Process

Turning Information into Assets

A key to turning content into electronic formats (assets) is to catalog and file such content. In ECM, we must create information infrastructures that allow us to answer the sorts of questions that an asset manager would need to know, such as, what kind of assets do we have? How many of them do we have? How old are they? Of what quality are they? (In the case of information, this refers to source, accuracy, and authority.) Where are they, and how can we find them? Can we attach a value to them?

To create such an information infrastructure, we need meta-data structures to describe content and a filing structure to place it in.

The filing structure is reflected in an ECM folder, or workspace, hierarchy. This structure must be a durable reflection of the business, to avoid changing the organization and location of workspaces and content later. It must be modeled on the processes in which the business engages. Organizational structures and titles tend not to be durable, and so are rarely the best basis for creating a file structure.

Meta-data is frequently associated with search ability, so its asset management potential can be overlooked. Here is an example of how meta-data assumes asset management capability. Consider these meta-data tags: Document type, Expiry date, Value, Product type, Region, Third-Party (supplier, customer, partner), and Document number.

Given these meta-data tags, we can answer the following questions:

• How many Sales contracts with Customer A do we have, and with what total value?

• How many come up for renewal this year and during the next quarter?

• How many at what value relate to product Y?

• How many contain clause (K), which, due to upcoming supply problems, we must renegotiate?

• When should we dispose of contract No. 327?

> Barnardo's

Who: Barnardo's is the UK's largest children's charity, supporting 100,000 children and their families through more than 300 projects in England, Northern Ireland, Scotland, and Wales. The organization employs around 5,000 staff, 3,500 of whom work directly with young people in 300 locations across the UK. Barnardo's runs more than 357 services, and its projects focus on a range of issues, including Homelessness, Young Offenders, Fostering, and Adoption.

Business Objective: To improve the lives of children and young people through enhanced document and collaboration management.

Business Needs: Replacement of a data-centric CRMS with a solution tailored to the specific needs of the organization with a focus on recording all ongoing interactions.

Solution Overview: An ECM-based collaboration tool that enables electronic recording of ongoing interactions with children, young people, and their families, as well as intra-organizational communication to facilitate enhanced knowledge-sharing. The solution also serves as a general document management tool and is flexible enough to be used by all of the over 300 unique services that Barnardo's runs across the UK.

Benefits: Employees can share case knowledge across the organization and get expert knowledge from all sources, while the recorded information is reusable and always up to date. The improved collaboration, flexibility, and ease of use of the ECM system provide support for the general objectives of the organization, enabling Barnardo's to work with an increased number of children, young people, and their families.

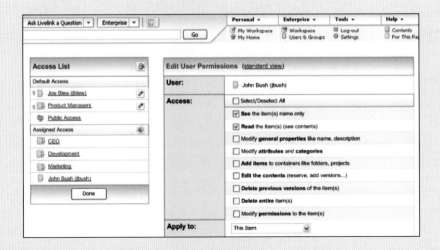

Figure 11.3: An Example of Access Permissions Setting in ECM

Barnardo's deals with human lives—and human lives can be very complicated! The challenge for an information system is to understand these complexities and offer solutions that support the organization's services without taking away from the work that is done directly with children, young people, and their families.

More than a decade ago, Barnardo's deployed an electronic customer relationship management system (CRMS) to record all ongoing interactions. The system implementation was driven by a need to collate management statistics and improve recording practices. The system was data-centric and inflexible, creating mounting difficulties from a practical and recording point of view. Very few employees found the system compatible with their service processes.

The organization decided to replace the system with a customized ECM solution for general document management. Throughout the decision making and system selection processes, Barnardo's involved the stakeholders—ranging from administrators to senior managers. Development of the customized system was closely monitored by a reference group—a small membership from various regions and roles—and overseen by system coaches who had previously trained users on the old system and were aware of the problem areas. When the time came to pilot the customized solution, a wide variety of business areas and services was chosen to ensure immediate engagement with the new processes across the organization. Regional implementation teams were created and given three days training in business analysis processes and in developing filing forms and structures. The first pilot was led by the ECM system provider with a few members of the next pilot's implementation team observing as a further training opportunity. This cascade type of training was used so that all implementation teams were monitored by someone who had previously undergone an implementation process.

Three months after the initial pilot, Barnardo's conducted a formal review of the pilot services. Following this review, various changes were agreed on and the implementation date changed. Although this was an unpopular decision, it ensured a successful rollout. The implementation process consisted of an initial familiarization day when several service managers were given a demonstration of what the new system could achieve. During the implementation week, data from the previous system were converted to text documents. Eventually, data from the old CRMS had been converted to the ECM solution for 259 open services and 38 closed services, along with several new services and planned separations of services.

Change management was successful because Barnardo's involved the end users from the beginning, listened to their requirements, and referred back to them throughout the process. The managers were also involved; they ensured that people used the system during and after the development stage, and monitored the quality of recording for each unique service.

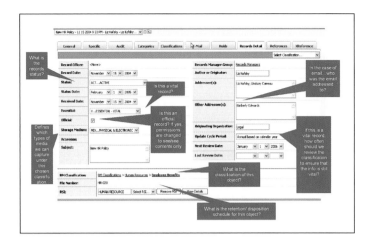

Figure 11.4: Behind the Scenes of Records Management – How Rules are Adhered to and Classifications are Inherited

This sounds good, but people don't like entering meta-data, and they can get it wrong or simply fail to do it. Therefore, we must deploy and configure intelligently so that the system takes care of the drudgery of information management. We need a system that enters the meta-data for you, puts it in the right place, prompts the right user to do the right thing with the content at the right time, manages the retention cycle, and generates the reporting you need for your information assets.

A good ECM platform will let you do this if you deploy intelligently and interpretively.

Process Enablement – Driving Operational Events

How many "process failure problems" in major organizations happen because there is no process? How many are because the process is not followed properly or in a timely fashion? Do process failures primarily relate to machines or systems failing? How many relate to people passing on information and acting on it? To companies whose filing cabinets bulge with process documents, these questions are painfully rhetorical. ECM is great at facilitating information-based process in workflows and has the reporting capabilities to track, audit, and report failings and successes. ECM does not just enable, but it drives and accelerates key information processes and the resulting operational events that represent vast numbers of process instances. Furthermore, when the people stop actively managing information, ECM doesn't. So large organizations with thousands of people who move from job to job can still successfully manage the content lifecycle, including creation, search, archive, and disposal of content whose life may be a few months or decades or even infinite.

Capitalizing on ECM workflow technology, Siemens' Nexus project gained a rapid return on investment by speeding processes and stripping costs. The first application was a means of automating the travel management process and the second required the streamlining and automation of authorization processes. Both of these applications needed to be paperless processes to eliminate non-value added activities and their costs (i.e. printing and photocopying). The processes also needed to be made electronic so as to provide a complete electronic record of all approvals to help ensure accountability. The Nexus project paid for itself in six months.

Initially, Siemens was using Nexus only in Singapore. However, following a series of tests as part of the pilot stage, Siemens' corporate operational procedures called for the rollout to be extended to its global development team at headquarters in Munich. From there, the global development team encouraged the rollout in other regions to facilitate the deployment of Nexus and the standardization of the ECM platform.

Collaboration Points

A group of people—and a "space" for them to work together—is a collaboration point. ECM takes this concept and enhances it with remote collaboration and a mobile library to manage content, discussion groups, task allocation, information distribution, and more. The right thought processes in deployment don't just enable this, they turbo-charge the whole process and can fulfill management intent across a large workforce, answering the following questions:

- How can I give teams of people a well-designed new workspace in less time than it takes them to book an office?

- How can I get 100 functionally identical teams to comply to standard best practices and processes?

- How can I roll out to large numbers of people with minimal training overhead?

- How can I minimize cases of inappropriate permissions?

Solution Design for the Enterprise Deployment

In the Enterprise deployment, "solution design" refers to the business model that is enabled. It is likely a roadmap, rather than a snapshot. This is because users must be recruited, processes and workflows enabled, and collaboration areas established—it will be a progressive, prioritized plan.

Also, if the intention is for genuine, organization-wide information sharing, searching and collaboration, the information infrastructure (folder or workspace hierarchy, meta-data structure) will also need to be designed from the start and implemented progressively. While it's vital to establish a high-level model for the enterprise as the basis of a workspace hierarchy, the detail will inevitably be completed by subject-matter experts.

The same principle applies to a meta-data structure. Two key conditions must be satisfied by this structure. First, it must be logically consistent—a subset of a meta-data field, such as "Document type" really must be a type of document. Second, it must use the language of the business. If employees don't understand the terminology used at the high level of the structures, something is wrong. To design the structures, you need either a librarian (taxonomy) or data modeler—don't take the risk of using a non-expert as a design authority.

The combination of information structures, workspace design, permissions design, and process enablement make up the solution design that must be translated into ECM functionality and its configuration, and sometimes its integration with other systems.

Retrospect – Constant Learning in the Deployment Cycle

As we've noted, successful enterprise deployment—getting registered and active users —is rarely about a "Big Bang." Rather it's about progressively achieving deployment, or more people using—and employment, or people using more functions. These let you use early rollout learning to improve later rollout practice.

Retrospect is a continuing perspective for enterprise deployment. It asks the questions, did we meet our objectives? Did our operational modeling prove right first time? Are our people using the deployment more or less than we thought? Are they using the functionality as we thought they would? Does the interface have good acceptance? Can they search or navigate as expected to find information easily? Knowing what we know now, what additional processes might be enhanced with ECM?

Program Management Office Now Crucial

Enterprise deployment and rollout involves different user groups, perhaps different functions, different information roles (information controllers, contributors, consumers) and perhaps a blend of straightforward system configurations, major information migrations, and process integrations. All of these may converge onto a single platform. Without an effective program office, the multiplicity of project work streams and occasional amendments to priorities is likely to unravel. The program management office must blend skill sets as diverse as business analysts, IT architects and employee communications experts into a single, efficient program.

Ask yourself one simple question: if a program office isn't coordinating the deployment, who is?

Ensuring the Receptive Enterprise – Organizational Readiness

Having done the groundwork—establishing the business case, defining the need, information structures and program management—another aspect of deployment is organizational readiness. It involves ensuring that, as we roll out to a broader audience, we've carried out the business and system management homework to ensure the organization is receptive to the new ECM capability.

Governance and People Structures

We must ensure we have the governance, management structures, teams, policies and sponsorship continuity needed for a successful business program. In ensuring this, we ask who sets direction and priorities for the program? Is the enterprise user base adequately represented? Who has overall program delivery responsibility? Many organizations create a Steering Group made up of authoritative stakeholders from both business clients and IT functions to help answer these questions.

Formulating policy guidelines and principles is another key aspect of organizational readiness. Examples of policy guidelines and principles are:

- How does ECM fit with legacy information provision (e.g., "the intranet")?

- What information do we use it for and not use it for?

- What's our corporate philosophy and policy on permissions and enterprise searching?

- How much admin can users do for themselves and how much should be done for them?

- How much do we let users develop for themselves (e.g., with workflows) and how much do we do for them at the System Administrator level?

- Have our sponsoring service consumers made their people's time available for training, admin, and so on?

- How will users be registered and how will workspaces or communities be formed?

- Have we lined up internal employee communications people to explain and support our program?

- Do we have the right user training in place, what is its scope, and how will it be delivered?

Continued Visible Sponsorship

As ECM is rolled out to the organization, users need positive messages from their senior managers concerning the rationale for deployment, the anticipated business benefits, and the desire of senior management to see it adopted. This, combined with messages from the Program team that give guidance and a clear message of personal benefit, will remind employees at all levels of the strategic relevance of the program.

Who: Northrop Grumman Corporation is a global defense company headquartered in Los Angeles, California. The company provides technologically advanced, innovative products, services, and solutions in systems integration, defense electronics, information technology, advanced aircraft, shipbuilding, and space technology. With 125,000 employees and operations in 50 U.S. states and 25 countries, Northrop Grumman serves national and international military, government, and commercial customers.

Business Objective: To develop a comprehensive solution for managing critical intellectual capital and sharing that information electronically.

Solution Overview: A shared information platform that includes an intranet and an extranet for electronic information sharing among employees, customers, partners, and suppliers, and that provides support for knowledge and business process management.

Solution Scope: Enterprise wide.

Benefits: Knowledge can be identified, captured, and shared across geographical and organizational boundaries. The company realized improved collaboration across the extended enterprise and with customers, suppliers, and remote teams.

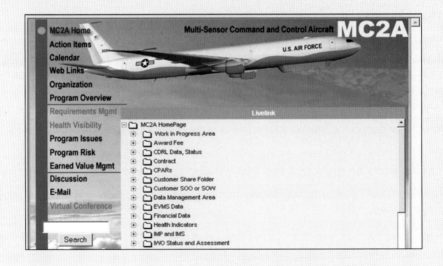

Figure 11.5: Knowledge Management at Northrop Grumman

Through ECM's shared technological infrastructure, Northrop Grumman is creating networks that build trust among its employees. Advancing collaboration as the Web-based medium for transforming business areas into product teams and communities of practice across geographical and cultural boundaries provides a documented process for innovation that is transferable and can be repurposed for future initiatives to reduce reinvention and rework.

Having deployed a successful enterprise-wide ECM solution, Northrop Grumman has learned first-hand various implementation processes to determine the rollout approach that worked best for its implementation team. Team members learned to set realistic goals and remain team-driven by communicating all project aspects. Having implemented the system in phases, the team learned to keep the tasks simple and plan for and document every step. An implementation structure and checklist, as well as a technical blueprint based on gathered requirements, were of utmost importance. The team encouraged users, managers, and technical staff to frequent the pilot and project site, communicating their efforts at every level and welcoming feedback. Thanks to end-user involvement at every project stage, and to training that began during the pilot phase, the implementation team managed to create familiarity with the system even before it was fully deployed.

Best practice usage at Northrop Grumman is considered a shared responsibility that ranges from senior to lower management and involves specially selected teams and technical staff. An ECM steering committee—a chartered committee with management representation—was established to oversee ECM coordinators and the technical team responsible for training. A multi-disciplined project team at Northrop Grumman establishes project requirements, expectations, and schedules; senior management directs usage policy and guidelines; the technical team recommends and implements solutions along with providing system administration; functional coordinators assist in day-to-day system usage; and functional management enforces system usage according to guidelines. In addition, the user training team is responsible for preparing in-house training material and conducting user classes.

Because the ECM system at Northrop Grumman involves both an intranet and an extranet, different content and permissions structures must be continuously set. By applying permissions to groups rather than individuals, decentralizing the permission control groups and centralizing control of group permissions, the organization has been able to streamline the process, save time, reduce mistakes, and increase stability.

"The knowledge management techniques we developed enable Northrop Grumman to identify, capture, and share knowledge across many geographical and organizational boundaries. Furthermore, our solution provides new and secure ways to collaborate across the extended enterprise, reaching customers, suppliers, and remote teams," concludes the Knowledge Management Program Manager, Integrated Systems Sector at Northrop Grumman.

IT Readiness – Ensuring a Successful Roll-out

IT Readiness connotes the readiness of all that IT provides—hardware, software, network and support in its various forms. Service providers, service consumers, and vendors work together to define and create an IT Deployment Roadmap to support the overall deployment.

Service Level Agreements (SLA) – Foundation of Satisfaction

The number-one task in IT readiness is to ensure there is an agreed-upon standard, or Service Level Agreement (SLA) for the user. A system that fails to perform at acceptable speed, a breakdown in the support chain, or a critical loss of availability can all deal major blows to the rollout of any system.

However, the highest possible standards do not come easily, so we must find the right balance between effectiveness and cost effectiveness in the SLA. Key variables of the SLA often include the following:

- Speed in performing transactions, taking account of hardware, software, networks, connectivity, and outside dependencies such as integration with another system. A key to acceptance is meeting existing standards. For example, one large organization had a "speed of access" criterion that said, "We'll match the existing intranet in performance terms."

- Business assurance and continuity – availability, resilience (redundancy), failover, and recovery of system functionality and content.

- Service and support – availability (from 24/365 down), response times, level of service (basic system, specific functionality, specialist applications), languages, support request process (e.g., Web-based issue registration and queuing) and fault categorization (from critical downwards).

- Systems administration and the delegation of functional deployment responsibility, e.g., do we allow users or their nominees to design and implement workflows or should that service be provided to them by IT?

- User registration and enablement.

- Security throughout the ECM service technology delivery chain—hardware, software, networks, and so on.

Skills

The skills required for deployment are comparable to those required for any major IT deployment. These include the skills of architects, data modelers, business analysts, business process engineering experts, database administrators, developers, and support providers. You must ensure that enough of their time is built into the deployment process, and that they have received adequate training on the ECM functions they'll be deploying. Typical training topics include ECM Administration, ECM Architecture, Security, Performance, and ECM End-User Support.

Getting the Infrastructure Right – Ongoing Partnership with Vendors and Users

The needs of our users will evolve over time. The infrastructure must also evolve to meet these needs, but it's not acceptable to overbuild just in case. Rather, we must form close partnerships with the internal IT organization, vendor solution architects, and representatives of end users. Some of the questions that must be answered regarding usership are, how many users will we have and when? What will they be using the system for, and how many transactions of what types are they likely to perform? At what times of day? How critical are the different applications?

Don't assume that history of usage is a good indicator of future usage. In one classic example, a major telecommunications company had a new application that involved thousands of engineers accessing documents around 1Mb in size, all perhaps within a 15-30 minute time span. Only close teamwork in such cases prevents a system impact that may be unexpected and unacceptable.

Interface is a key aspect of infrastructure. System "champions" or "super users" can act as an interface between users and service providers to develop an interface that increases acceptance and decreases the pain of the new user's learning curve. A number of ECM users set a tough standard in this regard. For example, some want the benefits of ECM without ever being aware that they are in an ECM environment.

Systems Administration and Usage

System administration and usage provides a clear link to organizational readiness. Your plans for systems administration should harmonize with your corporate policies for system usage. As well, you should receive appropriate input when formulating such policies.

In one organization, the corporate purpose of ECM as a knowledge sharing medium was always clear, but the capacity of users to see other applications was not always foreseeable. Only the appearance of some very large files alerted the IT team to request a policy that sizeable operational database owners not use the document management system as a backup medium!

Change Management

Making IT systems do things is not simple or easy, but it has one endearing characteristic—IT systems do as they're told (occasionally with distressing precision, if the instructions are wrong!), whereas people may or may not.

In some ECM instances, users may have no choice—the system they use to carry out a process changes, their instructions change, and the old system is no longer available. In other cases, participation is voluntary. In all cases, it pays to bring the people on side using communication and training.

Does this work? In a recent example, a major company ran a series of awareness sessions in which potential ECM champions were invited to understand why ECM was being deployed, see it demonstrated, and understand the challenge of becoming ECM community coaches. Ninety-three percent of attendees volunteered to do so.

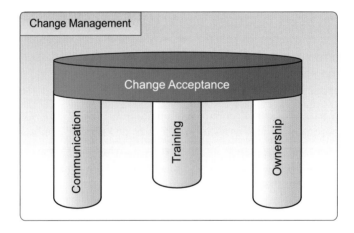

Figure 11.6: The Three Pillars of Change Management

Communication

"Not just what, but why"

Employees respond more positively when they understand management thought process. If they know why the ECM solution helps the organization that provides their livelihood, they are more likely to support it and involve themselves. Visible sponsorship from top management also encourages their involvement.

"What's in it for me?"

Generally, a well-designed ECM deployment makes people's working lives more productive, more fulfilling, and less stressful—make sure they know that it does and how it does it.

Training

The best ECM vendors offer a full range of training materials and services, however, some organizations choose to deliver all of the training in house. For a large rollout, mass customization of the training program is required. In developing a training program, the following questions should be asked:

- Who will use the system?
- What are the user roles that relate to the system and its content? For example,
    - information consumers are read-only users without autonomous access to content
    - information contributors may originate, modify, and distribute content
    - information controllers have total decision-making capability—they can create, change, distribute, make official, retain, archive, delete, and destroy
- What transactions must users perform to fulfill their roles?
- What training do users need to carry out these transactions?
- What is the most appropriate training medium?

In determining the best training medium, consider that a blended learning approach is often optimal, for example, classroom learning with Web-based refreshers on key transactions.

Change Management a Pre-requisite

The most common cause of failure of most IT deployments is a lack of clarity and agreement about expectations. In ECM, lack of a change management plan for the deployment is in the top-five cause of failure. If your major ECM deployment lacks a change management plan, put one in place without delay.

Sizing and Scaling your ECM System

By understanding and predicting the sum of system impacts resulting from the evolution of user's numbers, transaction types and volumes, time-of-day distribution, and SLAs, we can provide the raw materials required for sizing and scaling the ECM system.

As well as hardware performance, software licensing is important—plan ahead to optimize your purchases. Promising high deployment (number of users) and deployment (range of functions) can decrease unitary license costs.

Who: A subsidiary of the Jenoptik Group, M+W Zander is one of the world's leading companies in the fields of facility engineering, technical facility systems, and facility management. Based in Stuttgart, Germany, the organization has a workforce of nearly 8,000 at more than 40 sites worldwide.

Business Objective: To implement one collaborative platform for all needs—for internal end users as well as customers, subcontractors, and suppliers.

Solution Overview: A collaboration platform is the ECM foundation for a virtual work environment that facilitates effective project, document, knowledge and business process management, as well as online conferencing. Integrated with ERP technology, ECM-based Web content management provides support for news channels, a location finder, and a jobs portal.

Solution Scope: Enterprise wide, and an extranet for suppliers, contractors and customers.

Benefits: A single information platform for all needs has enabled information consistency across all business areas along with improved collaboration and knowledge sharing any-time, anywhere, and in any environment. M+W Zander has realized significant time and cost savings from reduced search/logistics time and decreased document controlling efforts, as well as reduced travel and relocation costs.

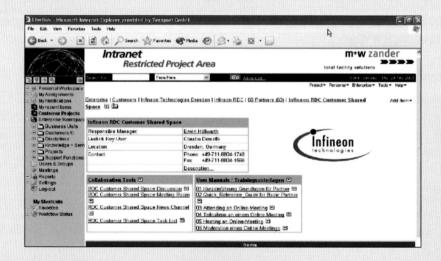

Figure 11.7: A Project Workspace at M+W Zander

m+w zander
▶▶▶▶
total facility solutions

A collaboration platform for all needs—at M+W Zander, a vision has become reality after the implementation of a Web-based, enterprise-wide, virtual work environment that supports internal employee collaboration as well as information sharing with partners, suppliers, contractors, and customers.

The realization of the dream began with a pilot implementation of an ECM-based knowledge management system. Although the rollout of the solution was initially attempted to be deployed on a wide scale, M+W Zander soon changed its strategy to focus on selected customer projects. Each project team was assigned a system expert whose job was to train other team members in how they could use the solution to save time and be more efficient in their project work.

Tangible benefits resulting from the implementation of any enterprise-wide information management system are oftentimes difficult to assess prior to the rollout. M+W Zander not only needed to overcome this particular management hindrance, but also had to convince future end users across the enterprise of the benefits of the solution.

At any time at M+W Zander, there could be several hundred globally dispersed engineers working on the same project that could last a year or longer. Because such projects require close team member collaboration, the support for online meetings was quickly adopted as employees realized that the collaborative tools enabled them to share knowledge and expertise across the enterprise. Once employees began using the collaborative platform, it soon became apparent that significant savings could be realized—team members could be brought together online instead of physically gathering at different locations. The same savings applied to meetings with customers and partners.

Having observed the benefits of the initial pilot, M+W Zander proceeded with a step-by-step rollout of the ECM system, deploying it to users based on project priority and then to all business areas. A user hotline was set up during the implementation where users could turn for help on any system-related matters. The hotline was supported by key users who had had more experience with the solution and, in case of unresolved problems, could turn to the key user support team for advice. On top of the support ladder was the ECM implementation team.

Following the successful enterprise-wide implementation, the deployed information platform had become the virtual work environment for effective project, document, knowledge, and business process management for all areas at M+W Zander—one platform for all needs. A vision was realized, but with the realization came the notion that reality could be taken even further than the idea. As a result, the company proceeded to implement an enterprise-wide Web content management system integrated with ERP technology. In the future, M+W Zander will continue to focus on expanding and improving their user-centric architecture.

Overall, sizing and scaling is as hard to get right first time as is usage forecasting, so the less predictable the latter, the more you need to regularly revisit the former. Examining the outputs of performance monitoring and building and re-running predictive system impact modeling are good tools for forecasting usage.

Your vendor's System Architects may be your best source of external advice here—their knowledge of their product architectures and their empirical experience add up to a knowledge base that's hard for their customers to match.

Systems Architecture – Partnership Not Optional

Systems Architecture is driven by a range of variables, some of which were discussed earlier in this chapter. They include user-base knowledge—who are your users, how many are there, where are they located, what mix of transactions do they perform and at what level, how are their transactions distributed, and so on. SLA(s) are also a factor in designing systems architecture. The legacy environment, including the existing software, hardware, other enterprise systems, networks, and user connectivity is a critical factor in systems architecture design. Finally, existing IT resources play a significant role in determining systems architecture, in terms of how many there are, where they are based, and so on.

A great deal of material could be written on this topic, and in each deployment, it usually is. Also, there is rarely only one approach that works for a given organization. However, we will amplify one key point; it's essential to combine client knowledge—of the current environment, of customer strategic systems, of networks, policies, internal standards for performance, and security—with the vendor's specialized knowledge of their products, architectures, software processes, and transaction demands on hardware and networks. Although every case is different, all organizations can benefit from the vendor's experience with other deployments.

Performance Monitoring – Vigilance Pays Dividends

The best ECM products provide comprehensive performance monitoring capabilities—use them. As a baseline, make sure your performance monitoring reports let you determine—and prove—that the terms of any SLAs are being met. The reports should also help you understand usage patterns and predict future usage levels.

Understanding usage patterns and levels can enable your ECM sponsors and system administrators to correct inappropriate usage or identify low usage levels and investigate them. It can also help them prevent performance bottlenecks and predict future usage levels, system capacity, the impact of new users, and the timing of upgrades.

Summary

The fundamental disciplines for ECM deployment will serve all levels of scale and complexity. ECM is about business—people and processes, creating, learning, sharing, and lifecycle management of information; IT implementation is just one part of the process. Finally, ECM deployment is about a partnership between IT and the business.

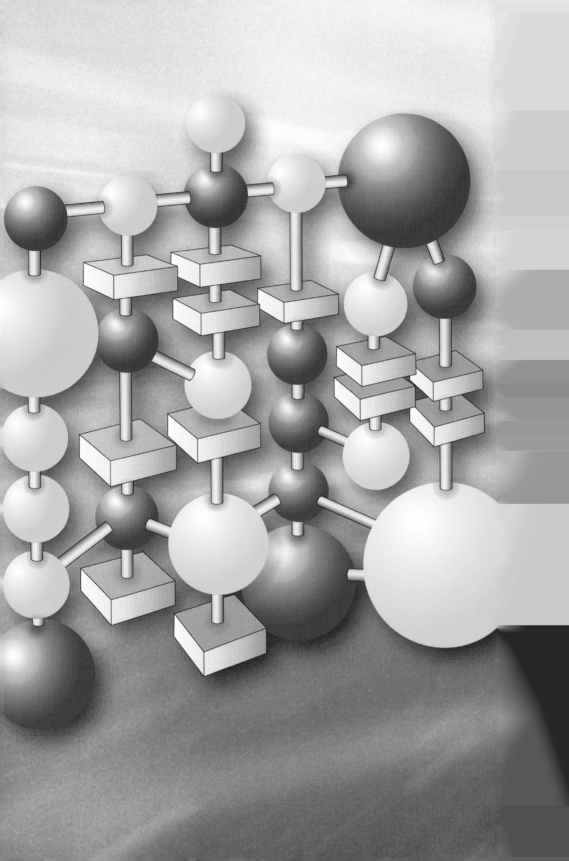

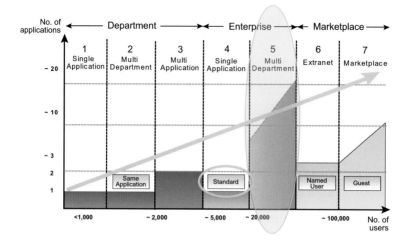

Figure 12.1: Stage 5 of ECM Adoption

Stage 5 represents the proliferation of the standard into multiple different applications throughout the enterprise. This stage is perhaps the most exciting and productive one for an organization since many benefits are achieved with very little incremental cost and at a rapid rate compared to the earlier deployments.

CHAPTER 12

ENTERPRISE DEPLOYMENTS STAGE 5

This chapter explores the characteristics of deploying a solution during ECM Stage 5 of ECM adoption. A fully developed version of Stage 5 is shown in Figure 12.2 below. At this point, there are multiple applications interacting across multiple departments.

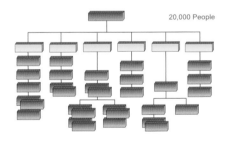
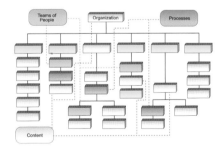

Figure 12.2: A Fully Developed Stage 5

As discussed previously, expanding ECM within an organization occurs iteratively by building upon on a series of incremental successes. To proceed to the next stage of adoption, you must make sure you have achieved success in the previous stage.

Based on our Deployment Framework, we will examine the necessary tasks and resources involved in the work streams of this stage.

First let's review the characteristics of Stage 5 adoption:

• An ECM standard is already set

• The ECM standard is rolled out into multiple different applications throughout the enterprise

• The number of users after the rollout is usually more than 20,000

• The rollout faces heterogeneous culture and organizational structures

• It's very likely that different countries and time zones are involved

Especially with a multi-departmental rollout, a clear understanding of the business drivers that justify the ECM solution being deployed is needed. ECM must be very closely aligned or be part of the corporate strategic vision. A key factor to success is the buy-in of departmental or regional middle and executive management.

In the case of Pfizer, a household name and global pharmacy organization, they started just letting people run their own areas and then realized that true enterprise deployment meant a true enterprise structure for deployment.

This chapter will provide an overview of deployment problems at Stage 5, followed by a deployment description. We've divided deployment into these sections: imperatives, scoping, corporate readiness assessment, IT readiness, infrastructure issues, and follow-on steps.

The proliferation of the standard into multiple different applications throughout the enterprise can be very exciting and successful. But problems can arise when you take your ECM deployment to Stage 5. The most common questions to be asked are:

• How do I know if we'll really benefit from ECM?

• How can I keep costs from spiraling beyond expectations?

• Which ECM components should be used for what kinds of content management, for example, which materials should be published to the Web and which should be placed in open document folders?

• How do we want people to work with ECM and which people do we want to do this?

• How can non-IT managers be part of the ECM decisions?

• Is the existing infrastructure sufficient for the new deployment?

Imperatives

The first task for any enterprise deployment is to understand organizational imperatives as drivers of the ECM extension. Imperatives, defined as the needs of the organization as expressed by senior managers, must be the drivers of deployment. These imperatives can be cost reduction, fulfillment of compliance needs, or faster decision making.

Defining the Strategic Vision

It is important to have a strategic vision and to identify your key business drivers. The vision must be shared by key program sponsors and the implementation team. A sure way of achieving deployment success is to quantify your success. You must have a clear understanding of the business problems you are trying to solve and an idea of what financial and non-financial benefits the solution will contribute. After the rollout, you must evaluate the results to determine whether the deployment was a success.

On-boarding

After defining the strategic vision, the next step is to schedule on-boarding. Given that in today's business world end users do not have time to try new things, users will embrace the ECM solution only if it meets their needs and solves their problems.

An on-boarding plan defines which user groups should be online first and which applications should be rolled out first. The priority should be to achieve the most benefits at the outset. In developing the on-boarding plan, consider benefits, complexity and investment size and evaluate them for each piece of the ECM deployment. It's a good idea to take small steps that result in quick wins. That's cost effective and ensures end user buy-in.

The environment for an ECM deployment is often multi-national as well as multi-cultural. Thus, the input of key managers, with appropriate sponsorship, must be engaged to ensure that the headquarters' vision meets the local needs.

Operational Modeling

Operational modeling is the next step. In it, we ask, what work patterns will our end users use when working with the ECM solution? If the answer is clear, you can decide how the solution should be configured to make these work patterns achievable. This is a key area where business meets IT.

The operational managers in any organization know what they want to achieve. ECM experts can point out the possibilities and the pros and cons of different approaches. The possibilities often exceed—and consequently expand—the ambitions of the business for managing and leveraging content.

> Kerr-McGee

Who: Founded in 1929, Kerr-McGee Corporation is an Oklahoma City-based company with assets of approximately $10 billion. The company is engaged in two global businesses: oil and gas exploration and the production and marketing of titanium dioxide pigment.

Business Objective: To implement an effective communications strategy across the enterprise.

Business Needs: An easy-to-use and self-service-oriented system that supports content re-use and timely access to information, and that could be used as a recruiting tool. A methodology was also needed to verify understanding and centrally track consumption.

Solution Overview: An integrated ECM-based solution made up of multiple components that incorporate document records and process management, workflow, and rich media delivery.

Solution Scope: Enterprise wide.

Compliance: Sarbanes-Oxley Act.

Benefits: ECM represents a critical component of the global knowledge management and information delivery program at Kerr-McGee. It enables the provision of timely, customer-friendly access to accurate information. Considerable resource and time savings have resulted in cost savings.

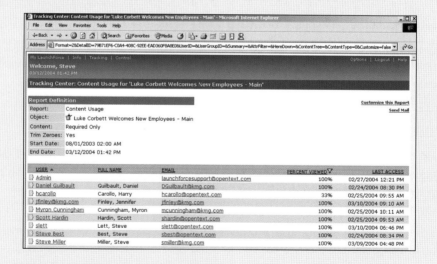

Figure 12.3: Tracking Center Reports at Kerr-McGee

Kerr-McGee faces the same problem that afflicts many companies today: how to attract and retain the best personnel. Studies show that the first 90 days of employment are crucial to establishing a sense of belonging, job satisfaction, and loyalty. Communication consistency that begins with new hires and reaches out to every corner of the globally dispersed enterprise often presents the solution.

An interactive, ECM-based Web site for employee orientation provides support for new hires during their first 90 days with the company. The site fulfils the self-service requirements for end users and Human Resources staff who keep it updated. Following the site implementation, Kerr-McGee integrated a rich media server into the solution as the primary platform for delivering interactive media to new hires. Videos can be produced in-house without bringing in a multi-media consultant and video crew. The media server also provided the required in-depth central tracking and understanding of consumption by allowing delivery of quizzes on important sections to the new hires. The key advantage for Kerr-McGee was the ability to verify delivery and understanding, and act on the results. For example, the company can send follow-up notes to individuals who scored below a certain score on a quiz or check the status of assigned requests and responsibilities. Kerr-McGee has also utilized ECM-based workflow that allows for tracking and task prompting for all parties involved. The system is integrated with ERP technology used by Human Resources.

One of the major challenges of implementing an enterprise-wide system is persuading people to change the way they work—this is just as true for new hires as it is for older employees. Kerr-McGee had already stumbled upon this obstacle when designing an ECM system that would support the organization's globally dispersed teams in their communication and project management efforts. In order to ensure effective system use, the organization had gathered user requirements and tailored the look and feel of the system using XML capability. An all-in-one user interface provides various navigational tools and links, including recent news releases and a list of project contacts, and supports easy access to collaborative tools such as discussions, task lists, and standard ECM system document management functionalities.

Having observed the success of the tailored user interface, Kerr-McGee re-applied the same method to the new hire orientation pages. In this case, the main driver was the development of an easy-to-use, intuitive user interface that anyone with basic Web browser familiarity could use. In addition to being visually inviting, the solution supports multiple learning styles by incorporating video and audio, while overcoming some of the bandwidth and latency realities of a global network.

Kerr-McGee also uses the system for communication needs, while the document management and collaborative tools support research and development.

In general, there are two ways to approach operational modeling. The preferred one is to conduct a multi-disciplinary workshop involving operational managers, IT, user groups, and other key managers. If the workshop is well moderated, the contributions of individuals will stimulate input from others and help participants gain a broader perspective. An alternative approach is to gather needs via interviews, arbitrate with IT to have the system configured to meet these needs, and then go back to seek acceptance. This is more time consuming and difficult, since the gatherer must be a proxy for others in representing their needs.

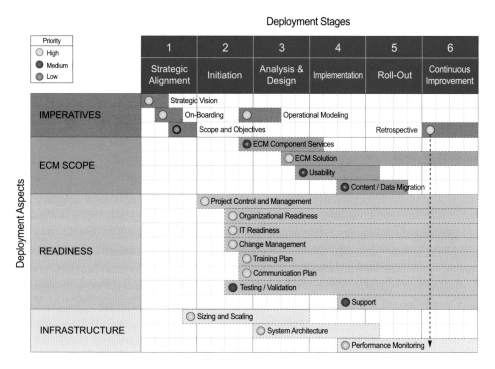

Figure 12.4: Deployment Framework

Corporate Readiness Assessment

After proving the ECM deployment can work and after planning what it could look like the next step is to make sure the organization is ready for success. Readiness can be divided into two main areas—Organizational Readiness and IT Readiness.

First we want to have a look at organizational readiness. It is extensively described in previous chapters of this book. But there is one piece that becomes increasingly important with enterprise deployments—the Program Management Office (PMO).

In the case of a multinational deployment you should already have a PMO as a competency center for ECM enterprise deployments. If not you should immediately establish one to manage budgets, schedules and resources.

Another important point is that the PMO also serves as a repository for Best Practices and Methodologies. Imagine all the guidelines, fact sheets, training material and checklists that have to be updated and translated in several languages.

This is exactly what Siemens set up as primary goals. They drew a KM roadmap outlining an overall corporate strategy and guidelines for establishing communities of practice. Siemens' Chief Knowledge Officer says "We, on a corporate level, can't coach every organization, but we can provide them with a KM implementation guide, something of a best practices sharing bible that helps with implementation."

In general any information produced in the earlier steps should be gathered in the PMO.

Other important questions of Organizational Readiness that are especially important in enterprise and multinational ECM deployments are:

• Who sets direction and priorities for the program—is the Enterprise user base adequately represented?

• What's our corporate philosophy and policy on permissions and enterprise searching?

• Have we lined up enough local internal (employee) communications people to explain and support our program?

IT Readiness

IT Readiness is often overlooked in this stage, since there is an existing ECM deployment and an existing IT environment, both of which are successful in conducting daily business. However, when IT creates the deployment roadmap, all partners, such as service providers, service consumers, and vendors must work together towards IT readiness.

IT must ensure that the resources assigned to the project are sufficient. The first step in resource planning is to identify the skills required for the deployment. The second is to ensure that enough people with the right skills are assigned to the project. Be careful with part-time resources. Often they are occupied with tasks that become urgent, and it's difficult to keep them up to date.

The next step is to establish a proper training schedule for the ECM deployment or the new ECM components. There should be separate classes for administration, architecture, security, performance and end-user support.

You must evaluate your existing hardware and infrastructure and order additional hardware early enough in the deployment cycle. Evaluating the physical equipment should include the network, network devices, and network services. The servers and storage devices must also be reviewed. Plan enough resources for additional development, testing, and training.

Business continuity is also part of IT readiness. There must be policies and back-up plans for errors such as end-user mistakes, hardware failures (e.g., losing sectors of disk, power loss), and disaster simulations (for example, loss of the entire data centre in the case of fire or earthquake).

A successful deployment also requires "ECM champions" in every business unit. These champions are the drivers of local user adoption. They must have the technical skills and understanding of the ECM solution, as well as the social skills to convince other users to use the new solution. And you must ensure that these champions have enough time to support the ECM project.

A well planned and well executed implementation is the key to realizing the maximum return on an ECM investment. Without adequate IT readiness, implementing a collaborative knowledge management solution can be hit or miss. Many ECM vendors provide an IT Readiness Assessment Checklist that can help you assess your IT readiness.

The goal of the IT Readiness Assessment is to gather and validate the information technology readiness of the infrastructure for supporting an ECM implementation. An IT readiness assessment focuses on Systems Management (Service Level Agreements, system availability), business continuity, Help Desk support, and change management.

The change management considerations include:

• Is the ECM Solution meeting the business imperatives?

• Are lessons learned captured for re-use for subsequent phases of the deployment?

• Are quality assurance plans in place to define the testing process for new
  applications or code changes?

Sizing and Scaling

Once you have a functioning ECM deployment, you know that the existing line capabilities are sufficient to support the deployment. But what about the next step?

The sizing and scaling work stream is needed to ensure that the system is sized for the system usage and number of users. You must ensure that the proper infrastructure is in place for the pilot and the roll-out phase. A proper design should ensure that the ECM deployment is scalable for future extended usage.

Systems design involves the analysis, design, and configuration of the necessary hardware and software components to support the solution architecture. Some vendors provide a Technical Architecture Questionnaire that they use to gather all the relevant information for sizing and scaling, such as current hardware, applications, user behavior, and server configuration. This information is used in the System Architecture work stream as well. This work stream focuses on fitting the system into existing infrastructure.

In a multinational and multi-departmental implementation, there is a greater need for setting standards than in a local or one-department implementation. The categories of standards that you must establish and/or adhere to are:

• Application Software Standards

• Environment Standards

• Infrastructure Security Standards

• Platform Standards

> With 434,000 employees around the world, Siemens has an exceptionally complex ECM deployment that provides streamlined processes, collaborative workspaces and shared content across the enterprise.
>
> As significant tangible and intangible benefits emerged as a result of departmental level ECM applications, Siemens' Information Technology group looked to extend those returns—improved team efficiency, enhanced productivity, time and resource savings—to the corporate level. The final step in the ECM implementation was the creation of an enterprise-wide knowledge strategy led by C-level management.
>
> ECM technology serves as the foundation for Siemens' worldwide intranet, project and knowledge management solution, providing extensive business process support, from selling products and solutions to quickly responding to customer requests and finding experts across the organization.

Follow-On Steps

After completing any deployment step, you should perform a retrospective. This is a process in which you identify the successes, failures, and lessons learned of the step. A retrospective also determines whether the metrics identified during the on-boarding process were met. Ask the following questions:

• Did the users and management get what they wanted?

• What went well?

• What could have gone better?

And (especially for international rollouts):

• What cultural or local traps did we fall into?

• Did we realize the estimated benefits/savings?

A proper retrospective assures senior management about the ECM decision and speeds up further deployment steps.

After the retrospective, the next step is performance monitoring. In this step, you determine whether the system is scaled for ongoing usage. You should measure the free capacities of server resources (RAM, CPU, etc.), operation system resources, the network, and the network services and of the application itself.

Summary

Let's review the problems identified in the beginning of the chapter and review how they were solved.

The problems identified were:

• How do I know if we'll really get benefit from ECM?

• You defined the business goals in the imperatives phase (for example, reduce headcount required for this task by 15 percent, speed up order processing by 10 percent). Conduct a retrospective to determine whether you met your goals.

• How can I keep costs from spiraling beyond expectation?

• Keep the ECM solution as near as the standard application as possible. Avoid too many vendors and too many interfaces.

• What ECM components should be used for what kinds of content management?

• Have ECM experts evaluate this.

• How do we want people to work with ECM, and which people do we want to do this?

• The answers to these questions come from on-boarding and operational modeling. Always verify your findings with the local management and user teams involved.

• How can non-IT people be part of the ECM decisions?

• Try to have the non-IT people look at prototypes or a test system.

• Is the existing infrastructure sufficient for the new deployment?

• Use a vendor's Technical Architecture Questionnaire and let them evaluate the results.

Summary of Next Steps

If you managed stage 5 you have reached the maximum of ECM within your company. You have interdepartmental and international information sharing and a common knowledge base. Furthermore, you proved the success of the ECM deployment in a retrospective against the metrics established in the imperatives phase.

The next step is to open your system to external users—customers, partners, or suppliers. The following and final chapters address this by discussing extranets and online marketplaces.

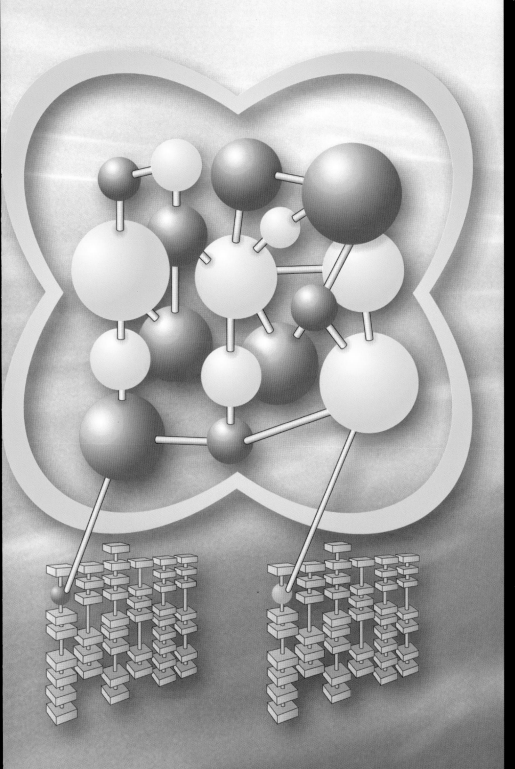

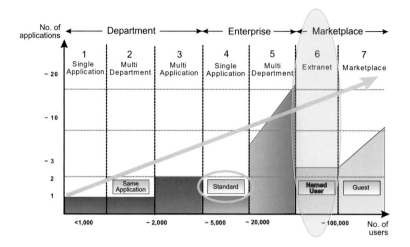

Figure 13.1: Stage 6 of ECM Adoption

The Extranet stage, shown in Figure 13.1 as Stage 6, is a natural evolution from an internal collaboration group that wants to extend the definition of "team member" to someone outside of the organization. This is typically done in limited cases in which the users are named users and well known to the organization. These groups are usually built around an existing internal application with a limited number of external users.

CHAPTER 13

EXTENDED ENTERPRISE DEPLOYMENTS STAGE 6

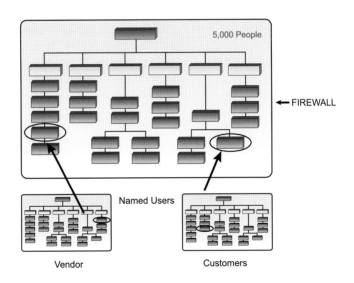

Figure 13.2: Stage 6 – Extranet

The key issues for this stage of ECM adoption are that the applications extend beyond the enterprise and may include competitors. Scaling is an issue, as an extranet often involves more users than an internal system and more users than the ECM system can handle. Each of these issues implies that there is a non-secure environment, which necessitates protective measures such as a firewall.

This chapter will cover these key elements and the methods used to deal with them.

> Dutch Refugee Council

Who: The Dutch Refugee Council (Vluchtelingenwerk) is an independent professional organization whose main goal is to protect asylum seekers and refugees. This work is mainly done by volunteers and entails personal support and the protection of refugees' interests during admission, reception, and social participation, primarily in the Netherlands.

Business Objective: To become the center for all expertise on refugee affairs and legislation in the Netherlands.

Business Needs: Geographically dispersed parties needed to access refugee files and legislation information regardless of time or location.

Solution Overview: A Web-based document management system enables information capture, storage, revision, and dissemination through an intranet and extranet, and provides support for secure, group-based access to confidential information.

Solution Scope: Enterprise wide and extranet.

Benefits: Internal efficiency has been optimized as staff and external groups have direct access to all essential documents. The number of phone-based requests has decreased, enabling employees to spend more time on direct work with refugees. As a result of the solution, the organization has realized significant cost savings.

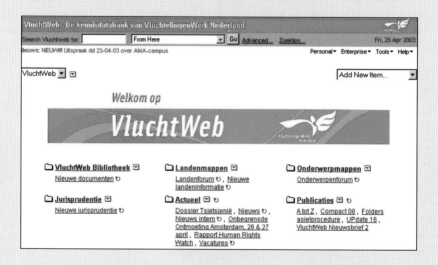

Figure 13.3: Document Management at the Dutch Refugee Council

An intensive exchange of information and knowledge defines the business day at the Dutch Refugee Council, ranging from refugee support done by dispersed branches within the organization to employees and social workers who work closely with the refugees. Information exchange necessitates access to refugee files and information on asylum and refugee legislation matters. In order to streamline this information, the Dutch Refugee Council has implemented an ECM document and content management system that has enabled it to become the center for all expertise on refugee affairs and legislation. The Web-based aspect of the solution was an absolute necessity, considering that the vast majority of users are not based at the council's head office in Amsterdam.

VluchtWeb is a Web-based document management system that enables information capture, storage, revision, and dissemination through an intranet and extranet. Prior to the launch of the solution, a large amount of information was scanned and integrated into VluchtWeb using imaging technology.

In addition to the staff dispersed among the many council branches, the VluchtWeb extranet must be accessed by many other user groups, including foreign court divisions, specialist law firms, and organizations such as Amnesty International and the Red Cross. As the Dutch Refugee Council needs to store and disseminate a lot of confidential information, content access must be carefully organized and easy to monitor. Consequently, VluchtWeb has been organized into folders and sub-folders, and user permissions have been organized based on user groups in order to enable access monitoring. Between all groups who need to access the information, 1200 licensees cover part of the costs by subscribing to VluchtWeb.

A user-friendly system was of great importance to the staff and the more than 8,000 volunteers the council works with, some of whom were not familiar with using a PC. The design of the user interface was thus kept as simple as possible, enabling everyone to easily access and find information. Some employees took the lead in this area, as they possessed the experience and the skills to turn VluchtWeb into a real knowledge management tool. Even so, the Dutch Refugee Council knows well that true organiza- tion-wide knowledge sharing is only possible if all VluchtWeb staff make an effort. To encourage such usage, the technical staff is continuously looking for ways to make the site more interactive by consulting users as well as working together and developing partnerships with customer groups. In order to keep the working environment attractive, a picture album is being integrated into VluchtWeb.

Internal efficiency has been optimized as staff and external groups have direct access to all essential documents. A recent user survey has indicated that 75 percent of participants believe they are more productive now that they use VluchtWeb.

Imperatives

The business drivers behind the decision to undertake an extranet project will vary depending on the type of application and the type of externals being included in the process. Typically, the imperatives include concrete benefits such as reducing the cost of interactions with suppliers, partners, and customers; and implementing formal communication processes and maintaining records of them for legal or regulatory compliance. The imperatives also include less tangible benefits such as maximizing the efficiency of collaboration or enabling partners, customers, and suppliers to communicate more effectively with the organization.

It is essential in this stage of ECM implementation that the strategic vision is clearly defined and understood up front. Only then can you effectively define the project scope and, perhaps more importantly, define the metrics that you will use to measure the project's success.

> As the systems engineer for total solutions, Siemens Building Technologies needs to collaborate and share information with seven locations and six divisions. Turning to an extranet solution, the organization manages all of the information related to building and construction projects online. ECM technology has enabled SBT to address productivity and customer satisfaction challenges caused by time-consuming searches for documentation, data and images during building projects.

Scoping

Defining the scope of the extranet project requires many of the same steps that have been described in previous chapters.

At the scoping stage, the obvious place to start is with the internal users who will be directly involved in participating in the extranet system. For example, in a customer care extranet, the first people to include in designing the scope would be the customer care representatives. Ideally, you should also try to include one or more representatives from the future external user group—in this case, some of the customers who would be using the service, in order to understand their requirements.

The scoping of an extranet differs from that of an internal ECM project in that you must include representatives from business areas that normally would not be involved for an internal project. Business areas such as Marketing and Legal are two good examples. The reason for these additional areas becomes clear if we take an analogy from the old fashioned way of doing business. Previously, customers who were visiting would see your office building and an impressive front door with your logo and a nice paint job. Perhaps they would have been invited into the reception area, or held meetings in executive boardrooms. Now however, you are opening up your front door and letting the customers into the back office, metaphorically speaking. You need to ensure that the people who usually only interfaced with customers over the telephone are now appropriately attired; that their desks are clean and that there are no confidential files from other customers lying around. Your face to the market has changed dramatically, and you need to ensure that the people responsible for looking after that face are involved in the change. So Marketing should be there to manage the brand—not only the look and feel of the Web pages, but also the design and structure of the communications. Legal should be there to ensure that customers have access to the right information, and only the information that they should have access to.

You must also consider the capabilities and characteristics of the end users when scoping the extranet program. When you work on an internal project, you know who those users are, their skill levels, their technical infrastructure, and their available tools. With an external project however, you can no longer assume that all the users will have the same standards (such as office software), or that their level of familiarity with Web sites equals that of your internal users. You probably won't be (or won't want to be) responsible for their training, and this is an especially important consideration when designing the functionality of the system—more functionality leads to greater complexity. If the typical external users are only going to be accessing the system occasionally, make sure that the most important functions are available to them in the simplest possible way. Don't try to offer too much functionality; it may confuse the occasional user. Forget about the "nice to haves" and stick with the "must haves."

Even basic assumptions such as language will be challenged when scoping an extranet. When Siemens was rolling out an extranet for Customer Care in their Automation and Drives division, they suddenly realized content that was previously internally focused was going to have to be repurposed and translated into multiple languages because the customers accessing this information came from all over the world. The content on the Automation and Drives Customer Care site is now available in six languages. Similarly, the British Council's Web site is available in multiple languages, as illustrated in Figure 13.5.

> Motorola

Who: Motorola is a Fortune 100 global communications leader that provides seamless mobility products and solutions across broadband, embedded systems, and wireless networks.

Business Objective: To provide a common tool across the enterprise to simplify information sharing and discovery in order to better leverage the intellectual capital of the company.

Business Needs: Reduce the costs and complexities of independent isolated information systems, while ensuring that all employees have the latest tools at their disposal.

Solution Overview: An ECM platform provides document management, search, desktop integration, workflow automation, online discussion forums, Web forms, and surveys.

Solution Scope: Enterprise wide.

Benefits: Improved collaboration and information reuse, reduced cycle time, and lower total cost of ownership.

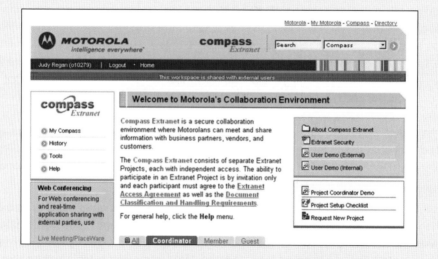

Figure 13.4: Folder and Additional Search Information at Motorola

When ECM technology was initially brought into the enterprise, Motorola began recruiting power users named 'Knowledge Champions' to help organize information in their subject areas. Soon after that, users were allowed to add their content to the system and the flood gates had opened… Fast forward eight years, and Motorola has one of the largest and most active ECM installations with more than 10 million documents, 9.5 TB of information, and more than one million transactions performed each day. Growth has been tremendous, with storage doubling every 12-14 months.

The solution—called COMPASS—has evolved to become an intricate part of the Motorola culture and a key business enabler. Encompassing more than 60,000 users worldwide, the system reaches all regions and disciplines across the enterprise. It is used in small workgroups to help collaborate and share ideas all the way to large-scale, enterprise-wide distribution of company policies and news. ECM has also extended beyond the enterprise walls and now enables collaboration with more than 4,000 extranet users, including customers, business partners, and suppliers.

COMPASS is trusted daily for some of Motorola's most critical and highly visible projects, such as sharing Sarbanes-Oxley Act documentation with outside auditors through the extranet. It is common practice to hear end users refer to their COMPASS location in meetings, on conference calls and in emails. The solution has also become integrated into many other corporate systems, such as the employee portal and distribution of engineering software builds for new handsets.

System performance and availability are critical issues at Motorola and performance is monitored continuously for any changes in the service level. Downtime is simply not an option—COMPASS includes business-critical documents and its end users are spread across the globe and time zones, requiring high system quality at all times. Despite increases in data and user load, Motorola has consistently improved performance and, over the years, has continued to push the boundaries of their ECM solution, leading the way in areas such as global load balancing and caching, content compression, and vertical scaling. For instance, content compression identifies content not being used on the system and compresses it, which decreases system data load. Continuous system improvements and performance monitoring result in a system availability rate of 99.9 percent, 24/7.

One of the main drivers for Motorola's IT organization has been to provide tools which are 'Common, Simple, and Global.' ECM has been a shining example of that— by standardizing on the technology, Motorola has been able to consolidate hundreds of other systems and reduce costs. COMPASS has also enabled Motorola to reduce complexity and provide a common shared toolset across the corporation, lowering training, increasing accessibility, and ensuring that all employees have the best capabilities at their disposal.

Figure 13.5: British Council's Multi-national Web Site

Corporate Readiness Assessment

The first step in achieving corporate readiness at this stage is to identify how the introduction of the extranet will impact interactions with external parties. How will it change the way your people work? Change management is key (see Chapter 6 for a discussion of change management). You must have the necessary training and incentive programs in place to ensure that the changes are accepted and welcomed by your internal users.

In the previous Siemens Customer Care example, the customers now have access to a corporate knowledge base, meaning that the number of calls to the Customer Care Centre may decrease. However, the calls that do come in may be more complex and more difficult to answer. Your staff needs to be prepared for this eventuality.

You must also assess how the new audience for the content and functionality provided by the extranet affects internal processes. Do you need additional approvals for validating content before it is published?

If customers and partners now have access to what were previously internal discussion forums or bulletin boards, you must ensure that all staff are aware of this fact—and that they do not use these platforms to make inappropriate comments about the company, their company's products, the customers, suppliers, or partners. It is critical that each staff member understands that when posting anything to an extranet, the information is in the public domain and affects your brand. The importance of a training and communications plan to ensure they understand cannot be overstated.

Infrastructure

Extending an internal system to external users could dramatically increase the demands on the infrastructure. For instance, the usage in terms of bandwidth and storage are much less predictable, with potentially many more extreme peaks and valleys. All of this must be anticipated and planned for, so ensure your infrastructure and IT department have the capacity and ability to scale quickly and effectively.

You must also ensure that the internal staff members who will be interacting with the system have the necessary tools to do so. It may sound obvious, but the basics are often overlooked. Staff interacting with customers, partners, and suppliers via an extranet will need the necessary hardware, software and connectivity to do their jobs.

Follow-On Steps

During the scoping phase, you will have defined the metrics to use to measure the success or failure of your extranet project. It therefore follows that you will need to monitor the achievement of your initial goals by tracking these metrics on an ongoing basis. Solicit feedback from your internal and external users. More importantly, act on this feedback, and ensure that your internal and external users see you acting on it. Gather usage statistics and monitor trends and changes.

Any extranet implementation will have far-reaching effects, so be sure to remember to monitor the effects on the areas of your organization that are not directly involved with the extranet. For example, are accounts paid in a more timely manner now that customers have access to their invoices online? Are customers receiving better service? Is Development producing more appropriate products as a result of monitoring customer feedback?

Finally, keep an eye on the competition and monitor the trends in your industry to ensure that your extranet remains something that your company and brand can be proud of.

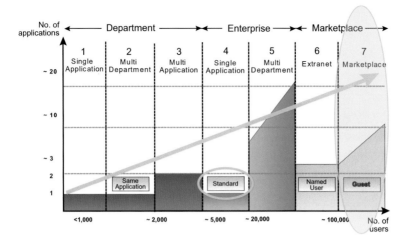

Figure 14.1: Stage 7 of ECM Adoption

The seventh and final stage of ECM Adoption is the online marketplace. In this stage, a series of extranets are extended to include a broad range of market participants, including competitors. An online marketplace functions as the main clearing house for all of the issues of a particular industry. The key difference with stage 7 is that the guest users are unknown, and this has security implications.

CHAPTER 14

ONLINE MARKETPLACES
STAGE 7

An online marketplace is a worldwide system of corporations and governments tightly integrated to provide real-time transactions and information. When a marketplace is created around a major organization, that organization acts as a "hub" and typically is responsible for the administration of that marketplace.

The health of the online marketplace depends on its flexibility to respond within minutes to any changes in the environment that may occur. ECM plays a key role in the online marketplace by facilitating the acquisition of information, the discussion of this information, and the re-distribution of the modified information.

This chapter explores the methods used to deal with the key elements characteristic of Stage 7.

Scoping

The change in scope when dealing with online marketplaces is that external parties become involved, and to accurately define the project scope, it is essential that you include more stakeholders than you normally would. You must also consider guest users (as opposed to the named users introduced in stage 6) at this stage. This has an impact on architecture, which requires a neutral area or De-Militarized Zone (DMZ) to permit the free flow of public information. The DMZ is very similar to the public Internet.

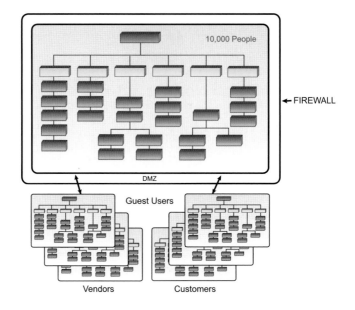

Figure 14.2: Stage 7 – Online Marketplace

Corporate Readiness Assessment

Corporate Readiness in the external environment follows the same basic principles as for any other ECM implementation—with some added pressure. In this case, your system is open to external users such as customers, partners and/or suppliers, and guest users. This means that any failure in the system or service will be a fairly public event, and can have far-reaching implications for your brand and corporate credibility in the marketplace. The assessment of your corporate readiness is therefore a critical stage in the deployment.

IT Readiness

An accurate assessment of the IT requirements for an online marketplace project is critical (the same can be said of an extranet project). The key issue is that any IT failures will be visible to your key stakeholders—the customers, partners, suppliers, or guest users for whom the system is designed—and this will affect your credibility and their perception of your service levels overall. Therefore, the IT requirements for the online marketplace should be handled with military precision; you must dot every 'i' and cross every 't'. Whether you decide to host the application internally or to outsource the hosting, ensure that you have a comprehensive Service Level Agreement (SLA) in place and ensure that the support level is appropriate to the application and the audience.

If your audience is geographically dispersed, their working hours will likely not match those of your IT department. If the system provides customer self service, it must be available 24 hours a day, 365 days a year. Your SLA must reflect and support this requirement.

Remember that the audience for this application is no longer restricted to your trusted internal users. You will need to safeguard your other internal systems, including adding security features such as firewalls, a De-Militarized Zone (DMZ), the appropriate authentication and authorization technologies, and more. Does your IT department have the necessary skills? Don't underestimate the level of investment required to provide the >99.9 percent availability required for a business-critical system.

The "DMZ"

Allowing external (untrusted) access to a trusted resource requires understanding and care: understanding of what the technical requirements are to facilitate such a situation, and care in limiting the exposure and potential threats that are inherent in such a system. The goal is to have the correct initial architecture to allow for access, with trained personnel capable of continued maintenance and monitoring (system load and traffic, security holes, and so on).

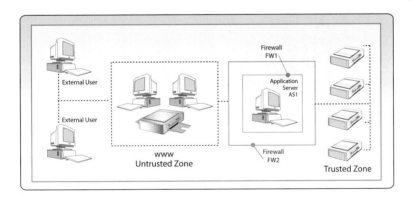

Figure 14.3: Traditional DMZ – Logical Architecture

Figure 14.3 shows a technical representation of the general architecture that deals with external access from an untrusted environment to a trusted zone. Between the untrusted and trusted zones, shielded by two firewalls is the "De-Militarized Zone," or DMZ. The DMZ is a semi-permeable boundary, otherwise known as a firewall. These firewalls have rules defining which traffic is allowed; i.e., which servers may be contacted, and on which port. When a communication request arrives at the firewall from some machine, the firewall examines its own rules to determine whether the communication is allowed and accepts it or denies it accordingly.

> Federal Ministry of the Interior

Who: The Procurement Agency is the principal buyer for 26 federal authorities within the portfolio of the German Federal Ministry of the Interior. In 2002, it managed an annual budget of €422.6 million. This makes the agency the second largest purchasing body in Germany's federal government sector.

Business Objective: To comply with the 2003 legislation of the German Federal Government requiring all federal authorities to use e-Tendering and the one-stop e-government shop by the end of 2005.

Solution Overview: The "Public Purch@sing Online" project is an innovative alternative to traditional procurement practices: contracts for goods and services are now awarded via the Internet. Thanks to the ECM solution, every step in the procurement process is performed electronically, including the exchange of legally valid contracts.

Solution Scope: Intranet and extranet for suppliers in the private sector across the European Union.

Benefits: Everyone benefits from electronic procurement: industry, public authorities, and taxpayers. Online procurement creates transparency, which strengthens competition and leads to more favorable prices. The use of electronic documents enables integration in existing backend systems, and electronic tendering is cheaper, simpler, and more transparent than conventional procedures.

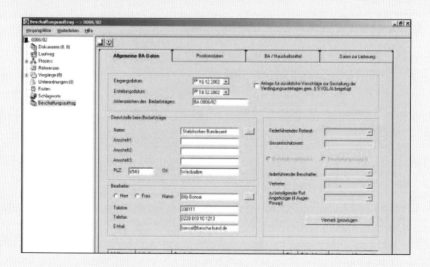

Figure 14.4: Overview of Received Procurement Assignments
at the Procurement Agency of the Federal Ministry of the Interior

Procurement by public authorities must follow the rules governing tendering procedures under the German law. Contracts for goods and services must be publicly advertised and all interested suppliers are sent contract documents upon request. The vendors use this information to calculate their prices and conditions. Once the deadline for submitting an offer has expired, vendors are bound by their offer. The awarding authority chooses the vendor with the 'economically most advantageous' offer. Where EU rules are followed, a failed vendor has the opportunity to request a review of the awarding authority's decision before Germany's Federal Tender Appeals Chamber. The tendering procedure must then be suspended until a final ruling has been made. For this reason, the awarding authority is very careful to avoid any procedural errors when awarding contracts.

The public procurement process should above all be fast, economical, and transparent. That is why the Procurement Agency of the Federal Ministry of the Interior is creating, with its "Public Purch@sing Online" project, an innovative alternative to traditional procurement practices: contracts for goods and services are now awarded via the Internet.

"Public Purch@sing Online" consists of three elements: the ECM-based Tendering Module facilitates the work of buyers at the Procurement Agency who invite tenders and award contracts; the e-Tendering central Internet platform enables suppliers in the private sector to call up all relevant information and submit their offers electronically without any paperwork; and the one-stop e-Government shop that enables federal authorities to procure materials from an electronic catalog where they can request items available from the suppliers with whom the Procurement Agency has made a framework agreement.

The electronic Tendering Module helps to establish a clear system for managing the placement of contracts and automatically assists staff by taking over certain procedural steps. This has been made possible by the deployment of an ECM-based workflow system, which not only performs document management, but also handles work operations. External consultants along with the system vendor had succeeded in technically modeling the Procurement Agency's internal workflows in an electronic Tendering Module. The workflow begins once an order form is received for an item not available in the e-Government shop. The data from the form is automatically input into the system's database and the order form is scanned into the solution for easy archiving. Subsequently, the electronic tendering procedures follow all the customary steps to be performed by the Procurement Agency on the basis of the legal requirements for the award of contracts. Thanks to the ECM system, every step in the procurement process is performed electronically.

"Public Purch@sing Online" puts the entire electronic tendering process online—from the preparation of a contract notice to the awarding of a contract. The entire electronic contracting process is legally watertight.

The most obvious benefit of the DMZ is that requests from the untrusted zone, which could be any user on the Internet, must first pass through the firewall to a limited number of servers—those that have been installed with specific solutions. However, once the request is in the DMZ, there must still be a process to pass that request through to the trusted zone (if appropriate). With an enterprise solution where the service runs in the trusted zone, using the DMZ as a stepping point is imperative. The untrusted machine calls an application server in the DMZ, which, if accepted, creates its own request through the second firewall to the trusted machine. This new request will be a different protocol, different port, and potentially calling a machine running a different operating system. External machines must not have direct access to the trusted zone.

The premise behind a DMZ is that machines that are the first connection point from an untrusted environment are at a security risk—these include items such as mail servers and Web servers. With the ever-expanding list of security warnings, it's not palatable to allow these services to run in the trusted environment. By using a DMZ, the risk is minimized.

Determining the firewall rules can be done in several ways, though the most successful tends to be the "open-as-priority" approach. It closes all communication among the zones, only opening ports as required. Before any ports are opened, the security ramifications must be understood.

Examining the configuration for a Web-based extranet suggests a secure communication channel from the untrusted zone (WWW), typically through HTTPS (443) into the application server in the DMZ. A Java servlet is called on the application server, which communicates information to the ECM solution through a second firewall, with a different port and different communication protocol. This solution is the most common.

Summary

The online marketplace is a term given to Web sites where buyers and sellers find and exchange information, collaborate and trade. Marketplaces can be operated by independent third parties or by an industry consortium. Often, they focus on a particular industry, although they sometimes focus on a particular region, function, or process. The products most suited to this type of market are commodities. Examples include office supplies, automotive parts, building materials, chemicals, and metals. Processes and services offered by online marketplaces include messaging, publishing, ordering, paying, and integrating.

There are thousands of online marketplaces today, but few have the participation of the world's largest companies or handle large trading volumes. This final stage in ECM adoption has yet to achieve a wide acceptance, but it will certainly follow the trend set by the previous stages for which there has been broad acceptance.

CHAPTER 15

ECM AND THE FUTURE

In the future, all components of current ECM technology must be seamlessly integrated. The value will lie in the business solutions enabled by ECM technology, not the technology itself. The approach to these solutions will be revolutionized by advances in ECM, broadband and wireless technologies, and tighter integration with desktop productivity tools for information workers. In addition, the nature of ECM will change as content, collaboration, and processes begin to blur the traditional lines that separate applications.

When it comes to investing in technology, the rush to get on the Internet has been replaced by a more thoughtful and fundamental approach. Companies are asking themselves: What procedures must our company comply with to ensure that we can continue to do business as a trusted partner? Why is my company investing this much money? Where is the return on investment for this project?

These are valid questions that indicate the market is now entering a long-term, sustainable investment track for ECM-centric business solutions.

The future of ECM will also be driven by the growth and sophistication of enabling technologies such as rich media and mobile technologies. In the organization of tomorrow, creating a document will not happen in isolation and meeting with someone in an office on the other side of the world will be only a click away. In many ways, the combination of productivity applications is already occurring at the personal and group levels: content is currently being created and saved automatically to a company intranet and global meetings are coordinated from the desktop. By integrating the functionality required to create, share and distribute a document (or other forms of media), people can achieve the highest level of productivity and effectiveness.

Future Trends

All of these issues are driven by six fundamental trends that will greatly affect the future, not only in ECM but in computing and society as a whole:

Content Aggregation	Easy access to all enterprise information available in desktop productivity applications
Increased Legislation	Compliance and governance features as demanded by increased legislation and internal controls
Security	Server-based architecture models for safeguarding the quality, integrity and recoverability of intellectual property
Higher Bandwidth	Rich media collaboration made possible by increased bandwidth
Online Mobility	Presence-awareness within all ECM applications through "always on" online mobility

While each of these trends is important, their simultaneous occurrence represents an important period in the development of the ECM industry.

Content Aggregation

In recent years, enterprises have made large investments in IT infrastructure and enterprise applications, such as ERP, CRM, email and ECM. Information relating to core business processes is often spread across these multiple applications, but there is no single point of access. To streamline business processes, improve information worker productivity and reduce risk, there is increasing demand to provide easy access to all information from enterprise applications directly from desktop productivity tools and portals.

This aggregation of content is achieved through the ECM framework's "Enterprise Library." The Enterprise Library does not require content to be moved from its existing locations, but is a metadata layer that indexes and enables information workers to access content wherever it lives. The Enterprise Library layer makes it easy to retrieve information from multiple enterprise systems with a single search and to present the results in any interface, including Web-based portals and desktop applications. The Enterprise Library is connected to long-term storage devices to enable the use of records management rules to archive content for compliance purposes.

Increased Legislation

Perhaps the single biggest trend affecting ECM is the global increase in legislation. As discussed in the Chapter on Return on Investment and Compliance, new legislation has had a profound impact on many industries. Regulators are seeking good governance and accountability through transparency. Such transparency is achieved by the diligent recording of all decisions made, including the collaborative processes and documents involved. We will see this diligence extend across every form of corporate communication—from email to instant messaging (IM) and recorded online meetings. Virtually everything will be digitized and recorded with a proper audit trail.

Most organizations will need to demonstrate that they are compliant with all regulations, both old and new. The amount of work required to comply is enormous. The Sarbanes-Oxley legislation, for example, has created an immense change in the way public corporations monitor and record decision making and reporting. Increased regulation means that organizations will receive more inquiries in the form of discovery orders, audits and so on. The information required for the response can span multiple applications and storage devices. The Enterprise Library provides a consolidated window into all enterprise content, enabling a timely and cost-effective response to such requests.

Regulations increasingly specify how organizations store information, and are particularly concerned with ensuring that it is tamper proof. The Enterprise Library enables organizations to automate the process of storing content relevant to a particular regulation appropriately. For example, most inland revenue regulations require a ten-year retention period for all cost or revenue-related documents on non-rewritable storage media, such as WORM (write once, read many).

Many industries are now subject to old and new regulations that regulate digitized content in the same way that paper-based content was regulated in the past. Going forward, this means that ECM will be mandatory for running a business. In the future, ECM deployments must assist an organization in meeting governance requirements, in addition to the basic requirements for higher productivity and a better return on investment.

Security

Security is another factor that will dramatically impact ECM and the rest of the computer industry. Intelligence theft, virus attacks and internal tampering are all threats to the quality and integrity of an organization's intellectual property. We all know that information on the desktop can be vulnerable to electronic attack and theft, but this information is also physically insecure—for example, when a laptop is stolen. With laptops containing more than 100 GB hard drives, the loss of content can seriously compromise an organization.

Organizations must also store backup copies of content in secure, offsite locations for disaster recovery. The Enterprise Library automates the process of storing vital or official documents on high-availability media servers that are located at a specified minimum distance from a main office.

These security issues can be addressed most cost effectively by a server-based architecture, which consolidates all active data on secure central servers, where it can be shared via a document management system. With heightened awareness of security issues, this type of architecture—content stored on central servers with user access via desktop GUIs—will become the standard in the near future.

A server-based architecture also makes it easier to control the information needed for regulatory compliance. Many regulations require an audit trail of information and actions. This involves enforcing higher levels of security for content storage and access.

Higher Bandwidth

Bandwidth will reach a satisfactory level once reasonable resolution (100x100 pixels) and VOIP (Voice Over Internet Protocol) can be delivered reliably. When this occurs, virtually all real-time collaboration, along with a substantial amount of asynchronous collaboration (email or blogging, for example), will advance from document to audiovisual formats. Instead of writing letters or sending emails, we will be sharing our ideas in face-to-face conversations hosted by rich media technology.

This evolution will improve productivity as the technology becomes more intuitive and easier to use. As a result, ECM technology will be available on a mass level, heralding the final stage of ECM adoption throughout the computing world. Because rich media places greater demands on bandwidth, storage and CPU power than other forms of media, it will become an increasing challenge for organizations to manage.

As rich media develops, ECM architecture will be required to integrate "slow zone" collaboration with "fast zone" bandwidths until the transition is complete. The ability to search on these objects will also require further advances to be made in retrieval algorithms. While this is achievable, it remains a growing challenge in the implementation of ECM solutions.

Online Mobility

Perhaps the most revolutionary of all future trends affecting ECM is the advent of "always on" computing. In its earliest form today, personal digital assistants (PDAs) or cell phones with SMS are letting users always be connected to the Internet. The next step in managing these online users is to enable collaborative groups to be aware of the presence of other members online. This presence-awareness creates a transition for users, from individual productivity tools such as writing a document to the ability to instantly initiate a dialog with other parties online.

Users can invite others into a real-time meeting area to review and discuss material as if they had just gathered physically around a whiteboard. In the virtual world, there will be as many hallways and whiteboards as there are users in the system, bringing Metcalfe's Law one step closer to the ultimate value of complete interconnectedness.

A Better Way to Work

Perhaps the most complex issue that ECM users face is the demand to achieve compliance via the transparency of content and action, while simultaneously supporting a security structure that restricts access. Balancing these conflicting requirements with the ability to deliver features and remain cost-competitive will be the true measure of success for future ECM implementations. Implementing a secure and scalable infrastructure in the context of a larger ECM strategy will determine an ECM solution's effectiveness over the long term.

As more transactions become Internet based, accounting will be faster and more precise. Transparency and compliance with such regulations as Sarbanes-Oxley will simply be built into the system and take place almost effortlessly.

Sales and marketing departments will receive critical information in record time, so they will be able to influence their markets at just the right moment. Direct mail information will be automatically collected and combined with individual consumer buying patterns to create customer profiles that can be used in email or targeted direct mail campaigns.

Research and development departments will be able to stay in tune with the changing needs of customers by having access to tailored information, sent along with each sale or Web search that occurs. Collaborating online using rich media will enable global teams to brainstorm ideas on a shared whiteboard.

Collaborative bid proposals and contract administration will streamline development cycles and improve time to market. Suppliers will add significant value by understanding the context in which a material is to be used if it is easily accessible.

CEOs will have incredibly accurate and timely information and make better decisions to pilot their enterprises. They will know that their teams have the right resources assigned and will be able to make the best decisions autonomously. They can be assured that their accounting practices and fiscal reporting are compliant. They will recognize how research and new product development meets regulatory requirements. They will know what their risks are and manage them effectively. Most importantly, they will know what their opportunities are and the precise moment to seize them.

Today, the ECM industry has taken the opportunity created by regulatory compliance to extend its leadership within the IT world. Leveraging the information within the organization has never been more important. Businesses today have to deal with large amounts of internal and external information—much of this brought about by the growing importance of the Internet. Organizations have to turn information overload into competitive advantage. Downsizing during economic hardship, the retirement of experts, the need for flexibility in the workplace and critical demand to better service customers are factors that drive companies to adopt an ECM strategy. Soon, the impossible will become an everyday reality as we log into a seamless system to find relevant information, meet online with colleagues from all over the world, collaborate on critical projects, share best practices, and effortlessly manage processes and the lifecycles of corporate information. ECM solutions will evolve in parallel with progressive Internet technologies. People will be more productive; companies will be more efficient. Because it defines a better way to work, the ECM industry will continue to expand the scope and scale of ECM solutions. In the future, millions of ECM users will become hundreds of millions of users as ECM solutions become commonplace.

So now you know that the next great idea, the next breakthrough, the next innovation, resides within the collective knowledge of connected people. This is the motivation that has driven ECM innovations from the start. By enabling great minds to work together across organizational and geographical boundaries, ECM unleashes potential and gives businesses room to grow. It ensures that companies evolve according to defined procedures and in accordance with standards and regulations. For this reason, ECM will be used by every sector of the economy, by all industries and by firms of all sizes. It will make global companies as nimble as start-ups and give small firms the global reach to deliver sophisticated, professional products and services using virtual networks.

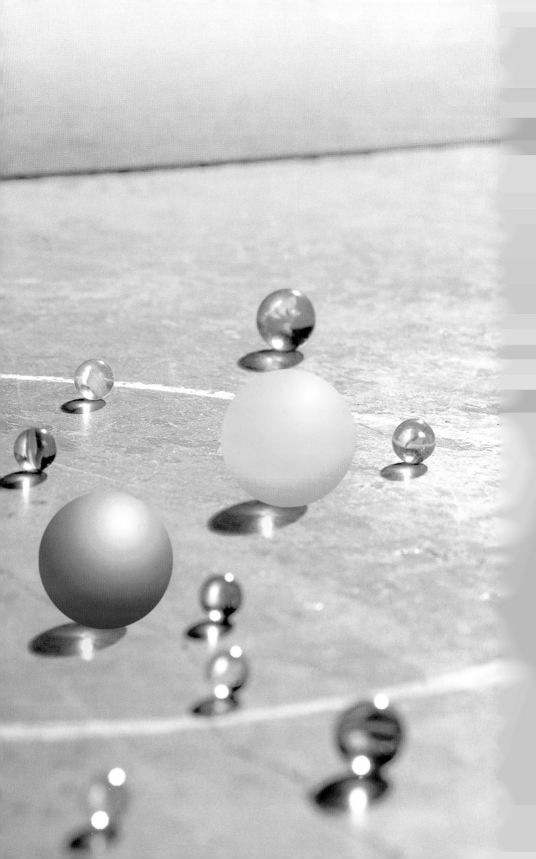

GLOSSARY

Application – Software or programs used to execute tasks on computers.

Architecture – The design concept for a software system that describes the overall philosophy of how the components interact.

Archive – A component of ECM. Systematic transfer to alternate storage media of digital data that is no longer required to be immediately accessible. Often stored via Computer Output to Laser Disk (COLD) systems. Also a collection of historical records and documents, especially about an institution.

Archiving & Retrieval – See Records Management.

ARMA – The trade association of information management professionals.

Asset Management – The tracking of physical assets.

Attributes – Specific fields and values of metadata.

Automated Classification – The technology and methodology of automating the classification of information to improve retrieval accuracy.

Basel II – A set of regulations for risk management that is due to come into force in 2006. Its application will have implications on IT security due to the stringent requirements imposed on systems handling sensitive data, particularly in the banking industry.

BLOG (Web Log) – A Web site that provides updated headlines and news articles of other sites that are of interest to the user. Also may include journal entries, commentaries, and recommendations compiled by the user.

Business Applications – Software programs used to solve business needs such as word processing, accounting, or customer relationship management.

Business Practice Improvement – A part of continuous improvement in management which involves the flow of work in order to achieve an objective.

Business Process Management (BPM) – A component of ECM. Refers to aligning processes with an organization's strategic objectives, designing and implementing process-centric tools or architectures, and developing measurement systems for effective process management. BPM also refers to automation efforts, including workflow systems and ERP systems.

CCICT – Now known as the ITU-T (Telecommunication Standardization Sector of the International Telecommunications Union). The primary international body for fostering cooperative standards for telecommunications equipment and systems. Located in Geneva, Switzerland.

CFTC – Commodities Futures Trading Commission. The United States regulatory body that protects market users and the public from fraud, manipulation, and abusive practices related to the sale of commodity and financial futures and options.

Case Management – The management of case books in an organization.

CFR – The Code of Federal Regulations maintained for every U.S. government agency and usually updated annually.

Claims Processing – The processing of customer-driven requests for action by an organization. Typically found in industries such as insurance.

Clinical Trial – A research study involving human subjects, designed to evaluate the safety and effectiveness of new therapeutic and diagnostic treatments.

Collaboration – The technology and methodology of supporting work among people.

Collaboration Points – Electronic meeting spaces where teams can work together and pool content (information).

Collaboration Software – A component of ECM Programs that link processes and individuals across different locations and time zones to create an environment where team members work together to share ideas, experiences, and knowledge.

Collaborative Knowledge Management (CKM) – Software that allows users within an organization to manage documents, projects and processes, and transparently store the by-products of collaboration in a knowledge base.

Committee Management – The governance and support structure of a formal committee. Often associated with NGO or trade associations.

Communities of Practice – The process of nurturing communities of employees having like interests. A method of sharing information from a common Web site instead of using email. Also referred to as a "virtual water cooler."

Compliance – Adherence to a body of regulations, government legislation or standards (for example, ISO 9000).

Content Management – Storage, maintenance, and retrieval of HTML and XML documents and all related elements. Content management systems may be built on top of a native XML database and typically provide publishing capabilities to export content to a Web site, CD-ROM, or print.

Corporate Governance – The relationship between all the stakeholders in a company. This includes the shareholders, directors, and management of a company, as defined by the corporate charter, bylaws, formal policy, and rule of law.

COSO – Committee of Sponsoring Organizations of the Treadway Commission. A set of definitions that describe an organization's controls environment.

Cross-Departmental Application – The implementation of a corporate activity that crosses over between major reporting departments and whose leadership is shared among departments within the organization.

Curriculum – The set of materials and lessons that constitute a set of knowledge to be taught on a particular subject.

Customer Relationship Management (CRM) System – Enterprise-wide software applications that allow companies to manage every aspect of their relationship with customers. The goal of these systems is to assist in building lasting customer relationships, and to turn customer satisfaction into customer loyalty.

DAM – See Digital Asset Management.

Database – A collection of data (normally numeric) arranged for ease and speed of search and retrieval.

Demilitarized Zone (DMZ) – The area of a network between the Internet and the internal network. This zone is not in the internal network, and is not widely open on the Internet. A firewall or a router usually protects this zone.

Digital Asset – Any subdivision or collection of content and metadata that holds value to the owner. Digital assets may include photos, video, audio, Web page, text document, Microsoft® PowerPoint, or graphics.

Digital Asset Management (DAM) – A component of ECM. A set of coordinated technologies and processes that allow for the efficient storage, retrieval, and reuse of digital content files independent of the medium to which they may be deployed. DAM provides the business rules and processes needed to acquire, store, index, secure, search, export, and transform these assets and their descriptive information.

Discovery Search – A type of ECM search used to locate all relevant documents in response to a legal or regulatory enquiry. For example, "Provide all documents and emails that may relate to your business activities with company <xxx> from 2002-2005."

Document – A piece of work created with an application, such as by a word processor. A computer file that is not an executable file and contains data for use by applications.

Document Management (DM) – A component of ECM. Involves the capture and management of documents within an organization. The term traditionally implied the management of documents after they were scanned into the computer. Today, the term has become an umbrella under which document imaging, workflow, text retrieval, and multimedia fall.

Document Repository – A component of ECM. A database that includes author, data elements, inputs, processes, outputs, and interrelationships.

Due Diligence – The process of carefully confirming all critical assumptions and facts presented by one party to another usually as a condition of finalizing an agreement.

ECM – See Enterprise Content Management.

ECM Applications – Applications that are usually tailored to address line-of-business problems or customized for specific vertical markets. Core technology elements include an RDBMS, a suite of component services, and an access layer (Web browser or rich client). In addition to the platform infrastructure, solution components can encompass a combination of software, hardware, or even a process methodology.

e-Learning – The technology and methodology to support the online learning objectives of an organization.

Email – One of the first and most popular uses for the Internet, email (electronic mail) is the exchange of computer-stored messages by electronic communication.

Email Archiving – The technology and methodology used to manage the exponential growth of email storage.

Email Management – A component of ECM. The technology and methodology used to manage emails as business records.

Email Monitoring – The technology and methodology used to monitor email traffic passing through an organization.

Employee Accreditations – The practice of ensuring that employees have mastered a subject area by having them take an online test.

Engineering Change Management – The process of controlling changes to an engineered product or infrastructure, enabling approved changes with minimum disruption.

Engineering Document Management – The technology and methodology used to manage engineering documents.

Engines – Software that performs a primary and highly repetitive function such as a database, graphics, or search engine.

Enterprise – Typically refers to the entire organization.

Enterprise Applications – The contextual integration of unstructured information with structured numerical data.

Enterprise Content Management (ECM) – Systems that capture, store, retrieve, print, and disseminate digital content for use by the enterprise. Digital content includes images, text, reports, video, audio, transactional data, catalog, and code.

Enterprise Resource Planning (ERP) – Any software system designed to support and automate the business processes of medium and large businesses. This may include manufacturing, distribution, personnel, project management, payroll, and financials. ERP systems are accounting-oriented information systems for identifying and planning the enterprise-wide resources needed to take, make, distribute, and account for customer orders.

Expertise Location – The technology and methodology of locating experts within an organization.

Exploratory Projects – Those projects initiated by an organization to investigate and explore a topic of interest.

Extended Enterprise – The ecosystem of suppliers, customers, and partners surrounding an organization.

Extranet – A private network that uses Internet protocols and the public telecommunication system to share a business's information, data, or operations with external suppliers, vendors, or customers. An extranet is usually viewed as the external portion of a company's intranet.

FASB – Financial Accounting Standards Board. The rulemaking authority for financial accounting and reporting.

FDA – The Food and Drug Administration in the USA. Responsible for protecting public health by assuring the safety, efficacy, and security of human and veterinary drugs, biological products, medical devices, the food supply, cosmetics, and products that emit radiation.

FDA Compliance – The steps required by the Food and Drug Administration in the USA prior to marketing a drug for use by patients.

Firewall – A physical boundary that prevents unauthorized Internet traffic crossing from one area into another.

FOIA – The Freedom of Information Act. Protects the rights of the public to information and makes provisions for individuals to obtain information on the operation of federal agencies. Adopted in the USA in 1966.

GAAP – Generally Accepted Accounting Principles. The common set of accounting principles, standards, and procedures.

GICS – Government Information Communication Network. A UK agency that brings together all the communication professionals working in UK government departments and agencies.

Guest User – Any user who is logged onto a system that they do not normally use or have access to.

HIPAA – The Health Insurance Portability and Accountability Act. Passed in 1996 to help people buy and keep health insurance, even when they have serious health conditions. The law sets basic requirements that health plans must meet.

Hosting – The service offered to organizations to house, equip, secure, and maintain a Web presence for an organization.

ILM – A component of ECM. Information Lifecycle Management.

IM – A component of ECM. Instant messaging.

Imperatives – Issues, challenges, or opportunities an organization needs to achieve its corporate objectives.

Index – A component of ECM. In data management, the most common method for keeping track of data on a disk. Indexes are directory listings maintained by the operating system, RDBMS, or application. An index of files contains an entry for each file name and its location.

Information Infrastructure – Combination or Workspace hierarchy and content meta-data schema to assist in finding content, managing its life cycle, and managing it as an asset.

Information Lifecycle – Total life of content, from its inception and creation to eventual archiving or disposal.

Instant Messaging (IM) – A component of ECM. Exchanging messages in real time between two or more people. Instant messaging (IM) requires that both parties be logged onto a network, such as the Internet and their IM service, at the same time in order for an exchange to occur.

Intellectual Property (IP) – The general term for intangible property rights which are a result of intellectual effort. Patents, trademarks, designs, and copyright are the main intellectual property rights.

Internet – An interconnected system of networks that connects computers around the world via the TCP/IP protocol.

Intranet – An "internal Internet" configured behind a firewall, potentially connecting departments, customers, and trading partners.

ISO – International Standards Organization.

Joint Venture – An agreement between two or more firms to undertake the same business strategy and plan of action around a specific business initiative.

Knowledge Management (KM) – A component of ECM. An umbrella term for making more efficient use of the human knowledge that exists within an organization. The major focus is to identify and gather content from documents, reports, and other sources and to be able to search that content for meaningful relationships.

Knowledge Repository – A database of information about applications software that includes author, data elements, inputs, processes, outputs, and interrelationships.

Language of the Organization (or business) – Terminology describing the organization, including its products, processes and people, that is widely understood by employees.

Libraries & Archives – see Knowledge Management.

Metadata – Data that describes data, e.g. ,"document type, contract" or "Termination date."

Multimedia – Integration of text, voice, video, images, or some combination of these types of information. See also Rich Media.

NIST – National Institute of Standards and Technology.

Online – Connected to or accessible via a computer or computer network. Typically refers to being connected to the Internet or other remote service.

Online Marketplace – The stage of ECM deployment in which an organization extends a series of extranets to include a broad range of market participants, including competitors. An online marketplace functions as the main clearing house for all of the issues of a particular industry.

Operational Event – A process instance, e.g., the fulfilment of a single order for a specific customer.

Oracle – An enterprise software vendor providing ERP applications.

OSHA – The Occupational Safety and Health Administration of the U.S. Department of Labor or Occupational Safety and Health Act.

Patriot Act – USA legislation passed in October 2001, in response to terrorist attacks, that required an increased set of compliance rules surrounding the handling and provisioning of information.

Permissions – Management of who can access information on a computer or network. The Access Control List (ACL) is the set of data associated with a file, directory, or other resource that defines the permissions that users, groups, processes, or devices have for accessing it.

Personal Digital Assistant (PDA) – A lightweight, hand-held, usually pen-based computer used as a personal organizer.

Pharmaceutical – An industry that researches and produces drugs for health care patients.

Portal – A component of ECM. Within the enterprise, software that provides access via a Web browser into all of an organization's information assets and applications. Portals provide services including Web searching, news, white and yellow pages directories, free email, discussion groups, online shopping, and links to other sites.

Process Automation – The orchestration of work activities having a specific sequence.

Production Document Management – A component of ECM. The technology and methodology supporting a high-volume, low-touch production process (e.g., claims processing).

Production Imaging – The technology and methodology of capturing paper to digital images.

Productivity – A measure of the efficiency of a particular individual, business practice, or organization.

Program Management – A structured repeatable business process that is often cross-functional, multi-disciplinary, operated from a program office, and owned by a program manager.

Project Selection – The assessment and decision process for advancing projects or new product ideas.

Real-time Collaboration – A component of ECM. Collaborating simultaneously in real time. The primary data collaboration tools are electronic whiteboards, which is a shared "chalkboard," and application sharing, which lets remote users work in the same application together.

Records Management (RM) – A component of ECM. Refers to the creation, retention, and scheduled destruction of an organization's paper and film documents. Email and computer-generated content also fall into the RM domain.

Regulatory Compliance – Adherence to laws, regulations, and established rules over-seen by various governmental agencies throughout the world. Examples relevant to content management applications include: U.S. FDA 21 CFR Part 11, U.S. DoD 5015.2 Standard, U.S. Sarbanes–Oxley Act, Basel II, KONTRAG, DOMEA, and HIPAA.

Relational Database – A database (typically numeric) in which all the data and relations between them are organized in tables. A relational database allows the definition of data structures, storage and retrieval operations, and integrity constraints.

Report & Output Management – A component of ECM. The process of verifying delivery of business reports and output to target groups.

Return On Investment (ROI) – Traditional financial approach for examining overall investment returns over a given time frame (supports indexing and scoring).

Rich Media – Information that consists of any combination of graphics, audio, video and animation, which is more storage- and bandwidth-intensive than ordinary text.

Rights & Permissions – Identifies the circumstances under which an asset may be used. For instance, indicates who legally owns the asset, in what mediums it may be used (Web, print, TV), and the financial liabilities incurred to include the asset.

SAP – An enterprise software vendor providing enterprise resource planning (ERP), CRM, and business applications.

Sarbanes-Oxley Act – Legislation passed by U.S. Congress to protect investors from the possibility of fraudulent corporate accounting activities. Also known as SOX. This act prescribes actions such as controls and the transparency of reporting that all major public companies must adhere to when reporting their financial results.

Search – A component of ECM. To look for specific data in a file or an occurrence of text in a file or on a page. Implies sequential scanning of content or indexes to find the results rather than a direct lookup.

SEC – Securities and Exchange Commission. Established by Congress to help protect investors by administering the Securities Act of 1933 and the Securities Exchange Act of 1934.

Security – The act of restricting access to certain information or programs. See also Permissions.

Siebel – An enterprise software vendor providing customer relationship management (CRM) software.

Service Level Agreement (SLA) – A formal document that sets out an agreed-upon standard of service for users of an IT application.

Social Networks – The process of modeling how people really work together by identifying patterns of interaction among individuals.

Solution Design – A design for the intended business process or "work-style" – what will people do to or with information, and how.

Stage-Gate – A business process, often used for new product decision making, broken into stages and specific gate criteria to advance to the next stage.

Standard Operating Procedures (SOP) – Documents describing how to perform routine operations.

Storage Management – The technology and methodology used to optimize storage requirements to storage devices.

Storyboarding – The process of creating a rough outline of what your video will look like from a selection of video clips. This process helps the user to visualize the whole video and how it will look when it is completed.

Structured Data – Data that resides in fixed fields within a record or file. Relational databases and spreadsheets are examples of structured data.

Subject Matter Experts – Individuals with specialist knowledge or expertise relating to a particular subject or domain.

Supply Chain Management (SCM) – The combination of art and science that goes into improving the way your company finds the raw components it needs to make a product or service, manufactures that product or service, and delivers it to customers. The following are five basic components for supply chain management: Plan, Source, Make, Deliver, and Return.

Taxonomic Classifications – Laws or principles of classification; systematic division into ordered groups or categories.

Taxonomy – A hierarchical classification.

Team Support – The technology and methodology to support effective teaming.

Transactional Applications – Systems that manage and record the transactional activity of the organization. See also CRM and ERP.

Unstructured data – Data that does not reside in fixed locations. Free-form text in a word processing document is a typical example.

Value Chain – A collection of business entities, each of which adds value to a product or service that makes up a finished good (or service) purchased and used by an end-use customer.

Versioning – A feature of ECM platforms that keeps track of versions or revisions of a document and enables any given version to be retrieved.

Web Content Management (WCM) – A component of ECM. Systems designed to drive Web sites by separating content from presentation and providing the following capabilities: capacity planning, site design/layout, look/feel navigation, content development, production, delivery, session tracking, and site evolution.

WIKI – A community Web site where both the content and organization are open to editing by the community.

Workflow – A component of ECM. Using applications and technology to automate the execution of each phase in a business process. For example, a workflow may contain the automatic routing of documents and tasks to the users responsible for working on them.

Work Space or Folders Hierarchy – Hierarchy of work spaces (collection of folders) or individual folders designed to facilitate navigation, not just search, to both content and its owners or creators.

Work Orchestration – The orchestration of work activities lacking a specific sequence.

World Wide Web (WWW) – An HTML-based Internet system developed at the European Center for Nuclear Research (CERN) in Geneva. Also relates to the complete set of documents residing on all Internet servers that use the HTTP protocol. The Web is accessible to users via a simple point-and-click system.

BIBLIOGRAPHY

Cain, Matt. *Mapping Collaboration Maturity*. META Group Report. © October 16, 2003.

Chapman, Merrill R. <u>In Search of Stupidity: Over 20 Years of High Tech Marketing Disasters</u>. Apress. © 2003.

Cotton, Bob and Oliver, Richard. <u>Understanding Hypermedia</u>. London, UK: Phaidon Press Ltd. © 1993.

Frappaolo, Carl. <u>Knowledge Management</u>. Oxford, UK: Capstone Publishing. © 2002.

Hanser, Kathleen. *Amazing Technology Facts from Boeing Commercial Airplanes*. http://www.boeing.com

Hashmi, Naeem. *ERP and Content Management: Harmonic Convergence*, <u>Intelligent Enterprise</u>. July 2004.   http://www.intelligententerprise.com/print_article.jhtml?articleID=22102269

Hayward, Simon et al. *Hype Cycle for e-Workplace Technologies*. Gartner Report. © June 6, 2003.

Logan, Robert K., and Louis W. Stokes. <u>Collaborate to Compete</u>. Canada: Wiley © 2004.

McGrath, Michael E. <u>Product Strategy for High Technology Companies, Accelerating Your Business to Web Speed</u>. New York: McGraw-Hill Book Co. © 2001.

Moore, Connie and Markham, Robert. *Market Leaders Emerging in Enterprise Content Management*. Forrester Research. © August 2003.

Moore, Geoffrey. <u>Inside the Tornado, Marketing Strategies from Silicon Valley's Cutting Edge</u>. HarperBusiness: Reprint edition © 1999.

Moschella, David C. <u>Waves of Power, The Dynamics of Global Technology Leadership 1964–2010</u>. New York, NY: American Management Association. © 1997.

Open Text Corporation. <u>Ten Years of Innovation: 1991–2001</u>. Canada. © 2002.

Open Text Corporation. <u>LiveLinkUp Conference Proceedings. Volumes 1-7</u>. Canada. © 1999–2001.

Peters, Tom. *The Wow Project, Excerpts*. <u>Fast Company</u>. Issue 24. © 1999.

Rao, Ramana. *Bridging Structured and Unstructured Data*. <u>Knowledge Management Online</u>. Line56 Media. © April 1, 2003.

Saint-Onge, Hubert and Wallace, Debra. <u>Leveraging Communities of Practice for Strategic Advantage</u>. New York: Butterworth-Heinemann. © 2003.

Santosus, Megan. *Don't Put Your Company in a Purple Haze*. <u>CIO.com</u>. January 7, 2005. http://www.cio.com/research/knowledge/know.html?ID=1206

Stewart, Thomas A. *The Case Against Knowledge Management*, <u>Business 2.0</u>. Vol. 3, pp80-83. February 2002.

USER CASE STUDY BIBLIOGRAPHY

Barnardo's. *Barnardo's*. LinkUp Europe London Proceedings 2004. Open Text © 2004.
http://www.opentext.com/ecmtrilogy/methodsbook/innovator/barnardos

Booz Allen Hamilton. *Livelink Enterprise Server Integration with PeopleSoft at Booz Allen Hamilton*.
LinkUp Phoenix Proceedings 2004. Open Text © 2004.
http://www.opentext.com/ecmtrilogy/methodsbook/innovator/booz_allen_hamilton

British Telecom. *Scaling up virtual communities in BT*. LinkUp Europe London Proceedings 2004.
Open Text © 2004. http://www.opentext.com/ecmtrilogy/methodsbook/innovator/bt

British Telecom. *ECM in BT—Vision and Realisation*. LinkUp Europe London Proceedings 2004.
Open Text © 2004. http://www.opentext.com/ecmtrilogy/methodsbook/innovator/bt

Capital One. *Nature vs. Nurture: Livelink Usability Research and Planning at Capital One*.
LinkUp Phoenix Proceedings 2004. Open Text © 2004.
http://www.opentext.com/ecmtrilogy/methodsbook/innovator/capital_one

CARE International. *Tackling world problems*. Success Story. Open Text © 2003.
http://www.opentext.com/ecmtrilogy/methodsbook/innovator/care

CARE International. *CAREing enough to manage world problems*. Success Story. Open Text ©
2003. http://www.opentext.com/ecmtrilogy/methodsbook/innovator/care

CBC Radio Canada. Open Text © 2005.
http://www.opentext.com/ecmtrilogy/methodsbook/innovator/cbc

Dutch Refugee Council. *A centre of expertise*. Success Story. Open Text © 2004.
http://www.opentext.com/ecmtrilogy/methodsbook/innovator/dutch_refugee_council

E-Plus Mobilfunk. *IXOS Services Optimizes Processes at E-Plus*. Success Story.
IXOS SOFTWARE © 2002. http://www.opentext.com/ecmtrilogy/methodsbook/innovator/e-plus

Federal Ministry of the Interior. *Federal Government Procurement Goes Online*. Procurement
Agency of the Federal Ministry of the Interior © 2003.
http://www.opentext.com/ecmtrilogy/methodsbook/innovator/fmoi

Federated Investors. Transitioning from linear work habits to efficient, parallel processes.
Success Story. Open Text © 2005.
http://www.opentext.com/ecmtrilogy/methodsbook/innovator/federated_investors

General Dynamics. General Dynamics © 2005. All Rights Reserved.
http://www.opentext.com/ecmtrilogy/methodsbook/innovator/gdc4

Giant Eagle. *Compliance through content management*. Success Story. Open Text © 2003.
http://www.opentext.com/ecmtrilogy/methodsbook/innovator/giant_eagle

HP Singapore. Open Text © 2005. http://www.opentext.com/ecmtrilogy/methodsbook/innovator/hp

Kerr-McGee. *Closing the Gap on Communication & Understanding at Kerr-McGee*. LinkUp Phoenix
Proceedings 2004. Open Text © 2004.
http://www.opentext.com/ecmtrilogy/methodsbook/innovator/kerr-mcgee

Kerr-McGee. *Using XML Skins to Enhance Usability and Time to Market*. LiveLinkUp Orlando
Proceedings 2003. Open Text © 2003.
http://www.opentext.com/ecmtrilogy/methodsbook/innovator/kerr-mcgee

LawPro. *Achieving a (Mostly) Paperless Office*. LiveLinkUp Orlando Proceedings 2003.
Open Text © 2003. http://www.opentext.com/ecmtrilogy/solutionsbook/innovator/lawpro

LVA Rheinprovinz. *Banking on electronic files and digital signatures*. Success Story. Open Text © 2005. http://www.opentext.com/ecmtrilogy/methodsbook/innovator/lva

M+W Zander. *ECM-Strategie von M+W Zander: von der Vision zur erfolgreichen Einführung*. LiveLinkUp Europe Munich Proceedings 2005. Open Text © 2005. http://www.opentext.com/ecmtrilogy/methodsbook/innovator/mw_zander

M+W Zander. Collaborative Engineering im internationalen Anlagenbau. LinkUp Europe Munich Proceedings 2004. Open Text © 2004. http://www.opentext.com/ecmtrilogy/methodsbook/innovator/mw_zander

Motorola. *Consolidating Content and Collaboration Across the Enterprise. Motorola Compass: Availability, Scalability and Performance for the Enterprise and Beyond*. LiveLinkUp Orlando Proceedings 2003. Open Text © 2003. http://www.opentext.com/ecmtrilogy/methodsbook/innovator/motorola

Motorola. *Motorola Extends use of Open Text's Livelink*. Press Release. Open Text © 2003. http://www.opentext.com/ecmtrilogy/methodsbook/innovator/motorola

Motorola. *Using COMPASS to find the way*. Success Story. Open Text © 2003. http://www.opentext.com/ecmtrilogy/methodsbook/innovator/motorola

Murphy Oil. *J.D. Edwards Integration Case Studies*. VIP Conference 2003. http://www.opentext.com/ecmtrilogy/methodsbook/innovator/murphy_oil

Northrop Grumman. *Ensuring a successful Livelink Implementation*. LinkUp Phoenix Proceedings 2004. Open Text © 2004. http://www.opentext.com/ecmtrilogy/methodsbook/innovator/northrop_grumman

Novo Nordisk. *Scaling Livelink with Remote Cache at Novo Nordisk*. LiveLinkUp Paris Proceedings 2005. Open Text © 2005. http://www.opentext.com/ecmtrilogy/methodsbook/innovator/novo_nordisk

Sasol. *Integration options between Livelink and SAP Enterprise Portal*. LiveLinkUp Paris Proceedings 2003. Open Text © 2003. http://www.opentext.com/ecmtrilogy/methodsbook/innovator/sasol

Siemens. *Global Network of Knowledge*. Live LinkUp Chicago Proceedings 2002. Open Text © 2002. http://www.opentext.com/ecmtrilogy/methodsbook/innovator/siemens

Siemens. *Siemens Achieved Efficiency with Livelink an SAP R/3 Integration*. Case Study Interview. Open Text © 2002. http://www.opentext.com/ecmtrilogy/methodsbook/innovator/siemens

Siemens Automation & Drives. *Instantly accessing archived documents*. Success Story. Open Text © 2004. http://www.opentext.com/ecmtrilogy/methodsbook/innovator/siemens

Siemens Business Services. *Tools for Knowledge Management and Communities of Practice—the Siemens Experience*. Live LinkUp Chicago Proceedings 2002. Open Text © 2002. http://www.opentext.com/ecmtrilogy/methodsbook/innovator/siemens

Siemens Enterprise Networks. *EZ-A (Easy Access to Customer Contracts, Engagement, Solutions, and Services)*. LiveLinkUp Orlando Proceedings 2003. Open Text © 2003. http://www.opentext.com/ecmtrilogy/methodsbook/innovator/siemens

Siemens Enterprise Networks. *Siemens Communications Enterprise Content Management using Livelink, e-publisher and Web Content Manager*. LinkUp Phoenix Proceedings 2004. Open Text © 2004. http://www.opentext.com/ecmtrilogy/methodsbook/innovator/siemens

Siemens Financial Services. *Technical Solution—Archiving with Livelink and IXOS*. LinkUp Phoenix Proceedings 2004. Open Text © 2004. http://www.opentext.com/ecmtrilogy/methodsbook/innovator/siemens

Siemens Netherlands. *Enterprise Content Management at Siemens Netherlands*. LinkUp Europe Proceedings 2004. Open Text © 2004.
http://www.opentext.com/ecmtrilogy/methodsbook/innovator/siemens

Siemens OSRAM. *OSRAM GmbH: ROI 201%*. Return on Investment Study. Open Text © 1998.
http://www.opentext.com/ecmtrilogy/methodsbook/innovator/siemens

Sinclair Knight Merz. *Global Collaboration Using Distributed Livelink Servers*. LiveLinkUp Orlando Proceedings 2003. Open Text: © 2003.
http://www.opentext.com/ecmtrilogy/methodsbook/innovator/skm

SONY Global Treasury Services. *Faster return on a SAP investment. Success Story*. Open Text © 2005. http://www.opentext.com/ecmtrilogy/methodsbook/innovator/sony

South East Water. http://www.opentext.com/ecmtrilogy/methodsbook/innovator/south_east_water

Swiss Air. *Swiss.com—ein wachsender Vertriebskanal*. LiveLinkUp Europe Munich Proceedings 2005. Open Text © 2005. http://www.opentext.com/ecmtrilogy/methodsbook/innovator/swiss

Transport Research Laboratory. *Livelink in Four Months*. LiveLinkUp Europe London Proceedings 2005. Open Text © 2005. http://www.opentext.com/ecmtrilogy/methodsbook/innovator/trl

Transport Research Laboratory. *Transforming into an open information environment*. Success Story. Open Text © 2005. http://www.opentext.com/ecmtrilogy/methodsbook/innovator/trl

T-Systems. *Collaborative Environment bei der T-Systems International: Erfolgsfaktoren bei der Einführung von myWorkroom*. LinkUp Europe Munich Proceedings 2004. Open Text © 2004.
http://www.opentext.com/ecmtrilogy/methodsbook/innovator/t-systems

T-Systems. *T-Systems MyWorkplace*. LiveLinkUp Europe Munich Proceedings 2005. Open Text © 2005. http://www.opentext.com/ecmtrilogy/methodsbook/innovator/t-systems

UBS. *An Interactive Information Platform*. Case Study. Open Text © 2006.
http://www.opentext.com/ecmtrilogy/methodsbook/innovator/ubs

United Nations High Commissioner for Refugees. *Email Integration into Livelink*. LiveLinkUp Europe Munich Proceedings 2005. Open Text © 2005.
http://www.opentext.com/ecmtrilogy/methodsbook/innovator/unhcr

Unilever. *Unilever Bestfoods Netherlands—Creating a live link to a dynamic brand*. Success Story. Open Text © 2004. http://www.opentext.com/ecmtrilogy/methodsbook/innovator/unilever

Vintage Petroleum. *Vintage Petroleum Improves Financial Processes, Advances Sarbanes-Oxley Compliance with Open Text's Livelink*. Press Release. Open Text © 2005.
http://www.opentext.com/ecmtrilogy/methodsbook/innovator/vintage_petroleum

VSP. Open Text © 2005.
http://www.opentext.com/ecmtrilogy/methodsbook/innovator/vsp

INDEX

Get the complete set of Enterprise Content Management (ECM) books for your reference library.

The ECM book trilogy (Solutions, Technology, Methods) covers all the important aspects of identifying and deploying ECM solutions. The books explain how to turn content into competitive advantage.

ECM Solutions

The ECM Solutions book is the first in the trilogy. It is intended for the non-technical reader who has a business challenge involving electronic information such as email or Web pages. The issues described in this book mainly concern regulatory compliance and increased productivity. Learn about effective ECM solutions for every major department in your organization and benchmark the most effective deployments by industry.

ECM Technology

The second book in the series describes the primary technologies that comprise ECM. Technologies discussed include search engines, knowledge management, workflow, collaboration, Web publishing and email archiving. Find out which ECM technologies are appropriate for a particular problem and discover the most effective deployments.

ECM Methods

The third book in the trilogy reviews the most effective methods for deploying ECM applications. Methods are described for every type of situation from a simple deployment to the creation of a large online marketplace. One of the key aspects of any ECM deployment is the management of people in a changing environment. Establish your competitive advantage by modeling your ECM solution on some of the most innovative organizations in the world.

For more information about these books visit www.opentext.com or www.amazon.com.